INVESTMENT
OPPORTUNITIES IN
RUSSIA AND THE CIS

D0880356

Russian and CIS
Programme | ⬤ THE ROYAL INSTITUTE OF
INTERNATIONAL AFFAIRS

David A. Dyker, *editor*

INVESTMENT OPPORTUNITIES IN RUSSIA AND THE CIS

Published by The Brookings Institution, *Washington, D.C.*
for The Royal Institute of International Affairs, *London*

Published by
THE BROOKINGS INSTITUTION
1775 Massachusetts Ave., N.W., Washington, D.C.

for the

ROYAL INSTITUTE OF INTERNATIONAL AFFAIRS
Chatham House, 10 St. James's Square, London SW1Y 4LE
(Charity Registration No. 208 223)

Library of Congress Cataloging-in-Publication Data

Investment opportunities in Russia and the CIS / David Dyker [editor].
p.   cm.
"The contributions to this volume were originally published in the form of papers by the Post-Soviet Business Forum (PSBF) at the Royal Institute of International Affairs, London."
Includes bibliographical references and index.
ISBN 0-8157-1999-X (pbk.)
1. Investments, Foreign—Former Soviet republics—Congresses. 2. Business enterprises, Foreign—Former Soviet republics—Congresses. 3. Former Soviet republics-Economic conditions—Congresses.   I. Dyker, David A.
II. Brookings Institution.
HG5572.I58   1995
332.6'732247--dc20   95-41795
                                                                               CIP

9 8 7 6 5 4 3 2 1

The paper used in this publication meets the minimum requirements of the American National Standard for Information Sciences—Permanence of Paper for Printed Library Materials, ANSI Z39.48-1984.

Typeset in Times Roman

Composition by Blue Heron, Inc.
Lawrence, Kansas

Printed by Edwards Brothers Inc.

The contributions to this volume were originally published in the form of papers by the Post-Soviet Business Forum (PSBF) at the Royal Institute of International Affairs, London. The PSBF has supported publications and meetings between academics, businessmen and officials for the Russian and CIS Programme at RIIA since January 1992 with generous support from the following companies:

B.A.T. Industries plc
Ente Nazionale Idrocarburi
Mobil Corporation
Nissho Iwai (Europe) plc
NM Rothschild and Sons Ltd
RTZ Corporation plc
Shell International Petroleum Co. Ltd
Statoil
The World Gold Council
Zeneca

About the Authors

William E. Butler, MA, Ph.D. (Johns Hopkins), JD (Harvard), LL D (London), FSA, is Professor of Comparative Law in the University of London and Director of The Vinogradoff Institute, University College London; Partner, White & Case (London/ Moscow/Almaty); and Academician of the Russian Academy of Natural Sciences and of the Ukrainian Academy of Sciences. He has been Visiting Professor at New York University School of Law, Ritsumeikan University, and Harvard Law School and has lectured at The Hague Academy of International Law. He has advised on the drafting of legislation for the former USSR, the Russian Federation, Ukraine, Kyrgyzia, and Kazakhstan (among them oil and gas, pledge, company law, privatization, finance leasing, and trusts), The World Bank, the United Kingdom Know-How Fund, the EBRD, and others, and in 1992 was a member of the EC Joint Task Force for Law Reform in the CIS. He is the author of more than 700 books, articles, translations, and reviews on international and comparative law, with particular reference to the former USSR.

Julian Cooper is Director of the Centre for Russian and East European Studies, University of Birmingham and Professor of Russian Economic Studies. A specialist on the defense industry and science-technology policy of the former Soviet Union, he is the author of a Chatham House Paper, *The Soviet Defence Industry: Conversion and Reform* (Pinter/RIIA, 1991), and many other publications on the former Soviet defense sector and conversion.

David A. Dyker is Reader in Economics in the University of Sussex and Senior Fellow of the Science Policy Research Unit of that university. He has published widely on the economics of Eastern Europe, including in this series, *After the Soviet Union: the International Trading Environment* (1992) and *Monopoly and Competition Policy in*

vii

Russia (1994) with Michael Barrow. He was also series editor to the second series of the Post-Soviet Business Forum.

David Humphreys received his Ph.D. from the University of Wales. He worked for nine years in government service, initially at the British Geological Survey and later in the Cabinet Office and Ministry of Defence. Since 1986, he has been Deputy Chief Economist with The RTZ Corporation plc in London, in which capacity he has lectured and written extensively on the mining and metals industries. He is Vice-President of Euromines, the Brussels-based industry federation, and Associate Editor of the journal *Resources Policy*.

Sergei Manezhev, Section Head in the Moscow Institute for the Study of the Far East, Russian Academy of Sciences, is one of Russia's leading specialists on the country's most easterly region, and has published widely in Russian and English. His "Free economic zones in the context of economic changes in Russia" appeared in *Europe-Asia Studies* in 1993.

Jonathan Stern is an independent researcher and consultant specializing in the energy situation of the former Soviet Union and Eastern Europe, and also in natural gas issues worldwide. From 1985 to 1992 he was Head of the Energy and Environmental Programme at the Royal Institute of International Affairs and remains an Associate Fellow of that Programme. He is Vice-President of the consulting firm Gas Strategies.

Contents

Part 5

Introduction

David A. Dyker

To say that the investment opportunities in the former Soviet Union are unlimited is merely to state a tautology. Investment opportunities are *bound* to be unlimited in a region of nearly 300 million people, with very substantial reserves of natural resources and (in most of the successor states) a comparatively high level of human capital endowment. There can be no dispute, therefore, that there is a domestic market to be penetrated, resource endowments to be accessed and exploited. But when we pass from the general to the particular, from the dimension of economics to that of business, we discover a very different picture. At the level of specific projects, foreign companies are hard pressed to find prospective investments in the CIS region which will, risk factors apart, generate a competitive rate of return over a period of years.

The big apparent exception to this generalization is the hydrocarbons sector, where, as Jonathan Stern documents in his chapter below, Western investment interest—and commitment—has been serious and stable. But oil is less exceptional than it appears. In the international petroleum industry, as in other sectors where market structures have become globalized, major players do not have the option of staying out of major new developments—unless they are prepared to risk loss of their status as major players.[1] Short-term profit rates on oil investments in the CIS countries are quite marginal (gas, it must be said, is a different matter). Thus in mid-1994, with the existing structure of taxation and tariffs, foreign investors were losing $2.70 on every barrel of oil they took out of Russia. The half-dozen joint ventures which were granted exemption from the export duty on oil at the end of 1994 would have been able to turn this into a profit, per barrel, of around $2[2]—still less than the profit rate on

1. Sharp (1992, p. 250).
2. Economist Intelligence Unit (1994a, pp. 14–15; 1994b, p. 16).

1

Middle East oil. The sustained interest of the oil majors in the CIS region is, therefore, less a function of short- to medium-term profit maximization than of long-term strategic thinking, aimed at furnishing those companies with options in the next century, by which time almost everything—including, most important, the international price of oil—may have changed. The fact remains that, as of 1995, investing in CIS oil is no more a gold mine than investing in CIS manufacturing.

A more genuine exception to this general pattern of modest prospective profitability is provided by specific consumer goods and consumer durables sectors. American-style fast-food outlets, luxury car imports, international hotels, to mention only the most prominent, are making good money for Western and CIS partners alike. But while some of these developments do address the mass market, none of them seek to access the specific resource endowments of the CIS countries. Thus we are still left trying to answer the question: why is it so difficult to make money out of the things the CIS countries have to offer? The chapters of this book provide a mass of insights into this critical issue. Let us list the major points that emerge.

The legal frameworks of the successor states to the Soviet Union are anything but user-friendly for the Western investor. Investors are often poorly briefed on peculiarities of local commercial law stemming from the Soviet inheritance, or from local usage. Tax regimes, regulations on repatriation of profits etc. are less uniformly hostile than unstable, confused and confusing, with different members of the same government often saying quite different things on key issues to the Western business audience (as happened in the case of Russia in 1994).

Attitudes on the part of the political and managerial elites of the CIS countries (in particular Russia) remain inimical to the very notion of profit-taking by foreign investors. In the extractive industries especially, a residual Marxist mentality seems to engender a "zero-sum game" orientation to joint-venture investments, whereby any profit transferred to the foreign partner is viewed as a direct and equivalent loss to the CIS partner. In its crudest form, this attitude boils down to the rhetorical question: "Why should foreigners make a profit out of our resources?" It often goes along with quite unrealistic assessment by local elites of the strength of their own technological capabilities. The possibility that Western investment, through the technology transfer it engenders, may increase profits *for both sides* seems to present severe conceptual difficulties. In the case of the gas industry, these modes of thought have produced an explicit ruling by the management of the Russian Gazprom that foreign firms should only be allowed to invest in poor or difficult fields, leaving the cream to domestic Russian organizations.

The peculiar political conditions prevailing in the CIS region create special negotiating problems. Corruption is a major factor throughout the region, particularly in the south, but this is perhaps a less critical obstacle than the bizarre pattern of "economic warlordism" that has developed, particularly in Russia. In a situation where local leaders have a great deal of effective physical power, if only as a function of their distance from the capital and the general poverty of communications, but little constitutional power to raise, or share in, revenue, "gate-keeping" behavior becomes universal. Local leaders may be looking for a bribe, a favor, a commitment to investment in local infrastructure—but in every case the existence of multiple levels of gate-keeping makes the negotiating position of the prospective Western investor infinitely more complex than it would be, say, in relation to a typical Third World country. That helps to explain why Western companies are often happier doing business in Transcaucasia and Central Asia, with all the local difficulties that exist there—because the countries are smaller and the power structures simpler.

Local managers and politicians tend to have a systematically distorted perception of the resource endowments of their own economies. (Again, this applies particularly to Russia.) They tend to an inflated view of the value of their natural resource endowments. This comes through particularly strongly in the mining and minerals sectors. As David Humphreys shows, managers in CIS mining industries have found it difficult to break free from the typically Soviet notion that sheer physical endowment, irrespective of extractive conditions and/or location, is what counts. As a result, they continue to view as "unique" deposits which, to a Western company, present quite modest commercial prospects and are uncompetitive with alternative investments. There is, at the same time, a general tendency to undervalue human capital resources (with some of the elements of the old Soviet defense industry presenting a striking exception, as Julian Cooper demonstrates). While politicians make general statements to the effect that "something must be done to save Russian/Ukrainian/Kazakh etc. science," the reality is that many of the former Soviet Union's world-class scientists and designers (along with a large number of mediocre ones!) have been effectively thrown out of a job by the transition process. Some of them have clawed their way back by making deals with Western companies which have brought FDI into the given CIS country, and set up two-way technology transfer flows.[3] But these deals have mostly been made by isolated, enterprising individuals, working against a largely hostile environment. The experience of the smaller East European countries is that effective development of these precious human capital resources is critically de-

3. Dyker and Stein (1993).

pendent on the existence of a favorable climate and regulatory framework in which the small and medium-sized enterprises (SMEs) can flourish—so that isolated, enterprising individuals can develop into entrepreneurs and employers.[4] The reality in most of the CIS countries is that the business sector is dominated by monopoly elements, and it is extremely difficult for new firms to break into any sector.[5]

As a corollary of the tendency to neglect the importance of human capital endowment, CIS managers and politicians tend to underestimate the importance of soft management technology. They are often poorly aware of the critical importance of managing technology transfer, and, in insisting on the maintenance of local management control over joint ventures, often throw away the biggest advantage FDI can bring. There is a marked contrast here with the experience of the smaller countries of Eastern Europe, where there is generally a very clear understanding of the critical importance of Western soft technology in the context of FDI.[6]

To the extent that there has been restructuring in the industries of the CIS countries, it has tended to be primarily supply-driven. Thus even the more enterprising managers of the region rarely have any clear idea of the need to structure a new business venture around a potential market.

Organized crime is a major problem in all the successor states. Protection racketeering is the most widespread form of organized crime, and local businesses do, in many cases, pay protection money. Big international companies are in a better position to resist extortion, though often at the cost of hiring bodyguards for all their own management personnel. In any case, protection racketeering has a knock-on effect which increases costs for all businesses.

When businessmen talk generally about the problem of medium-term political risk they are, as William Butler points out, to an extent simply summarizing the points made above—in relation to taxation, profit repatriation, law and order, negotiation difficulties. They are also thinking of something rather broader—of the fact that this part of the world, but newly emerged from seventy years of oppressive and stultifying dictatorship, has not yet settled down. For that reason, there is still a multitude of nightmare scenarios—ranging from a revival of communism or the coming to power of fascism in Russia, to the advent of Muslim fundamentalist regimes in the south, which could wipe out international business altogether in the given country. Of course Western companies are quite accustomed to considering, and bearing, such generalized

4. See Jakupovic (1994).
5. Dyker and Barrow (1994).
6. Inzelt (1994, pp. 146–48).

medium-term political risks in other parts of the world. What is unique about the CIS, and what largely explains the poor flow of FDI into that region, is the *combination* of general medium-term political risk and the whole host of specific factors enumerated above. Where (other things being equal) initial estimates of expected rates of return are very high, a hefty discount to take account of general medium-term political risk may still leave the project looking attractively profitable. Where the undiscounted estimate of likely profits is already on the modest side, a realistic adjustment to take account of general medium-term political risk may leave the given project looking marginal in the extreme.

Yet with all this, most forecasting services predict that FDI in the CIS as a whole (not necessarily in every single member-state) will pick up toward the end of the century. They base this largely on the assumption that most of these countries will, in practice, continue to settle down, that political extremes and apocalyptic regimes will be avoided, and that the whole region will not turn into a giant Yugoslavia. At time of writing this seems like a reasonable assumption. (But note that Jonathan Stern delivers something of a minority report on this issue!) Indeed the Russian military action in Chechnya, distasteful though it has been to the West, should probably be interpreted as an element of settling down, rather than a harbinger of new instability. The settling down, certainly, is in this case in terms of a rather traditional Russian pattern of politics, in which holding on to the empire (reduced though it may be in extent) is a paramount goal, uniting the great majority of Russians (and a fair proportion of the non-Russians within Russia). In the same way, politics in Transcaucasia and Central Asia will settle down (indeed to some extent have already settled down) in terms of a mixture of the traditional pre-Soviet and the classically Soviet types of authoritarianism, with elements (in some cases significant elements) of Western-style democracy or Muslim radicalism thrown in. On this basis, the general medium-term political risk discount factor will have fallen substantially by around 1997–98. That alone would lead us to posit a modest increase in the flow of FDI as a baseline prediction. If that modest increase grows into something more like a flood, it will be because changes have occurred under the more specific headings enumerated above, changes which are making prospective investments in the CIS countries look more profitable right from the start. Any such changes would have to be initiated largely by the governments and business leaders themselves. So what are the prospects for a significant evolution in the medium term of the factors that tend to depress the return on investment?

If we expect Russia to settle down in general political terms, then we must also expect it to settle down in relation to specific factors affecting investment business. In particular, the reassertion of physical control by the center over the geographical periphery of the Russian Federation is likely to produce some simplification of the negotiation process for foreign companies. But it would be wrong to be too sanguine on this count. As Sergei Manezhev points out, many of the center-periphery difficulties in the Russian polity arise because there is no stable revenue base for local government. As long as the general fiscal situation remains unregularized (see below), this problem is unlikely to be fully resolved. And however much Moscow succeeds in reasserting physical control on the periphery, local political leaderships will always be able to obstruct, even veto, specific economic developments. Thus gate-keeping will continue to be both possible and necessary.

The general process of settling down in the CIS countries will not be accompanied by any final resolution of the budgetary problems which presently afflict all of them. Budget deficits will in all cases remain above five per cent—in most cases above ten per cent—of national income. This will, of course, mean that inflation rates will remain high, which creates its own problems—certainly not insoluble—for foreign investors. More important, it means that governments will continue to live in a state of permanent fiscal crisis. That in turn will almost certainly mean continued fiscal instability, as successive finance ministers improvise and juggle with taxes to try to square the circle and to cut the budget deficit without disturbing major vested interests. Foreign capital is unlikely ever to be regarded as such a major interest, so that foreign investors must always be prepared for nasty shocks in relation to their tax burden.

General settling down will be accompanied by a process—stuttering and incomplete—of regularization of commercial law systems. Significant progress will be made on many of the difficult points highlighted by William Butler. So while companies will have to continue to be prepared for the worst on the strictly tax side, they will find that on issues of contract and company law, the CIS countries will become more like Western countries.

The trend toward more muscular political regimes could mean the turn of the tide for organized crime in the CIS countries. It is particularly striking that in the eyes of ordinary Muscovites, the war in Chechnya is as much a war against gangsters as against rebels. Yet at the same time it would be dangerous to overgeneralize from the case of Chechnya. The downside risk is that some, if not all, of the CIS countries degenerate further into a Latin American scenario, where political authoritarianism goes hand in hand with escalating organized crime. On balance, the chances are that gangsterism will be less of problem for foreign business in five years' time than it is right now. But there is a big margin of error here, and there could be substantial variation between countries.

The mind-set problem is likely to ease with the passage of time. Sociological surveys indicate that both traditionalists and liberals are to be found in the management structures of most industries in the CIS.[7] Traditionalists, with their inherent hostility to outsiders, are currently generally in the ascendancy, even where given enterprises have been privatized and marketized. They are also, on the whole, from the older age groups. By the same token, the younger cohorts of management are predominantly liberal, evincing a much more neutral attitude to outsiders, and with a much better grasp of the complex counterpoint of management, finance, technology and marketing that characterizes contemporary life, and of the need to start every business calculation from the demand side. So it is a demographic certainty that the average CIS manager will, by the turn of the century, be much closer to the standard Western executive type.

A number of the CIS countries, notably Russia, have government programs for the development of SMEs. It would be rash to place too much faith in their rapid and energetic implementation. But the monopoly problem in the CIS economies is, to a considerable extent, a legacy from the old system, a dimension of the *nomenklatura* capitalism which has, with its peculiar forms of insider dealing, perhaps inevitably dominated the early transition period. Like the mind-set problem, the monopoly problem is, therefore, likely to ease for purely demographic reasons, although it will not disappear. Organized crime —protection racketeering in particular—is also a big disincentive to small business. So to the extent that CIS governments are able to clamp down effectively on gangsterism, the conditions for new, dynamic enterprise should improve.

In terms of conditions in the CIS countries themselves, then, the situation is fairly clear. General medium-term political risk discounts will fall, and the specific factors which tend to depress the rate of return on investment will be likely to ease. In principle that should lead to a substantially increased flow of FDI into the region. But that substantial increase will, of course, occur only if Western companies react to improved conditions in the former Soviet Union. So let us now try to list the main areas in which prospective investors will have to be proactive.

While regulatory frameworks will tend to stabilize, they will remain com-

7. Kharkhordin and Gerber (1994).

paratively complex and volatile, even inconsistent. Prospective Western investors will have to be prepared to invest more in in-depth investigation of local legal structures, in order to avoid the kind of mistakes that, as William Butler documents, have been made in the past. As overall prospective profitability on direct investments rises, it should be possible to do this without destroying the net present value of the project.

If the most valuable local resources to be accessed through investment in manufacturing are human resources, and if these resources are now increasingly being channeled through start-up firms of one kind or another within the CIS countries, Western companies will have to devote more of their resources to intelligence work on these new developments, the more so as local regulatory and political structures are likely to remain less than wholly congenial to the full flowering of SMEs. Sun Microsystems have already demonstrated that this kind of head-hunting is perfectly feasible and produces profitable results.[8] But they were lucky, in that their quarry actually made the initial contact. If Western companies are not prepared to put time and money into active research into the human capital resources of the countries of the former Soviet Union, they will be left with a small self-selecting group of confident and articulate post-Soviet scientists and designers who may be good, but will not necessarily be the best, and who will perceive no personal interest in helping their Western partners broaden their CIS contacts.

Finally, what can Western governments and international organizations do? The experience of Western Europe over the past four decades has demonstrated graphically how close is the connection between trade flows and investment flows. To the extent that the European Union remains the main extra-CIS trading partner of all the CIS countries, liberalization of trade with the Union will be a critical factor of future investment prospects, particularly since it will open up new potential markets for the fledgling manufacturing export sectors of the CIS countries. In the medium-to-long-term future, liberalization of trade with East Asia and North America may become at least as important. For the time being, however, it is the CIS-EU nexus which dominates the trade agenda. The hope must be that all the CIS countries will sign Partnership Agreements with the EU, on the model of the one signed between Russia and the EU in 1994, and that Russia itself, and eventually the others too, will be able to progress to the kind of comprehensive free trade agreement which all the Baltic countries have had with the EU since 1 January 1995.

But one of the most interesting things to come out of the experience of the

8. Dyker and Stein (1993).

Visegrad countries in relation to their association agreements with the EU is that free trade deals can create as many problems in relation to FDI as they solve. For in signing their individual association agreements with the European Union, Poland, Hungary and (originally) Czechoslovakia created an anomaly. It would now be easier for, say, a Polish company to do business with the EU than with neighboring Czechoslovakia. That in turn meant that an EU company, considering the alternatives of siting a given new plant in the EU, or in one of the Visegrad countries, and in the absence of a strong cost advantage one way or the other, would rationally choose the EU location—because in this way it would have access to the whole EU market, plus the markets of all the Visegrad countries. If it sited its plant in, say, Hungary, it would have access only to the EU market plus the Hungarian market.

This anomaly was quickly spotted by the Visegrad governments, and corrective action taken through the creation of CEFTA—the Central European Free Trade Area—which established from April 1993 the same free-trade regime between the Visegrad countries as that operating between those countries and the EU, through the Association Agreements. It would be rash to suggest a direct link between the coming into force of the CEFTA agreement and the big kick in the flow of FDI into Hungary and Poland in the second half of 1993.[9] But the creation of CEFTA has done much to clear the level playing-field that investors require and expect in that part of the transition region.

Trade liberalization between individual CIS countries and the EU will create the same trading anomaly as did the Visegrad countries' Association Agreements, and with the same, perverse, knock-on effects in relation to investment. The difference between the two cases is that whereas in the Visegrad case the governments concerned were able to use the existing framework of political cooperation to put in place a subregional free-trade agreement almost immediately, the CIS record on economic cooperation is one of repeated failures. A CIS Economic Union was set up on paper by agreement of the member states in September 1993. It was stillborn. A further agreement of October 1994 set up an interstate committee of economic union, dedicated to the pursuance of the goals of free trade and a payments union, and ultimately a customs union. The new agreement also targets the issue of joint investments between the CIS countries, particularly in the area of infrastructure and energy grids. All of this is precisely calculated to create the single investment space which both CIS countries and interested Western companies need, if investment opportunities are to be fully exploited. The problem is that the chances

9. Economic Commission for Europe (1994, p. 118).

of anything like full implementation of the October 1994 program are, by common consent, virtually zero. The strong probability is that CIS governments will continue to pursue essentially autarkic goals, moderated by occasional bilateral agreements between individual CIS countries. To the extent that there is trade, it will be largely barter trade. And the barriers to free movement of goods between CIS countries, in terms of customs duties, quotas and obstructive and corrupt officials, will remain formidable.

Western free-trade initiatives vis-à-vis the CIS countries will, then, play a significant role in opening up investment opportunities in the CIS region. But the impact of these initiatives will be greatly reduced by the likely failure of the CIS countries to match such inter-regional initiatives with intra-regional free-trade agreements. So the international dimension eventually leads back to the basic issues of capacity for domestic policy articulation discussed earlier. As in the sphere of domestic commercial regulation, we should expect slow and halting progress towards a more rational ordering of CIS economic space. But for some years to come, a prospective investor in, say, Uzbekistan, will have to assume that it may be easier to export from Uzbekistan to Western Europe or North America than to other states of the CIS.

The papers that follow fill out the framework outlined in this introduction and give depth to the key points that have been noted briefly above. Jonathan Stern and David Humphreys look at key individual sectors. Julian Cooper evaluates the prospects for conversion of the former Soviet defense industry—the sources of the bulk of the high-value human capital resources of the successor states. William Butler gives an authoritative account of the special legal problems. Finally, Sergei Manezhev presents a study of the Russian Far East, one of the most important—and far-flung—regions of the Russian Federation. For the investor who would be wiser rather than sadder, all of this is surely essential reading.

References for the Introduction

Dyker, David A., and Barrow, Michael (1994). *Monopoly and Competition Policy in Russia*. London: Royal Institute of International Affairs, Post-Soviet Business Forum.

Dyker, David A., and Stein, George (1993)."Russian software: adjusting to the world market,"*RFE/RL Research Report*, vol. 2, no. 44 (5 November), pp. 50–53.

Economic Commission for Europe (1994). *Economic Bulletin for Europe*, vol. 46. New York, United Nations.

Economist Intelligence Unit (1994a). *Country Forecast. Russia. 2nd Quarter*. London.

Economist Intelligence Unit (1994b). *Country Forecast. Russia. 4th Quarter*. London.

Inzelt, Annamária (1994). "Privatization and innovation in Hungary: first experiences," *Economic Systems*, vol. 18, no. 2 (June), pp. 141–58.

Jakupovic, Esad (1994). "Procvat male privrede," *Ekonomska Politika* (Belgrade), no. 2219, 17 October, p. 22.

Kharkhordin, Oleg, and Gerber, Theodore P. (1994). "Russian directors' business ethic: a study of industrial enterprises in St Petersburg, 1993," *Europe-Asia Studies*, vol. 46, no. 7, pp. 1075–1107.

Sharp, Margaret (1992), "Changing industrial structures in Western Europe," in David A. Dyker, ed. *The European Economy*. Harlow, Longmans.

Part 1

OIL AND GAS IN THE FORMER SOVIET UNION: THE CHANGING FOREIGN INVESTMENT AGENDA

Jonathan Stern

The current problems and prospects of the former Soviet oil and gas industries present very different pictures. The oil industry has experienced a major crisis; production fell by some 45 percent and exports by nearly 50 percent in the pe-

I would like to thank Neil Malcolm for suggesting that I write this paper. Thanks also to those who attended the Chatham House study group in April, especially Alan Smith for his help with statistics. Thanks to Shyama Iyer and Matthew Tickle for their organizational skills and forbearance toward my general ineptitude on dates and deadlines. Finally thanks to David Dyker for his constant encouragement and editorial skills.

This paper was revised in early 1995 to take account of the significant events which had occurred since it was drafted two years earlier. The text has been revised only minimally. Significant effort has focused on updating the tables, and particularly the appendix to chapter 3, which has been extensively revised and considerably expanded. Many of the conclusions reached in the original text have been allowed to stand. There remains, accordingly, an emphasis on "great expectations" from foreign investment, which is perhaps more a reflection of the post-Soviet euphoria of the early 1990s than of the more skeptical views that have come to predominate as that euphoria has dissipated. To have changed the perspective radically would have needed a much more extensive reworking of the paper.

riod 1988–94. By contrast, gas production peaked in 1990 and fell by just 10 percent in the period up to 1994, mostly owing to lack of markets for gas. Organizational structures may account for some of the difference—the oil industry having fragmented and gas having remained a centralized monopoly. However, the serious problems of the oil industry, which were certainly already apparent in the 1980s, have been exacerbated by the breakup of the Soviet Union and the subsequent Russian economic collapse.

There is an urgent need to focus on the demand side of the energy balance. If modest successes in energy conservation and efficiency can be achieved in the context of economic restructuring and reform, then there seems to be no reason why Russian oil exports should not be maintained at current levels if production can be stabilized over the next year. The potential exists to increase gas exports significantly. However, realization of that potential is highly dependent upon a satisfactory solution to transit problems, especially through Ukraine. The Energy Charter Treaty could make a contribution to the solution of this problem.

By the end of 1994, foreign companies had become involved in more than 200 oil and gas ventures in CIS countries, a figure which had more than doubled during a two-year period. Although actual investment volumes are difficult to estimate, it might be reasonable to suppose that around $1.5 billion had been invested in the Russian oil industry and about the same in the Russian gas industry. However, the Russian oil investments relate to literally dozens of projects, whereas the Russian gas investment is for a single project. Elsewhere in the former Soviet Union, total investment in the oil and gas industries is even more difficult to estimate. A figure of $2 billion might be a reasonable guess, of which the Tenghiz oil project in Kazakhstan might account for around $1 billion.

There has been a discernible trend away from big exploration and production projects requiring substantial up-front capital investments. Smaller projects involving refurbishment and enhanced recovery, as well as study/cooperation projects, are providing a low-risk learning experience for a considerable number of foreign investors. Many companies which showed a preference for investing in the Caucasus and Central Asia, as opposed to Russia, have discovered that political instability and problems of oil and gas transportation to hard-currency markets are major complicating factors. It is clear that those who decide to make an investment in the former Soviet Union (FSU) must be prepared to put up with political, legal and fiscal uncertainty and instability for an indefinite period.

In 1994, oil from joint ventures accounted for only 4 percent of total Russian production. While it is possible that foreign investments could yield up to 50 million tons of additional annual Russian production in the period up to 2000, the actual figure may be rather lower. In the context of the dramatic fall in annual Russian oil production by more than 250 million tons since 1988, this seems like a major disappointment. It should not be seen in this way. The role of foreign investment has been remorselessly "hyped" by governments and press alike, in both the former Soviet Union and the OECD countries. The reality is that there are no "quick fixes." While foreign investment can make a contribution, the institutional chaos in Russia which lies at the heart of most of the problems can only be addressed by the Russian government and oil industry.

In this situation, the biggest danger (especially in Russia) is mutual disillusion—Russians believing that foreign investors are simply not serious, and investors believing that the Russians are incapable of getting their political and economic act together. Looking ahead, a large number of small ventures in Russia and other CIS states will undoubtedly succeed. However, there will be only a very small number of multibillion-dollar investments over the next decade, and these are as likely, possibly more likely, to involve natural gas as oil.

Gas and Oil Fields in the Former Soviet Union

Arctic Ocean

East Siberia

Yakutia Fields

Sakhalin
Island

Khabarovsk ●

● Nakhodka

Sea of Japan

Mongolia

China

0   400   800 Kilometres   ▲ Gas Fields

0   400   800 Miles   ■ Oil Fields

CHAPTER ONE

Introduction to Part One

The aim of this paper is to provide some thoughts for the agenda of foreign investors who are considering the opportunities in the oil and gas industries of the former USSR, and the impact that such investments may have over the next few years.

The theme of the paper evolved from conversations which revealed that—despite the availability of large amounts of data and analytical material from a range of studies by academics, multilateral lending agencies and consultants—those in the corporate sector responsible for Russia and other CIS countries remain profoundly uncertain as to how to advise their top management on the potential risks and rewards of oil and gas investment opportunities in the region.

The corporate issue of whether a company should be "doing something" in a country where the political and economic uncertainties are considerable is not new. The unique feature of the former Soviet Union is that the potential opportunities which present themselves to investors are of a magnitude unlikely to be matched anywhere else in the world.

—Upstream: this is perhaps the final opportunity for companies to acquire a stake in one of the world's remaining undeveloped "super-giant" gas fields, and to discover and develop oil fields which, while not in the "super-giant" category, would make headlines anywhere else in the world.

—Downstream: privatization may provide an opportunity to purchase a stake in one of the world's biggest energy markets—a market which may grow enormously following the marketization of the economy.

—Service contracts and refurbishment: these services may allow an investor access to a share of additional oil and gas deliveries, or a share of oil and gas saved as a result of conservation/efficiency measures.

However, despite the lure of massive reserves, major markets and access to significant volumes of oil and gas, a huge question mark remains over the advisability of any such investments

—in a region undergoing fundamental economic and political change and racked by instability;

—where, to add to the uncertainty, the end-product may have to be transported across several countries in the region;

—when conventional wisdom suggests that oil prices will not rise appreciably in real terms over the next five to ten years.

Even supposing a company has several billion dollars to invest, is it wise to place them in a region undergoing such fundamental changes, however big the promise? And if this is not the time to invest, then will next year, or the year after, be better, and, if so, why?

This paper does not pretend to provide definitive answers to these questions. The intention is to provide a perspective which will continue to retain some validity in a complex and fast-moving situation.

Systemic change

By the beginning of 1995, the degree of macroeconomic decline and political instability in Russia (and many other former Soviet republics) had become so great that they dwarfed the problems of any one individual industrial sector—even ones as important as oil and gas. It would indeed have been possible to concentrate a very large part of this paper on problems of political stability, central-regional-local political relationships, economic reform (including price reform) and industrial restructuring. I have chosen not to devote a great deal of space to these issues (which are, it should be said, all treated at length in the companion volumes to this), but simply to sketch them in as background in the context of the future of the oil and gas industries. The paper is thus focused specifically on the problems, prospects and investment opportunities in these industries, rather than on systemic change. The danger of this approach is that, if the political and economic situation continues to worsen, the perceptions of foreign investors may become increasingly dominated by systemic problems rather than the opportunities which the oil and gas industries may have to offer. By taking this risk, however, we are able to focus quite clearly on key sectoral issues.

Geographical coverage and terminology

As far as geographical terminology and coverage are concerned, the breakup of the Soviet Union has left energy analysts (among others) trying to make sense of a region which, with the emergence of fifteen sovereign states, can less and less be treated as a single entity. Each of the former republics requires separate analysis with regard to its political and economic outlook, resource endowment and geographical location in respect of current and potential energy flows. A combination of these (and a range of other) factors will inevitably lead to different conclusions about the future energy options of, and foreign investment opportunities in, each of the new states of the FSU.

The present work does not pretend to be more than a minor building block in a monumental undertaking. The aim is to provide a backdrop for one specific aspect of a very complex picture, rather than to attempt any kind of comprehensive coverage. The first two chapters use the former Soviet Union as a reference point for a brief historical overview as well as a discussion of the current and future energy outlook. Thereafter, the paper focuses principally on Russia, in its discussion of potential foreign investment opportunities. Mention is made of Central Asia (Kazakhstan, Uzbekistan and Turkmenistan) and also of the Caucasus (Azerbaijan, Georgia and Armenia) and Ukraine. These states encompass the principal current and potential production locations for oil and gas, as well as the principal transit routes for exports of hydrocarbon fuels to Europe. While this author is not impressed by the current or likely future institutional relevance of the Commonwealth of Independent States, the term CIS is used in the paper to provide some relief from the clumsy formulation "former Soviet Union."[1]

---

1. The CIS excludes the Baltic states, and for many purposes Azerbaijan.

CHAPTER TWO

Oil and Gas and the Overall Energy Outlook

So many "disaster stories" have been written about the oil and gas industries of the former Soviet Union that it is easy to forget that these were among the most successful industrial sectors of the final two decades of the Union's existence, albeit in the context of a relatively unsuccessful economy. Indeed the oil and gas industries were crucial for the ability of the Soviet economy to continue to industrialize, and to purchase the equipment and technology it needed from world markets. There is every indication that these industries are likely to play a similar role in the post-Soviet era. It is absolutely essential at the outset, however, to make a sharp distinction between the two industries. For despite their evident interrelationship, the future prospects of the oil and gas industries are as different as their past performance.

The oil industry

Soviet oil production grew steadily in the 1960s and 1970s, only beginning to show signs of a slowdown in the latter part of that period.[1] In the late 1970s, accordingly, there was a major controversy in Western academic and govern-

---

1. For the background to this situation and some of the details of the controversy in Western literature, see Marshall I. Goldman, *The Enigma of Soviet Petroleum: Half-Empty or Half-Full?* (George Allen and Unwin, 1980), Leslie Dienes and Theodore Shabad, *The Soviet Energy System* (V. H. Winston, 1979); Ed A. Hewett, *Energy Economics and Foreign Policy in the Soviet Union* (Brookings, 1984); Thane Gustafson, *Crisis Amid Plenty: The Politics of Soviet Energy under Brezhnev and Gorbachev* (Princeton University Press, 1990).

Table 2-1. *Crude Oil and Condensate Production in the Former Soviet Union, 1988–94*

Republic	1988	1990	1991	1992	1993	1994
Russia	568.8	516.2	461.2	394.6	339.9	317[a]
Western Siberia	418.5	378.9	339.3	276.8	233.8	...
Volga-Urals	115.6	104.8	99.1	92.5	84.3	...
Komi	22.8	19.0	17.1	16.5	15.4	...
North Caucasus	7.9	7.2	6.7	6.2	4.5	...
Kaliningrad	1.5	1.4	1.2	1.0	0.7	...
Sakhalin	2.5	2.0	1.8	1.7	1.2	...
Ukraine	5.4	5.2	4.9	4.4	4.1	...
Belarus	1.9	2.0	2.1	1.9	1.8	...
Central Asia	34.7	33.4	35.0	35.2	32.6	...
Turkmenistan	5.8	5.6	5.4	5.2	5.1	...
Uzbekistan	2.4	2.8	2.8	2.8	3.3	...
Kazakhstan	25.5	25.8	26.6	27.2	24.2	...
Azerbaijan	13.7	12.5	11.7	11.1	10.3	...
Georgia	0.2	0.1	0.1	...[b]	...[b]	
Total FSU	624.2	569.3	514.8	448.7	392.9	

Source: 1988–93 figures from David Cameron Wilson, *CIS and East European Energy Databook,* Eastern Bloc Research: 1994.

a. Estimated; different assumptions about joint venture production have produced an alternative estimate of 309 million tons.

b. Negligible.

ment writings concerning the future of Soviet oil production and exports. The actual outcome during the 1980s was relatively unspectacular: production increased slowly, dipped around mid-decade, and increased to a peak of 624 million tons in 1987–88.

SUPPLY, DEMAND, AND TRADE. Tables 2-1 and 2-2 give some basic data on oil production and exports in the former Soviet Union during the period 1988–93. At the beginning of the 1990s production went into a tailspin as the crisis affecting the entire country engulfed an industry which was already experiencing severe problems. Export performance in the 1980s was spectacular and largely unexpected: the steady increase in Soviet oil exports was temporarily halted in 1985, but instead of the expected ensuing decline, volumes surged again to a peak of more than 200 million tons in 1988. But they dropped sharply thereafter as the production decline began in earnest. In 1993, oil production in the former Soviet Union fell to 393 million tons, more than

Table 2-2. *Crude Oil Product Exports from the Former Soviet Union,*
1988–93

Million tons

Year	Export	OECD	Eastern Europe	LDCs	Total
1988					
	Crude	55.34	72.07	16.79	144.20
	Products	42.89	5.34	12.76	60.99
	Total	98.23	77.41	29.55	205.19
1990					
	Crude	55.34	39.27	13.94	108.55
	Products	35.92	4.13	9.94	49.99
	Total	91.26	43.40	23.88	158.54
1991					
	Crude	36.9	18.2	5.4	60.5
	Products	38.3	2.3	3.3	43.9
	Total	75.2	20.5	8.7	104.4
1992					
	Crude	46.1	20.7	5.3	73.1
	Products	30.4	1.8	1.7	33.9
	Total	76.5	22.5	7.0	107.0
1993					
	Crude	53.5	23.8	5.1	82.4
	Products	35.1	1.6	1.1	37.8
	Total	88.6	25.4	6.2	120.2

Source: Eastern Bloc Energy, August 1992, p. 18; January 1995, p. 22.

30 percent below the peak reached in 1988. Exports declined to just over 100
million tons, around one half of their 1988 total.[2]

Table 2-1 shows the dominance of Russia in the oil industry of the former
USSR. Virtually all former Soviet production comes from Russia and Central
Asia–Kazakhstan. Within Russia the importance of Siberia is clearly evident,
as is the continuing role of the Volga-Urals region—although the latter has
been in long-term decline as a major producing area.

As far as exports are concerned, Russia is once again overwhelmingly
dominant, with just a few million tons of crude oil and products reaching the
world market from Kazakhstan. Thus other former Soviet republics are heavily dependent on Russia for oil supplies, while Russia is dependent upon other
former republics for equipment (deliveries in support of the industry), refin-

2. So many rival statistics are now being published that it is difficult to know which sources to
believe. Even "official" figures are no longer consistent, with the principal problems being how to
deal with joint venture oil production and exports. Many claim that production and exports are
substantially higher than apparent, and that official figures do not take illegal "leakage" sales of
oil into account.

ing, and transit to export outlets. The commercial ramifications of this interdependence—particularly regarding transit to export outlets versus sales to former republics—have become extremely complex. In the case of oil, this is particularly important for the Baltic countries, Ukraine and Azerbaijan. How to resolve these issues—which parties should pay what level of prices and in what currency, what leverage each party can exert if satisfactory payment is not forthcoming—represents a crucial problem in the economic relations between Russia and the other former Soviet states. The Intergovernmental Council on Oil and Gas, established at a CIS Conference in Surgut in March 1993, seems to have been of limited significance in this respect.[3] In any event, the other republics are facing major cutbacks in Russian crude oil (and oil products) deliveries, with 1994 volumes less than one-third of those received in the final year of the Union's existence (see table 2-4).

Table 2-2 shows the pattern by geographical destination of FSU oil exports to world markets since the peak in 1988. It is immediately evident that Eastern Europe and developing countries have borne the brunt of the rapid decline, their shares of the total falling from 38 percent and 14 percent in 1988 to 21 percent and 7 percent respectively in 1992. This clearly demonstrates the evaporation of the Soviet political and strategic imperative of maintaining intra-CMEA relationships, and the primacy of hard-currency payments in determining contemporary export markets. While by 1993 the picture appeared to have stabilized with regard to total oil exports, product exports continued to decline in that year, with crude sales increasing to compensate.

The demand side of the former Soviet energy balance has always been extremely difficult to evaluate, with a lack of data on end-market sectors and a general reliance on "apparent consumption" figures.[4] On this basis, table 2-3 shows that Soviet oil consumption peaked in 1986 and declined slowly until 1991, only moving down sharply in 1992 as Russia sought to maintain exports to world markets, and the other former Soviet republics were forced to bear the brunt of the whole of the production decline.

Table 2-4 attempts to chart the development of Russian oil demand during the period 1985–94—a task which requires a number of tricky assumptions. Some allowance needs to be made both for inaccuracy of statistics, especially

3. Of the fifteen former Soviet republics only Latvia and Turkmenistan did not attend the conference. *BBC Summary of World Broadcasts*, Part 1, Former Soviet Union (henceforth *SWB*), SU/WO271 A17-19, 5 March 1993. See also Chrystia Freeland, John Lloyd, "Tensions Hinder Oil Deal with Russia," and Deborah Hargreaves, "Uniform CIS Pipeline Rules Urged," *Financial Times*, 2 March 1993; 9 March 1993.

4. For an analysis which attempted to go further than this see David Wilson, *The Demand for Energy in the Soviet Union* (London: Croom Helm, 1983).

Table 2-3. *Oil Production, Trade and Demand in the Former, 1985–92 Soviet Union*

Million tons

Category	1985	1986	1987	1988	1989	1990	1991	1992
Production	595	615	624	624	607	570	515	449
Exports	167	186	196	205	184	159	104	107
Imports	14	17	16	22	15	11	10[a]	10[a]
Apparent Consumption	442	446	444	441	438	422	401	332

Sources: 1985–90, Alan Smith, *Russia and the World Economy* (Routledge, 1993), table 8.2, p. 181. 1991–92 figures from tables 2-1 and 2-2.

a. Estimate.

on deliveries to former Soviet republics, and on stock changes from year to year. In general the data probably understate actual demand; for example the Fuels and Energy Minister Shafranik gives a 1992 Russian oil demand figure of 240 million tons.[5] The 1985 data may not be comparable with the later figures since they are drawn from a different source; an intuitive estimate for 1985 would give a figure of around 250 million tons or even higher. Nevertheless, the overall conclusion is clear: Russian oil demand certainly did not fall appreciably in the period 1985–91, and may indeed have risen slightly. Demand appeared to decline by around 10 percent during 1992. Thus domestic oil consumption did not respond to the collapse of Russian industrial production to the extent that would have been expected. Shafranik notes that the 20 percent industrial decline in 1992 produced a decline in industrial energy demand of only 6-7 percent.[6]

For Russia, 1993 provided the acid test for oil demand. With production falling to 340 million tons, exports to world markets could not have been sustained without a major drop in demand. In the event, demand declined by more than 20 percent and this was followed in 1994 by another fall of more than 10 percent. However, exports to world markets were also sustained by huge falls in exports to former Soviet republics, which have dropped to one-third of the level seen at the close of the Soviet era.

PROBLEMS AND PROSPECTS. The problems of the oil industry are relatively well known and will merely be outlined here. Prior to the political and economic crisis of the former USSR, it was already well known that the costs of the industry were increasing rapidly, owing to exhaustion of the more easily

5. *SWB*, SU/W0271 A/17, 5 March 1993.
6. Ibid., SU/W072 A/16, 12 March 1993.

Table 2-4. *Russian Oil Balance, 1985–92*

Category	1985	1990	1991	1992	1993[a]	1994[b]
Production	542	516	461	395	340	317
Exports	356	294	230	186	175	169
Rest of world (ROW)	157[c]	133	91	91	113	126
crude		100	56	66	78	88
products		33	35	25	35	38
FSU	199	161	147	95	62	43
crude		123	119	76	48	39
products		39	28	19	14	6
Imports	28	30	28	26	20	20
ROW (re-exports)	14	11	10[b]	10[b]	10[b]	10
FSU[d]	14	19	18	16	10	10
Demand	214	238	244	233	185	168

Sources: 1990–93 FSU figures from *Eastern Bloc Energy*, January 1993, p. 16. 1990–93 rest of world figures from David Cameron Wilson, *CIS and East European Energy Databook*, Eastern Bloc Research (1993), table 126, p. 32. 1985 figures from *Materialno-Tekhnicheskoe Obespechenie Narodnogo Khozyaistva SSSR* (Moscow: Goskomstat, 1988), p. 145.
a. Official projections.
b. Estimate.
c. 6 million tons hard currency export from Kazakhstan assumed.
d. From Kazakhstan.

accessible resource base, particularly that portion located in relatively large fields. According to Bykov, although the former USSR has 2,314 oil fields which have been explored, only 83 (19 giant and 63 large fields) account for 72 percent of production and 62 percent of remaining explored reserves.[7] The future of the industry is dependent upon bringing into production a relatively large number of smaller fields in regions with minimal infrastructure. Poor oil field practice (principally overrapid exploitation of the resource base, to the detriment of future recovery factors) and a lack of advanced technology (mainly for secondary and tertiary recovery) have hampered the industry's ability to maximize production from maturing oil provinces.[8] Inability to retain labor in Siberia because of poor living conditions, and complete disregard

7. V. F. Bykov, "The Resource Base of Russia's Oil Industry," *Oil and Gas Russia, Central Asia and the Caucasus*, (henceforth *OGR*) vol. 2, no. 1, Spring 1993, pp. 18–23.

8. The most common issue cited here is the use of water flooding of deposits at an early stage of development. Bykov notes that in Tyumen the water cut rose from 48 percent in 1985 to 78 percent in 1991 and will rise to 83 percent in 1995. There have been major disagreements between Soviet specialists on the benefits of water flooding. For a general discussion of Soviet oilfield practice see Gustafson, *Crisis Amid Plenty*, chapters 3 and 4.

for environmental devastation (particularly in Siberia) have also been significant issues, which have led to major complications for the development of the
industry.

These problems were inevitably compounded by the economic and political fragmentation of the former Union, which caused severe disruption of materials and equipment supply to the Russian industry, particularly for the
maintenance and servicing of wells and pipelines. This situation was graphically outlined by the vice-president of Rosneftegaz in February 1993. In Russia, he said, "we have 2,000 fields. One thousand of these are being exploited. . . . Those which are operational we are exploiting to the extent of
about 67 percent. 12 percent of those which have been opened up are lying
fallow and about another 10–12 percent are ticking over but only just. . . . In
1988 there were 7,000 abandoned oil wells. There are now 32,000."[9]

Low morale caused by inadequate incentives to work in the more isolated
regions, against a background of erratic wage payments and a lack of basic infrastructure, have also played their part in the accelerating decline of production. Technical opinion is divided as to whether the very large number of idle
wells could be restarted and could produce significant quantities of oil on a
sustained basis. Some believe that as much as 50 million tons per year could
be produced from these wells; others think that, having been shut down for a
protracted period, they are worthless as far as sustained future production is
concerned.

An important issue for future students of the Russian and former Soviet oil
industry will be whether the sharp production decline was inevitable, even if
there had been no general domestic upheaval. An answer to this question
would give us a clue as to whether the decline can be, at least partially, reversed, if and when the political and economic situation begins to stabilize. It
is certainly clear that in the years since 1990 the collapse of central investment
allocation has been principally responsible for the speed of production decline. Leshchinets notes that capital investment in 1992 amounted to 7 billion
rubles (in 1988 prices), compared with twice that figure in 1988. He refers to
1992 as "a lost year."[10] On the other hand, simply throwing increasing investment at the industry is not the answer, even if sufficient resources were to become available. The pattern of the 1980s, with vast increases in investment in

9. Ilya Leshchinets, "Capital Requirements—Domestic and Foreign Dimensions," in *The
Russian Oil Industry: Foreign Investment Opportunities*, 2d Annual Russian Oil Conference, 11-
12 February 1992. Proceedings available from the Royal Institute of International Affairs, London.
10. Ibid.

the industry yielding smaller and smaller returns in the form of increased production, are only too well documented.[11]

Many different figures are quoted in the Western press for the investment requirements of the Russian oil industry, of which "$4–5 billion per year needed just to stabilize production" and "$30 billion over a five-year period" are the most common. Such statistics are probably meaningless in aggregate unless applied to a specific production program. Leshchinets has given the following statistics for programs considered by the Russian government:

> The idea they put forward was that in 1993 we would produce 350 million tons, in 1994 330 million tons, in 1995 320 million tons. Then we would gradually go up again until the year 2000, when we would get back to 350 million tons. On the basis of this . . . there would be about 76,000 wells in operation, including 30,000 which would be brought on line in 1993. Of course the necessary . . . finance [and] . . . the necessary equipment has not been found . . . [and] we are not going to be able to carry out this plan. So there is an alternative plan, a more modest one . . . that . . . over the next three years we should bring on line about 40,000 wells, including 15,000 in 1993. The idea was that 160 new fields would be opened up, including 47 in 1993, 53 in 1994 and 60 in 1995. [This] amount of drilling [and] opening up of new fields . . . meant that 50 billion rubles in 1984 prices ($75 billion at the exchange rate for that year) would be spent on . . . investment. [12]

It goes without saying that even that amount of investment is likely to be beyond the means of the industry in the short term. Nevertheless, by the end of 1994, it seemed that the stabilization of Russian oil production could be in sight, with the previous six months of deliveries having matched the 1993 figures. It remains to be seen whether this is a real stabilization or a false dawn, but in any event the seemingly relentless slide appears to have slowed dramatically.

The natural gas industry

Soviet natural gas production grew strongly and steadily throughout the period 1970–90, more than doubling from 198 billion cubic meters in 1970 to 435 billion cubic meters in 1980, and nearly doubling again to 815 billion cubic meters in 1990.[13]

11. Gustafson, *Crisis Amid Plenty.*
12. Leshchinets, *Capital Requirements.*
13. All figures in this section are Russian cubic metres measured at 20 degrees Celsius. In order to convert to standard European cubic metres (9,500 Kcal) the figures need to be multiplied by 0.935.

Table 2-5. *Natural Gas Production in the Former Soviet Union, 1988–94*
Billion cubic meters[a]

Republic		1988	1990	1991	1992	1993	1994[b]
Russia		589.8	636.7	642.9	640.4	617.7	607.8
	Siberia	514.0	562.2	571.7	583.4	573.7	...
	Volga-Urals	52.3	54.1	52.9	40.6	30.3	...
	Komi	15.6	14.2	13.1	11.5	9.4	...
	North Caucasus	7.9	6.2	5.2	4.9	4.3	...
Ukraine		32.4	28.7	26.2	22.7	20.2	...
Central Asia		135.6	139.4	134.3	104.8	122.5	...
	Turkmenistan	88.3	89.1	84.3	57.2	67.5	...
	Uzbekistan	39.9	43.0	41.9	39.5	40.4	...
	Kazakhstan	7.1	7.0	7.9	8.0	7.6	...
Azerbaijan		11.0	9.3	8.0	8.0	6.9	...
Belarus		0.3	0.2	0.2	0.1	0.1	...
Total CIS		769.7	815.5	810.5	788.0	760.9	...

Source: 1988–93 figures from David Cameron Wilson, *CIS and East European Energy Databook*, Eastern Bloc Research, 1994.
a. Soviet billion cubic metres measured at 20 degrees Celsius. To convert to European standard cubic meters, multiply by 0.935.
b. Estimated.

SUPPLY, DEMAND, AND TRADE. The program of pipeline building connecting Siberia to the western part of the USSR, including the export pipelines, permitted huge annual production increases of the order of 30–40 billion cubic meters in the 1970s and early 1980s. While production increases slowed in the late 1980s, it was not until the first quarter of 1991 that a minimal decline in total Union output became apparent. While gas production in 1994 had declined by 5.6 percent in comparison to its peak in 1991, it is clear that this is due primarily to a lack of demand for gas, rather than to problems in the industry.

As table 2-5 shows, the former USSR was rather less dependent on Russia for gas than for oil. Nearly 20 percent of former Soviet gas is produced in Central Asia: Uzbekistan and Turkmenistan are currently predominant, but there are expectations of Kazakhstan, where large reserves have been located. On the other hand, Russian gas production has barely faltered, in contrast to some Central Asian countries, notably Turkmenistan. The fall in 1992 production levels in that republic was mainly due to an organizational dispute with Gazprom of Russia and a price dispute with Ukraine which severely curtailed gas deliveries (see chapter 4). Turkmen production recovered significantly in 1993, but fell again in 1994, probably below the 1992 level.

Natural gas exports (table 2-6) have also maintained a relatively stable pattern of increase over the past two decades, rising from only 3 billion cubic meters in 1970 to 57 billion cubic meters in 1980 and 109 billion cubic meters a

Table 2-6. *Natural Gas Exports from the Former Soviet Union, 1970–93*

Billion cubic meters[a]

Country	1970	1975	1980	1985	1990	1993
Austria	1.0	1.9	2.9	4.2	5.1	5.3
Germany	...	3.1	10.7	12.4	26.6	25.8
Italy	...	2.3	7.0	6.0	14.3	13.8
France	...	...	4.0	6.8	10.6	11.6
Finland	...	0.7	0.9	1.0	2.7	3.1
Turkey	...	...	...	...	3.3	5.0
Switzerland	...	0.3	0.4	...	0.3	0.4
Total	1.0	8.0	25.5	30.4	63.0	65.0
Eastern Europe	2.3	11.3	30.4	34.7	41.5	35.9
Former Yugoslavia	...	2.1	3.6	4.5	4.5	2.7
Grand Total	3.3	19.3	58.0	68.7	109.0	100.9

Sources: 1970–80: Jonathan P. Stern, *International Gas Trade in Europe* (Heinemann/RIIA: 1984), table 2.4, p. 65; 1985–90: *Vneshnyaya Torgovlya SSSR*; 1993 figures from Gazexport.

a. Estimate.

decade later. The stability in deliveries to Western Europe stems from the fact that gas has traditionally been traded on long-term (twenty- to twenty-five-year) contracts, and deliveries are, within limits, predictable. This has not been the case with deliveries to Central and Eastern Europe. With the disengagement of the former Warsaw Pact countries from the USSR, and the breakdown of the CMEA trading area, it emerged that the bulk of the gas sold to Eastern Europe was traded on annual contracts and that the USSR was reluctant to sign new long-term agreements with these countries.[14] For the former CMEA countries, the only remaining long-term contracts are those specified under the Yamburg treaty in return for work carried out in the former Soviet Union on pipelines and other gas installations. These agreements allow for a total of 25 billion cubic meters per year to be delivered to East European countries. But the contracts expire in 1998.[15]

Intra-CIS gas deliveries follow complicated patterns which make exact quantification difficult. In broad terms, Russia supplies gas to Ukraine, Belarus and Moldova, while Turkmenistan supplies other Central Asian states,

14. For a useful East European overview see Rudolf Safoshnik, *Gas Supplies to Poland, Hungary, Czechoslovakia, Romania and Bulgaria*, a paper to the Conference, "Transmission and Distribution of Gas in Emerging Markets of Central and Eastern Europe," London, 26-27 October 1992.

15. The figure of 25 billion cubic meters is the total commitment to Hungary, the Czech Republic, Slovakia, Poland, Romania and Bulgaria. In addition, there may be long-term commitments of up to 10 billion cubic meters per year to the former Yugoslavia. But with the breakup of that country the status of such commitments is uncertain.

Table 2-7. *Natural Gas Deliveries from Russia and Turkmenistan to Fsu and the Rest of the World (ROW), 1985–94*

Billion cubic meters[a]

	Russia		Turkmenistan		total
Year	fsu[b]	ROW	FSU	ROW	ROW
1985	151	...	74	...	69
1990	92	83	55	26	109
1991	90	90	54	14	104
1992	106	88	38	11	99
1993	79	90	46	11	101
1994[c]	78	101	45	...	101

Sources: 1985: *Materialno-Tekhnicheskoe Obespechenie Narodnogo Khozyaistva SSSR* (Moscow: GOSKOMSTAT, 1988), p.145., as table 3; 1990–91. *Ekonomika i Zhizn'*, no. 13 (March 1992). 1992–93, *BBC Summary of World Broadcasts*, SU/W0272 (March 12, 1993), p. A/9.
   a. Russian cubic meters (see table 2-5 for definition).
   b. Gross deliveries, not counting imports from Turkmenistan and other Central Asia Republics.
   c. Estimate.

the Caucasus and Ukraine, as well as parts of southern Russia. Following the breakup of the USSR, contractual relationships—in terms of volume, price and transit fees—immediately became a critical issue. Attempts to resolve these problems, particularly with regard to Russia and Ukraine and Turkmenistan and Ukraine, continue to dominate intra-CIS gas commerce, and have important ramifications for exports to Europe (see chapter 4). During the Soviet era, there was an agreement between Russia and Turkmenistan whereby the latter received a "quota" of the export trade to Europe, and this is shown in table 2-7.[16] The details of this arrangement have always been sketchy, and it appears to have been completely abandoned in 1994. However, information at the beginning of 1995 suggested a significant increase in Turkmen sales to Russia, which may suggest a revival of the hard-currency quota.

PROBLEMS AND PROSPECTS. In marked contrast to the situation in the oil industry, the problems facing the Russian natural gas industry are relatively straightforward. The resource base is well established, with some of the largest fields in the world located in northwestern Siberia, on the Yamal and Taz peninsulas, and offshore in the Barents Sea. While there are doubts about the commercial viability of opening up new fields at the international prices prevailing in the 1990s, the potential availability of gas is not in question. The

16. Whether actual Turkmen gas is received in Europe or whether the entire volume is consumed in Ukraine and Russia is not known. However, since all of the contractual arrangements with European customers are with the Russian Gazprom (specifically with its subsidiary Gazexport, formerly Soyuzgazexport), the latter has complete flexibility in its operations.

key issue for the gas industry is the condition of the pipeline (and related) infrastructure. This is a major subject in its own right, and we merely summarize the issues here:[17]

— many of the earliest pipelines built in the 1970s were inadequately protected against corrosion;

— many 1980s pipelines suffered from being built in haste;

— Russian compressor stations used on these pipelines can be unreliable and inefficient;

— there have been severe problems of under-investment in maintenance and servicing of the pipeline infrastructure since 1990 (in part because of lack of spare parts).

As a result of incidents well-publicized in the Western press, the Russian-CIS pipeline system has gained an international reputation for major and frequent breakdown, and leakage on a huge scale. The extent to which this reputation is deserved is not easy to determine. The continued extraordinary success of the industry in maintaining production levels amidst the chaos that surrounds it indicates that many of the apocalyptic stories circulating in Western industry circles must be apocryphal.[18] However, the evident lack of investment in the transmission system leads to the inevitable conclusion that deterioration must be taking place, and that this will lead to a loss of capability to maintain the flow of gas. In 1992, Gazprom began to take major steps to remedy this situation with a program of equipment imports said to cost a total of $8.7 billion.[19]

It is interesting that Soviet/Russian decisionmakers have continued to give investment priority to the opening up of new production capacity. While, as noted above, ample resources are available, the location of the major new fields—especially those on the Yamal Peninsula and offshore in the Barents and Kara Seas—means that they will require very significant investments, of the order of $10–15 billion, for a 56-inch pipeline to carry some 30–35 billion cubic meters annually to the west of the country. Recent indications from Gazprom suggest greater interest in developing smaller satellite fields in the

17. A detailed analysis of pipeline failure in the recent period can be found in O.M. Ivantsov, "Reliability of Northern Gas Pipelines," *OGR*, vol. 2, no. 1 (Spring 1993), pp. 51–58.

18. For example, the remark attributed to the energy policy director of the European Bank for Reconstruction and Development that 15 percent of Russian production leaks from the network. *Financial Times Energy Economist*, April 1993, p. 27.

19. In some accounts, this amount of investment is required just to refurbish existing infrastructure, in others it also covers the opening up of new fields. See, for example, "Hottest Game in Town," *Russian Petroleum Investor*, February 1993, pp. 32–33.

Urengoy region, which could utilize existing pipeline infrastructure as production from the larger fields declines in the late 1990s.[20]

While this appears more realistic—and certainly economically more attractive—than development of new multitrillion cubic-meter fields, there seems to be a continued assumption that gas production will, and should, continue to increase. There is still little serious discussion of the merits of conservation and efficiency improvements as opposed to investment in additional production. It has in the past been extremely difficult for Gazprom decisionmakers even to entertain the possibility that demand may decline, but with the 1992–94 period witnessing an accelerating fall in demand, attitudes have now begun to change. The period since 1992 has also seen an enormous increase in nonpayment of bills—a problem affecting more than half the gas delivered to Russian customers in 1994. As debts began to spiral out of control, so the political issue of disconnection began to loom large. In this context, it has become increasingly important that major government decisionmakers should develop some degree of "demand orientation"—particularly difficult for people whose formative experience has been in the supply-driven world of the centrally planned economy.

Organizational and administrative issues

The contrast in performance records between the oil and gas industries of the former Soviet Union over the past decade, and particularly since 1987, has been remarkable. The oil sector was in some difficulty prior to the present period of political and economic upheaval, which has added new problems and greatly exacerbated the difficulties it was already facing. The gas sector was the most successful industrial sector of the past two decades of the existence of the Soviet Union and, despite intensifying infrastructural problems, continues to defy the current industrial trend of plunging production levels.

Some part of this difference may be attributed to the contrasting organizational and administrative structures of the two industries. Even before the breakup of the USSR, the demise of the respective Soviet ministries for the different industries (and the abortive attempt to combine them in a single ministry) generated an increasingly chaotic structure. Since that time, the structure

20. Specifically: Zapolyarnoe, Komsomol, West Tarkalinskoe and Yubileinoe. See A. D. Sedykh, "The Gas Industry of the Commonwealth of Independent States (CIS)," *OGR*, vol. 2, no. 1 (Spring 1993), pp. 59–68.

of the Russian oil sector has become more and more confused and fragmented. The decree on the privatization of the Russian oil industry indicates
that in November 1992 the industry comprised three different types of organizations[21]—259 enterprises involved in production, refining and distribution;
three integrated companies (Lukoil, Yukos and Surgutneftegaz); and two
transportation companies for crude oil and oil products (Transneft' and
Transnefteprodukt).[22] By 1995 other integrated oil companies had been created: Slavneft, Sidanko, Vostochnaya oil company (VOC) and Orenburg oil
company (ONAKO).

The institutional structure of oil exports—the most important single for-
eign-currency earning commodity for Russia—has become similarly chaotic.
Soyuznefteexport originally held a monopoly, and this organization has remained the dominant actor. Following the breakup of the USSR, it was re-
named Nafta-Moskva in 1992. Oil export sales became diversified, through oil
exchanges, trading companies, integrated oil companies, production associations and foreign joint ventures. The subsequent "leakage" of exports through
semiofficial, unofficial and criminal outlets, as exporters sought to avoid the
bureaucracy of export licenses and the imposition of export taxes, led the government to try to recentralize exports in order to control the volumes and col-
lect taxes.[23] This in turn created difficulties for current and potential joint ventures which had been negotiating terms under a previous (less onerous) tax
regime. By 1993, 80 percent of exports were once again centralized through
the mechanism of "state orders", leaving 10 percent for producers and refiners
to sell on their own account and 10 percent for regional governments. Thus although there were 30 registered crude exporters and 83 registered product exporters, "the state order" exports of crude was handled by four companies
alone (Konex, Rosvneshtorg, Nafta Moskva, and Lukoil) and those of products by just five (Urals, Rosvneshtorg, Rosnefteimpex, Nafta Moskva, and
Neftekhimexport). By 1995, the creation of the Russian Union of Oil Exporters, comprising eight principal companies and chaired by the Minister for

21. Decree No. 1403, 17 November 1992.
22. The full list of enterprises in the oil industry, including those composing Transneft' and
Transnefteprodukt, can be found in *Oil and Gas: Russia and the post-Soviet Republics*, Hydrocarbons Brief, Newsletter 8, 15 March 1993.
23. By 1995 the issue had narrowed to the question of the Russian government's oil export
quotas, which had incurred the wrath of the IMF and other multinational lending agencies. While
the Russian government remains nervous that deregulation will lead to a flood of exports and an
oil famine at home, international pressure finally secured abolition of the quotas—along with liberalization of domestic energy prices—in March of that year.

Foreign Economic Relations of the Russian Government, seemed to indicate a major recentralization of exports under government control.[24]

In complete contrast, the gas industry—in its present incarnation of Gazprom—broke away from the former Soviet Ministry of Oil and Gas and remained in complete control of production and transmission in the USSR until the end of 1991. Following the breakup of the Union, the Gazprom organizations in each of the former republics maintained a relatively strong degree of coordination—with the exception of Turkmengazprom, which declared its independence. In Russia, the decree on the privatization of the gas industry foresees Gazprom continuing as a centralized monopoly organization owning all eight production associations and thirteen regional transmission companies. Although the production associations and transmission companies have aspirations to create an independent existence for themselves, and regional authorities in Siberia are also keen to become directly involved in gas commerce, no serious challenge to Gazprom's authority was visible by the beginning of 1995.

Following a November 1992 decree, all of the gas distribution enterprises, formerly owned by Rosgazifikatsiya, became independent joint stock companies.[25] The two city gas companies Mosgaz and Lengaz—in Moscow and St Petersburg respectively—have remained independent, municipally owned companies. Exports are controlled by Gazprom through its export division Gazexport (formerly Soyuzgazexport, which it inherited from the Ministry of Foreign Economic Relations). Since 1990, when Gazprom established a joint venture with the German company Wintershall—Wintershall Erdgas Handelshaus (WIEH)—Gazprom has established joint venture marketing companies in all the countries to which gas is exported (see chapter 4).

In summary, after the breakup of the Union, the oil industry fragmented as a result both of the breakdown of centralized authority, and of a deliberate attempt to move away from centralized planning and decisionmaking. Since 1993, there have been a series of measures seemingly aimed at recentralizing the industry under government control. By contrast, the gas industry maintained a centralized mode of organization, very little different from that of the Soviet period. It is relevant here to mention the role of Victor Chernomyrdin

24 The eight companies are: Lukoil, Nafta Moscow, MEC, Komi Tek, Konex, Alfar Eco, Balkar Trading, and Rosnefteimpex. A useful overview of the 1993 institutional change in oil export markets can be found in Stephen MacSearraigh, "Exporting from Russia: Rough Ride Ahead," *International Oil and Gas Technology*, vol. 1, issue 1, pp. 176–80.

25. *Privatization and Transformation of Enterprises, Associations and Organizations in the Gas Industry*, Decree No. 1559 of the President of the Russian Federation, 8 December 1992.

in the organizational future of the oil and gas sectors. Chernomyrdin was the Minister of the Gas Industry who made the bureaucratic power-play to set up an independent Gazprom—with evident success—and who was subsequently elevated to the position of deputy prime minister responsible for fuels and energy, prior to becoming prime minister.

At time of writing Chernomyrdin remains prime minister of Russia, and his views on the oil and gas industries (in which he has spent his entire career) are of some importance. While it would be too extreme to label Chernomyrdin "a centralizer" opposed to market forces, it would not be an overstatement to say that his elevation to high office owed much to a successful industrial career in the old, Soviet, centralized system. The decree on the privatization of Gazprom—which maintained the latter's structure and monopoly position—appeared to have Chernomyrdin's stamp upon it.[26] While the turnover of senior Russian political figures is likely to be relatively rapid for a number of years, two broad policy directions seem likely:

—Further attempts to recentralize the oil industry, perhaps by bringing the production associations into a relatively limited number of integrated oil companies, can be expected. The relatively tight central control on the gas industry is likely to continue.

—Falling demand and nonpayment problems (particularly in the gas industry) will have the effect of forcing a major shift of emphasis from supply-side to demand-side policy measures. However, because of political obstacles—principally the unemployment which is likely to result from closing bankrupt enterprises—progress is likely to be slow.

The overall energy context

Since most of the Western literature on the former Soviet energy balance concentrates on oil and gas (quite naturally in view of export potential and foreign investment interest), it is easy to overlook the other two supply industries—coal and primary electricity, particularly nuclear power. Indeed it is hard to avoid the conclusion that coal and nuclear power (even before the Chernobyl accident) constitute the real failure of the Soviet energy sector over the past two decades.

26. Since the special privatization did not conform to Russian legislation it needed to be endorsed by the Supreme Soviet. *SWB*, SU/WO256, A/8, 13 November 1992..

COAL. Soviet coal production recorded small but steady production increases until the first half of the 1980s, when a decline began to set in. Although this was reversed in the latter part of the decade and production hit a peak of 772 million tons in 1988, the industry has been severely affected by recent events, and production had declined by nearly 40 percent to 486 million tons by 1994.[27] The resource base is vast, in total and in terms of individual fields. The problems of the industry can be crudely divided into (a) older mines in poor condition and producing high-cost, deep-mined coal; and (b) newer mines—principally in Siberia and Central Asia—which are remote from centers of demand and which in many cases contain huge reserves of poor-quality lignite presenting very difficult characteristics for transportation and combustion. The strain on the railway network caused by moving increasing volumes of coal over long distances gave rise to intensive research into different options for coal/electricity transformation and transportation. In the 1970s and early 1980s the favored method appeared to be to build large-scale mine-mouth power stations generating power which would be carried to the west of the country via high-voltage, long-distance electricity transmission lines. As environmental issues began to move up the agenda, the effect of uncontrolled power station emissions on the fragile Siberian ecosystem added yet another negative element to the balance-sheet of such projects.

Both in Russia and in Ukraine, which account for nearly 80 percent of the coal produced in the FSU, the industry is likely to continue to decline, and governments are likely to encounter increasing problems from a recalcitrant work force which continues to imagine that its output is indispensable. The Russian minister of fuels and energy has called the situation in the coal industry "worse than in any other energy sector" and has produced the startling statistic that subsidies to the industry amount to 6 percent of the total Russian budget.[28] In 1994 the World Bank offered a package of loans which would have involved a huge closure program. While this was not accepted, the inevitability of major closures seems to have been acknowledged by all parties; it is the timing, and the issue of the social consequences of closure, remain to be resolved.

27. These are gross output figures. The net output figure is typically 7-10 percent lower. In addition, the calorific value of Soviet hard coal—which composes over three-quarters of total output—has declined significantly since 1980. David Cameron Wilson, *CIS and East European Energy Databook* (Eastern Bloc Research, 1993).

28. Gillian Tett, "The Fantasy-Land Economics of Russian Coal," *Financial Times*, 5 May 1993.

NUCLEAR POWER. The problems of the nuclear industry are probably greater than those of coal. It is ironic to recall that, prior to the Chernobyl accident, it was the graphite moderated (RBMK) stations, including Chernobyl, which had performed creditably—in terms both of speed of construction and reactor performance—in contrast to the pressurized water (VVER) reactors. In the aftermath of Chernobyl, a combination of public safety concern and pressure from international investigation teams resulted in both types of reactor being temporarily, or even (supposedly) permanently shut down; some of these received a reprieve when it was realized that it would be impossible to meet winter power demand without them. International efforts to raise large-scale finance in order to make essential repairs and modifications to existing stations have taken a very long time to get off the ground, and seem unlikely to be adequate to meet the requirements of the sector.[29]

The nuclear construction program ground to a halt, with little prospect of completion of partly constructed units, let alone commencement of new ones.[30] This was due in part to domestic and international pressures, but also to lack of investment and the chaotic political and economic situation, including huge problems of nonpayment. In fact, virtually all construction work on new power stations—nuclear and nonnuclear—appears to have stopped around 1990. In view of the continuing sharp decline in economic activity, this may not be a particularly serious problem. However, in December 1992 a presidential decree was issued, which anticipated the construction of more than 17 gigawatts of new nuclear capacity by 2010.[31] The Russian nuclear establishment continues to defend the safety record and the acceptability of its stations. The key conclusion regarding the coal and nuclear sectors is that any real upturn in their fortunes seems unlikely. Their problems appear greater, and the potential return on investment smaller, than for oil and natural gas.

LONGER-TERM ENERGY STRATEGIES AND THE CENTRALITY OF DEMAND. The 1994 *Russian Energy Strategy* breaks with past documents from the Soviet era, insofar as it makes a genuine attempt to come to terms with the imperative

29. Clive Cookson, "Russia, Ukraine in Reactor Pledge," and "West's Fears Delay Repairs to Reactors," *Financial Times*, 10 September 1992; 16 October 1992..

30. One exception to this trend was the final commissioning of the fourth unit of the Balakovo reactor in early 1993. *Eastern Bloc Energy*, April 1993, p. 8.

31. Although Deputy Minister Reshetnikov claims that the decree "does not deal with the construction of new nuclear power stations but with how to complete some existing stations using old plans," Western reports have details of the new stations and the timing of their commissioning. *SWB*, SU/WO266 A/14-15, 29 January 1993; *Eastern Bloc Energy*, March 1993, p. 9.

of reducing energy demand, as opposed to increasing supply. It remains very clear that this can only happen as macroeconomic policy and political will begin to make possible a greater degree of market-based pricing and closure of unproductive and inefficient enterprises. It still appears very difficult for Russians to understand that energy demand can genuinely fall, and that investment on this side of the energy balance will yield greater returns than supply investments. This is not, it must be added, particularly surprising, given that similar skepticism in many OECD market economies has curtailed energy conservation and efficiency programs in recent years to a fraction of their potential.

To summarize, there is good reason for believing that energy conservation and improved efficiency can make a very significant impact in Russia (and elsewhere in the CIS) during the 1990s as a result of a combination of:

— sharply reduced levels of economic activity and closures of industrial plants, with a likely concentration of plant closures in energy-intensive industries;
— modest investment in low-cost, low-technology conservation in all energy functions: production, transmission, distribution and end-use (mostly using existing plant and equipment);
— significant improvements in the efficiency of new plant being installed;
— modest energy conservation as a result of increased prices.

The quantification and timing of all of these elements is inevitably a matter of guesswork. Nevertheless, taken together, they may allow Russia to maintain its exports of oil at, and increase its exports of gas beyond, the levels achieved in 1994. This outcome is very much more certain in the gas industry than in oil. However, if sharp reductions in domestic oil demand can be maintained, and the decline in production has been halted, then the prospects for the oil industry should progressively improve.

CHAPTER THREE

Foreign Involvement and Investment Opportunities

Foreign involvement in oil and gas in the Soviet period was of two types. Exploration, production, transmission, and export projects, with American and Japanese companies, were universally unsuccessful. Many large-scale deliveries of equipment and "turnkey" project agreements, largely with European companies, were extremely successful.

The Soviet period

The Japanese initiatives date back to the mid-1960s, when proposals were made for Japanese companies to participate in developing oil resources in the Tyumen region, and oil and gas resources offshore Sakhalin. The Tyumen oil project foresaw 25–40 million tons of oil per year being piped to Nakhodka.[1] The Sakhalin oil and gas project (of which more below) proposed that oil and gas should be either piped or shipped to Japan on the basis of joint exploration of the deposits in the region.

The American initiatives were launched during the US-Soviet détente of the early 1970s and foresaw the possibility of two multibillion dollar liquefied natural gas (LNG) projects:

---

1. Jeremy Russell, *Energy as a Factor in Soviet Foreign Policy* (RIIA/Saxon House, 1976), chapter 11; Peter Egyed, *Western Participation in the Development of Siberian Energy Resources: Case Studies*, East-West Commercial Relations Series, Carleton University, Ottawa, Research Report, no. 22, December 1983.

— one taking gas from the Urengoy ("North Star") field to a liquefaction plant at Murmansk and thence by tanker to the United States;

— the other, involving cooperation with Japanese companies, pipelining gas from the Yakutia field to Nakhodka, where it would be liquefied and shipped to both Japan and the United States.[2]

These projects are principally of interest to historians of East-West relations and trade. With hindsight, they were doomed to failure because of the rapid deterioration in US-Soviet political relationships which followed the era of détente and continued in the aftermath of the Soviet invasion of Afghanistan and the arrival of the Reagan administration in the White House. As far as Japanese-Soviet relations were concerned, the failure to settle the Northern Territories issue, the generally poor climate of relations between the two countries (strongly influenced by the prevailing US-Soviet relationship), and the antipathy of many senior figures in Japanese utility companies to the Soviet Union, combined to restrict progress on these projects.

In fact, it seems unlikely, irrespective of the political situation, that (with the exception of Sakhalin oil and gas, which was to be exploited on a relatively small scale) any of these "mega-projects" requiring capital investments in the range of $3–10 billion (in money of the day) would have been economic when compared with alternative oil and gas supply projects, even when evaluated at the oil prices of the period 1973–86. With hindsight, it is clear that these projects appeared attractive to a small section of the energy business community that was seeking new sources of oil and gas, perhaps rather indiscriminately, at a time when the commodities in question were in short supply with rapidly increasing prices.

Central to the machinery and equipment programs of the Soviet period was the trade involving big deliveries of large-diameter pipe and compressor stations in exchange for natural gas imports. This was the mechanism that allowed Soviet natural gas exports to Western Europe to get under way. Complementarity was the key to success: European steel and engineering industries, perennially desperate for large-scale orders, found a near-perfect counterpart in a Soviet gas industry with huge potential surplus resources, but lacking the infrastructure to bring it to export markets. This is the basic reason why—for the past 30 years, despite frequent political problems and trade em-

2. Joseph T. Kosnik, *Natural Gas Imports from the Soviet Union: Financing the North Star Joint Venture Project* (New York: Praeger, 1975).

bargoes—gas has proved to be such a successful trading commodity.[3] The compelling logic, relative simplicity and long-term nature of the transactions were of considerable help in resisting pressure from politicians with shorter-term political agendas.

Two significant examples of equipment sales to the oil industry were the Dresser drill bit plant in 1978, which caused a furor on the US domestic political scene, and the gas reinjection program at the Samotlor oil field, for which the French company Technip supplied large amounts of equipment in the early 1980s.[4] The Dresser plant undoubtedly assisted the Soviet drilling effort (the extent of this assistance was debated endlessly in Washington), but the gas reinjection program was rather less successful. Delays in installation occurred, owing to the 1981–83 gas pipeline embargo (see box 3-1), which caused labor to be diverted to trunk pipelines, and much of the equipment does not appear to have been installed. Gustafson notes that the outcome was rather more successful at a similar project at Surgut.

The importance of these examples is that they illustrate how, during the Soviet period, relatively low-technology exchanges with a compelling commercial logic—as in the gas-for-pipe deals—worked well. Anything which required a significant organizational or technical input from the Soviet side—for example the Samotlor gaslift program—was much less successful. Despite convincing analytical work to the contrary, the US policy literature of the 1970s and early 1980s tended to conclude that only foreign technology stood between the Soviet economy and disaster.[5] By contrast, the typical conclusion of European academic work on East-West technology transfer was that:[6]

— assimilation took longer than in Western Europe;
— there was no sign of a reduction in lead times;
— subsequent manning tended to be on the high side and output levels on the low side;
— successful domestic diffusion and modification were limited.

3. For details of pipe and equipment deals see Angela E. Stent, *Soviet Energy and Western Europe*, The Washington Papers, no. 90 (Praeger/CSIS, 1982); for details of gas contracts, Jonathan P. Stern, *Soviet Oil and Gas Exports to the West: Commercial Transaction or Security Threat?* Energy Papers, no. 21 (Aldershot: Gower, 1987).

4. Marshall I. Goldman, *The Enigma of Soviet Petroleum: Half-Empty or Half-Full?* (George Allen and Unwin, 1980), pp. 159–63; Thane Gustafson, *Crisis Amid Plenty: The Politics of Soviet Energy under Brezhnev and Gorbachev* (Princeton University Press, 1990), p. 111.

5. Office of Technology Assessment, *Technology and Soviet Energy Availability*, US Congress, 1981.

6. Philip Hanson, *Trade and Technology in Soviet-Western Relations* (Macmillan, 1981).

Looking at Soviet imports of Western equipment and technology in the period 1960–90, we can draw two broad conclusions. First, how little the oil and gas industries availed themselves of equipment that Western companies were (in general) falling over themselves to provide, often with the financial assistance of their governments. In areas such as refining, very little equipment was imported, despite repeated demonstrations that it was desperately needed and that it could have a very positive effect on the performance of the sector.

Second, only a small number of foreign companies managed to make significant investments in the Soviet oil and gas industries. Traditional Soviet foreign trade policy dictated that no commodity should be imported from world markets unless it had been shown irrefutably that the domestic economy was unable to produce it. This resulted in a situation where even the transactions cited above required a great deal of time to bring to fruition, and were only sanctioned by the Soviet authorities after repeated attempts to manufacture similar equipment in Soviet factories had failed. To be successful, a company needed to devote significant resources to the Soviet market for a number of years, with little expectation of profits in the short to medium term. This deterred all but the most determined, and those who could see prospects of long-term, large-scale business. The Soviet Union was not the kind of market where an energy company could expect to make a quick buck. Those which were successful in making the cultural adjustment to the slow and painful bureaucratic processes reaped large rewards. But they were the few—perhaps as few as twenty energy companies worldwide.

It is useful to recall the lessons of the Soviet period. Many of the obstacles to greater trade were a product of the Soviet system, which demanded a degree of persistence in the face of bureaucratic obstacles, and a related expenditure of executive time and effort that few companies were either willing or able to expend. Nevertheless a significant number of obstacles were erected by Western governments. Because of ultrasensitivity over the technology content of machinery exports, there were important trading restrictions, such as special export licenses and withholding of most-favored-nation status. These restrictions periodically erupted into full-scale trade hostilities, as Soviet domestic and foreign policy actions caused OECD governments to try to exert economic leverage on Moscow. Such attempts often led to disarray among the Western allies—usually in the form of conflicts between the United States and major European countries—who were unable to agree on policy responses to Soviet actions (see box 3-1).[7]

---

7. Bruce W. Jentleson, *Pipeline Politics: the Complex Political Economy of East-West Energy Trade* (Cornell University Press, 1986).

Box 3-1. *The Urengoy Gas Pipeline Embargo, 1981–83*

The arrival of the Reagan administration in the White House, with a mission to halt the spread of Soviet influence, particularly in Europe, coincided with the negotiation of a large tranche of gas supplies from the Urengoy field to a number of West European countries. As usual, the gas contracts were to be accompanied by large and lucrative equipment contracts for large-diameter pipe and compressor stations. The Reagan administration, having discovered that it could not persuade European allies (specifically Germany, France, and Italy) voluntarily to withdraw from the project, sought to halt the construction of the pipeline by embargoing the sale of turbine components by General Electric to a number of European companies which had already contracted to supply turbines for the compressor stations. The affair caused a major rift in the Atlantic alliance, with even such staunch Reagan supporters as British prime minister Margaret Thatcher refusing to support the U.S. position. The Soviet Union gained an enormous propaganda victory, and completed the pipeline on schedule with more domestic compressor units than had been originally intended. European and American companies lost a large amount of potential business. American sanctions were finally lifted in late 1982 and a face-saving form of words was devised in the form of an International Energy Agency Communiqué to the effect that OECD countries would "avoid undue dependence" on a single source of supply and "give priority to indigenous (i.e., OECD) gas supplies."

The post-Soviet period

In the final years of the Soviet Union, joint venture (JV) legislation created the possibility of opening up the oil and gas sector to foreign investment on a much larger scale than had been conceivable during the Cold War period. Yet even following the 1987 JV legislation, progress in the energy sector was extremely slow.[8] At the end of 1989, out of more than 1,000 registered JVs, only two involved that sector.[9] Bearing in mind that the dramatic decline in oil production only began in 1989, we can see clearly that the Soviet authorities did not at that time believe that energy was a priority sector for JV activity.

The establishment in 1988 of the American Trade Consortium and a counterpart Soviet Foreign Economic Consortium was an important landmark. Although the plan was overambitious—it embraced a number of sectors, including food, pharmaceuticals, and energy, simultaneously—the March 1989 signing of an agreement between the consortia started a process of which one of the first stages was the involvement of Chevron in the Tenghiz region of Kazakhstan.[10]

---

8. Leonard Geron, *Joint Ventures in the USSR: the State of Play*, Royal Institute of International Affairs, Discussion Paper, No. 14, 1989.

9. Matthew J. Sagers, "Joint Ventures in the Soviet Energy Sector," *PlanEcon Report*, vol. 5, no. 40 (6 October 1989).

10. Ibid. The original idea was a grand conception for an integrated joint venture from oil production to vehicle manufacture, with Ford involved in the latter.

The years 1990–95 have witnessed great excitement, and discussion of a large number of projects. They have also seen the demise of the Soviet Union, and the ensuing chaos, confusion and crisis, both within Russia and between Russia and the other CIS countries, and both as regards oil and gas and general economic relations.

The appendix to this chapter represents an attempt to list the major oil and natural gas projects which may involve significant foreign investment, in progress or under serious consideration, in Russia and other CIS states. A very large "health warning" should be attached to this appendix. It is undoubtedly incomplete and inaccurate, since it is almost impossible to keep abreast of all the projects reported in the press. Moreover when projects are abandoned or where the project is in deadlock, this is rarely reported unless there is a major falling out between the parties. Classification of projects is also difficult. Some of those included in exploration and development also incorporate elements of refurbishment and enhanced recovery. The appendix lists more than 200 ventures in various stages of development from initial study to full production. This compares with around ninety ventures two years earlier. To put this into perspective, industry sources indicate that by the end of 1994 there were only forty-eight oil-producing foreign ventures in Russia, with some serious disagreements as to how much oil was actually being produced and exported.[11] A very major omission from the Appendix is the large number of pipeline projects to move oil and gas from Central Asia and the Caucasus to Europe. These projects require a separate study of their own.[12]

One of the most serious problems is the difficulty of determining whether projects have progressed beyond the study and negotiation stage to the point where foreign investors are spending significant sums of money that will result in appreciable additional production of fuels. Many studies (and the newspaper headlines which accompany them) give the impression that huge capital investments are being made in the hydrocarbon industries. Detailed investigation reveals that these are at best potential projects, likely to be realized only over many years and perhaps decades.[13] As far as this author has been able to

11. See *Russian Petroleum Investor*, December 1994/January 1995, p. 79. For a longer description of some of the major ventures than is contained in the appendix, see *Eastern Bloc Energy*, February 1995, pp. 2–5.

12. For an excellent summary see James P. Dorian, Ian Sheffield Rosi, and S. Tony Indriyanto, "Central Asia's Oil and Gas Pipeline Network: Current and Future Flows," *Post-Soviet Geography*, 1994, vol. 35, no. 7, pp. 412–30.

13. See for example, Frances Williams, "Oil Boom in CIS May Attract \$85 billion," *Financial Times*, 5 May 1993. This article purports to summarize a UN ECE study in *East-West Investment*, no. 1, January 1993.

ascertain, the total foreign investment in the Russian oil industry at the end of 1994 did not exceed $1.5 billion. By contrast, the Tragaz joint venture between Gazprom and an Italian consortium to refurbish gas pipelines and compressor stations was itself worth around $1.5 billion.

Having registered those caveats, we can identify general trends in foreign investment activity on the basis of this data:

— The majority of the projects listed are in the Russian oil sector. This may, however, be deceptive far as magnitude of foreign investment activity is concerned. The very large Tragaz joint venture has already been noted. In addition, if the Tenghiz and Karachaganak projects in Kazakhstan are fully successful, the volume of investment there could exceed $7 billion. By contrast, many of the projects currently under consideration in Russia involve investments of only a few million dollars.

—By the end of 1992, Russian companies had signed twenty-seven contracts with foreign partners to bring 5,000 of the 32,000 idle wells back into production (in addition to contracts for new fields).[14] However, in 1994 joint ventures involving foreign investment activity accounted for less than 12 million tons of oil production, or under 4 percent of total Russian production.[15] No gas was produced from joint ventures in 1994. Apart from the Chevron joint venture at Tenghiz in Kazakhstan, there is no single oil project currently under consideration which—by itself— would significantly increase CIS production by as much as 25 million tons (half a million barrels per day).[16] Nevertheless the projects listed in the Appendix would, in aggregate, certainly produce significant results. More precise knowledge about the stage of project development might allow some quantification of the additional oil and gas expected to be produced—and saved—by successful foreign investment.

14. Ilya Leshchinets, "Capital Requirements—Domestic and Foreign Dimensions," in *The Russian Oil Industry: Foreign Investment Opportunities*, 2d Annual Russian Oil Conference, 11-12 February 1992. Proceedings available from the Royal Institute of International Affairs, London.

15. These magnitudes are very difficult to calculate. One source puts JV production at 7.5-13 million tons plus 1.34 million tons from Yugansk-Fracmaster, but suggests total Russian production was 411 million tons. Rustam Tanyayev,"Official Statistics Underestimate Russia's Oil Production," *Russian Petroleum Investor*, February 1993 pp. 56–57. Another source suggested that joint venture oil would average only around 12 million tons in 1993. *Nefte Compass*, 19 February 1993, p. 2.

16. The Tenghiz and Korolev field developments are expected to produce around 35 million tons/year (700,000 barrels per day) in the early years of the next century. For a useful summary of the project see Mona Khoury, "Eastern Front Runner," *International Oil and Gas Technology*, vol. 1, no. 1, pp. 192–97.

— Over the past four years, and particularly since the breakup of the USSR, there has been a weakening of interest in Russian "mega-projects" and an increased interest in refurbishment projects for both oil and gas. This results principally from two factors: the desire to gain experience in certain regions while expending relatively small amounts of money; and the difficulty of negotiating a contract for a large project with any speed and continuity—is not necessarily a reflection of disillusion with the opportunities on offer, or of any reluctance to commit funds to the region. As another way of gaining experience without spending large sums of money, "studies" and "cooperation agreements" are arousing increased interest.

— The gas projects are smaller in number and generally lower in profile than the oil projects, but possibly have a greater chance of being implemented in that they are backed by foreign companies with a strong incentive to increase the volume and reliability of CIS gas supplies. With the European gas market anticipating major increases in demand over the next decade—and imports comprising an increasing proportion of this demand—gas companies have a more direct stake than their colleagues in the oil industry in ensuring a speedy and successful outcome.[17]

17. For detailed information on the development of European gas markets, see Jonathan P. Stern, *European Gas Markets: Challenge and Opportunity in the 1990s* (Royal Institute of International Affairs, 1990).

Appendix: Oil and Gas Foreign Investment Activity in Russia and Other Former Soviet Republics

Field/Project Joint Venture   *Foreign Investor(s)*

Russia

1. Exploration and Development/Production

Oil

Priobskoye field (Yugansknneftegaz)	Amoco
Romanovskoye field (Rostov regional administration)	Amoco
"Geoilbent" North Gubkinskoye, Prizklonnoye field (Purneftegazgeologiya)	Benton*
"Polar Lights," Ardalinskoye, Dosychevskoye, Kolvinskoye fields (Arkhangelskgeologiya)	Conoco*
Arkhangelsk Province (Arkhangelskgeologiya)	Conoco
Severo-Khampurskoye field (Purneftegazgeologiya)	Conoco
"White Nights" (Varyeganeftegaz)	Phibro/Anglo-Suisse*
Inchke More field (Dagestan)	Grynberg/Corpo/Premier
"Komi Arctic Oil" Vozney and Upper Vozney fields (Komineft)	Gulf Canada/British Gas*
Khariagina field (Komineft)	Total*
"Blue Kama" (Tatneft)	Panoco*
Mogotlor field development (Agarskgeologiya, Tyumen)	Pennzoil
Saratov/Volgograd exploration & development	ELF
Okruzhnoye field (Sakhalin Gov't/Sameko)	PetroCanada/Quantoo
"Golden Mammoth" (Varyegannneftgaz, Western Siberia)	Anglo-Suisse*
Verkhne/Zapadnoye-Salymskoye field development	Shell
Yuzhnoshapinskoye (Komineft)	Neste
Timan-Pechora (Arkhangelskgeologiya)	Texaco
"Parmaneft" (Ukhtaneftegazgeologiya)	Occidental*

This appendix is principally concerned with exploration and production, enhanced oil recovery, collection of associated gas and NGLs, refurbishment of pipelines, compressor stations and distribution systems. It does not include: petrochemical projects, simple sales of equipment, barter of oil for equipment, data collection and sale, joint venture marketing of oil and gas in foreign countries, or oil and gas pipeline projects.

* denotes oil producing joint venture

Field/Project Joint Venture	*Foreign Investor(s)*
(Orenburgneft)	Gardes Directional Drilling
(Stavropol'neftegaz)	Energy World Trade (EWT)
Kalmyk region	Hyundai
Kalmyk region	Premier Consolidated, Grynberg, Santa Fe
(Nizhnevarovskneftegaz)	Mustang Inv.
"Symskaya Exploration" (Yeniseineftegazgeologiya/geofizika)	Equity Oil, Leucadia National Corporation
"ROW," Zhigansk oil field (Zhiganskneftegaz)	Comco
"Volgodeminoil," Volgograd region (Nizhnevolskneft)	Deminex*
Chernogorskoye field (Chernogorneft)	Anderman/Smith, St Mary Land Exploration, Itochu
"Vanyeganneft" Vanyogan and Ayogan fields (Chernogorneft)	Occidental*
Okruzhnoye field (Sakhalin, PetroSakh)	Nimir Petroleum
"UrengoyTrace" (Urengoynefte-geologiya)	Tracer Petroleum, Dundee Bancorp, Con Brio, Euromin
"Permtex" (Permneft)	Snyder Oil
Khayankert and Goykt-Kort fields (Chechen Ministry of Oil/Gas)	Enforce Energy Corp
"Black Gold" Stavropol fields (Stavropolneftegas)	Genesis Eurasia Corp Beta Well Service
Khanti-Mansiisk region (Khantimansiiskgeologiya/geofizika)	Petro-Hunt, Dresser Industries
Pechora Sea (Arktikmorneftegazrazvedka)	Petro-Hunt
"Timan Pechora Company" oil exploration in Timan Pechora (Arkhangelskgeologiya)	Texaco, Exxon, Amoco, Norsk Hydro
"LukAgip" Vostochno-Pridorozhnoye field (Lukoil)	Agip
"LukAgip" (Kalmykneft, Astrakhanneft, Nizhnevolskneft)	Agip
"Amkomi" development drilling in Komi republic (Komineft)	Aminex
"Yeniseineft" Vankorskoye field, Eastern Siberia (Yeniseineftgazgeologiya)	Anglo-Siberian
Prirazlomnoye field, Pechora Sea (Gazprom, Rosshelf)	BHP Petroleum
Pechora region, Komi (Silur)	Bitech
Krasnodar region	Coplex Resources
"Yogan Oil," South Vat-Yoganskoye field (Lukoil, Sinco and Megioneftegazgeologiya)	TM Oil, Dana Exploration (Hardman Resources, Vanguard Petroleum)
"Sinco," Yuzhnoye production and pipeline development, Siberia	Eurosov Petroleum, Hardman Resources, Vanguard Petroleum

Field/Project Joint Venture	*Foreign Investor(s)*
Tatarstan, oil reserve development	Geos Ltd
Talakan oil field, South Yakutia	Handelsbank AG, Voest-Alpine AG, Lag Trade Vertribs, Voest-Alpine Intertrading
Pudinsko-Parabelskii oil region, Tomsk (Tomskneft, Tomskneftegazgeologiya)	IMEG
Oil field development in Nizhnevartovsk (Nizhnevartovskneftegaz)	C. Itoh, Slovnaft
Inchke-More field, Dagestan (Dagneft, Rosneft, Lukoil)	J.P. Kenny
Yelabuga, Bakhchisaraishkoye and Yelginskoye fields, Tatarstan (Tatneft)	Manx Petroleum
Yuzhno-Shapkinskoye field, Timan-Pechora (Arkhangelskneftegaz)	Neste
Krasnoyarsk region (Yeniseigeologiya-geofizika)	Petrofina
Urninskoye field (Western Siberia)	Ramco
"Tatoil," Talinsk field (Kondpetroleum)	Richmond oil and gas*
Khariagina field (Pechora Basin, Nenets region) (Komineft, Rosneft)	Total
Ruf Yeganskoye oil field (near Samotlor) plus pipeline connection (Magma Oil)	Vanguard Petroleum
"Oil Progress" (Komineft)	J. Weiss Int'l*

Gas

Novoport/Bovanenko fields, Yamal Peninsula (Nadymgazprom)	Amoco
Yakutsk (Sakha Republic) gas field and pipeline development (study)	Daewoo/Hyundai
"Takt" Otradnenskoye field in South Yakutia and other fields (Sakhaneftegaz)	OMV
Shtokmanovskoye field, "Rosshelf" (Gazprom)	Consortium of investors
Collection and processing of associated gas (Gazprom, Purneftegaz, Sibneftgazpererabotka)	Ruhrgas
Polyethylene pipe installation at Ishim (Zapsibgazpromstroi)	British Gas

Oil and Gas

Tomsk region	Naphtha Corp
Krasnoyarsk region, Eastern Siberia (Yeniseygazgeologiya)	Petrofina
Rogozhnikovskaya field (Khantimansiskneft) (Megionneftegaz)	Petro-Hunt Slovnaft/C Itoh
Timan-Pechora region (Severgazprom, Arkhangelskgeologiya, Ukhtaneftegazgeologiya)	Shell/Saga

Field/Project Joint Venture	*Foreign Investor(s)*
Anadyr and Kahtyrka Basins (Chukotneftegazgeologiya)	IPC
"NorthGas" North Urengoy field (Urengoygazprom)	Bechtel
Condensate production from Evo-Yakha and Samburg fields (Urengoygazgeologiya, Pripolyarburgaz, Neftekomlogaz)	Senega, Swift Energy
Vernechonskoye oil field and Kaviktinskoye gas field, Irkutsk region	Bitech, Rusia Petroleum
"Sakhalin I" Arkutu-Daginskoye, Odoptu and Chaivo fields	Exxon/Sodeco
"Sakhalin II" Piltun-Astokhskoye and Lunskoye (Sakhalinmorneftegaz)	Marathon, McDermott, Mitsui, Mitsubishi, Shell
"Sakhalin III" Kirinsky Block	Mobil, Texaco
Prizalivnaya block, Sakhalin (Vostokgeology)	Stirling Resources, Hardman Resources

2. *Refurbishment/Enhanced Recovery*

Oil

"Samotlorservis" Samotlorneftegaz (Nizhnevarovskneftegaz)	Fracmaster/PanCanadian*
"Vakhfracmaster" (Tomskneft)	Fracmaster/Shell*
"Yugansk-Fracmaster" (Yuganskneftegaz)	Fracmaster/Shell*
"Vasuygan Services Enterprises" Sobolinoe, Siginsk, Severo-Vasuygan fields (Vasuygannneft, Tomskneft)	Fracmaster/Norcen*
"Noble Oil," Usinsk field (Komineft)	Marc Rich*
(Kuibyshevneft/Pervomayneft Logovaz)	GHK
Dagestan, West Caspian Sea	J.P. Kenny
(Ukhtaneftegazgeologiya)	Total
(Stavrolpolneftegaz)	EWT
"Tatolpetro" Romashkino field (Tatneft)	Total*
"Komiquest," South and West Vosey, South Farman and Ufin-skaya fields (Komineft)	Quest Petroleum/Star Valley*
"Pur River," Severo-Komsomolskoye field (Purneftegaz) Kuibyshev	Quintana,Teikoku/Mitsui /Toyo/Santech*
Tatarstan (Tatoil)	Veba
Komi Republic, technical assistance with oil fields	Texaco
Timan-Pechora (Arkhangelskgeologiya)	Norsk Hydro
"Tatex" Onbysk field (Tatneft)	Global Natural Resources (GNR)*

Field/Project Joint Venture	*Foreign Investor(s)*
Khayankort, Goyt-Kort fields (Chechen Republic)	EnForce Energy
Raduzhny (Tyumen Region)	Baker Hughes
Raduzhny (Varyeganneftegaz)	Nowsco Well Service, Marubeni
"Joyludneft" Ulyanovsk region	Joy-lud Distributors Int'l
Sutormin field (Sutorminskneft)	Texaco
Kogalym, Western Siberia (Kogalymneftegaz)	Beta Well Services
Kechimavsk field, Langepas (Lukoil)	Bridas
Oil and condensate at Urengoy field (Tyumenegaztekhnologiya/Urengoygazodobycha)	Camco
"Catkoneft" (Kogazlymneftegaz, Langepas-neftegaz, Krasnoleninskneftegaz)	Catoil*
Tyumen region (Yugyskneftegaz)	DEB Industries
Tomsk region	Omani Oil
"Permtotineft" Garshukinskoye field (Permneft)	Totisa Ecuador*
"West Siberian Services" (Western Siberia)	Ina-Naftaplin, Marc Rich*
"Tatoilgaz" (Tatneft)	Mineral Rohstoff Handel*

Gas

"Tragaz," refurbishment of trunk pipelines/compressor stations (Gazprom)	Nuove Pignone, Snamprogetti
Refurbishment of distribution in St Petersburg (Lengaz)	Neste/Uponor/ British Gas
"Spbvergaz" refurbishment of distribution in St Petersburg (Lengaz)	Gaz de France
"Mosparteplogaz," refurbishment of Moscow distribution system (City of Moscow, Mosgaz, Mosteploenergo)	Gaz de France
"Rosfragaz," refurbishment of distribution in a number of Russian cities [incl: Saratov, Nizhni-Novgorod, Chelyabinsk, Smolensk] (Rosgazifikatsiya)	Gaz de France
Refurbishment of Russian distribution system (Rosgazifikatsiya)	Ruhrgas plus six other German companies

Refining, processing

Oil

Volgograd [modernization]	ABB Lummus Crest
Perm [modernization] (Lukoil/ Permnefteorgsintez)	ABB Lummus Crest
Krasnodar [construction] (Lukoil)	ABB Lummus Crest
Kirishi [hydrocracker construction]	Chevron, ABB Lummus Crest
Achinsk [modernization] and Industrial Co, Encon System	Bechtel, Chemical

Field/Project Joint Venture	*Foreign Investor(s)*
Volgograd refinery [modernization]	SNC Lavalin
"Volgooil," Volgograd [upgrading]	Total, Marc Rich
Khabarovsk refinery [expansion]	C Itoh
Ukhta, Lisichansk [modernization]	Marc Rich
Ryazan [upgrading, modernization]	John Brown
Tomsk region [construction]	Multinational Corp.
Yaroslavl [cat-cracker] (Yaroslavneftorgsintez)	Stone and Webster
Perm [desulphurizer, cat-cracker]	Texaco
Perm (distillation unit)	Ventech Engineers
"Petrolsakh" Sakhalin, construction of Pogranichnoye refinery	U.S. Petroleum
"Baltic Petroleum" St Petersburg [construction of refinery] (Baltic shipping co, Nefteorgsintex, Neftenalivnoi Rayon)	BP
Saratov [overhaul] (Rosneft)	Cepsa, Dragados & Construcciones
Novo-Ufimsky [reconstruction]	En and Son
Nizhnekamsk [modernization]	Lurgi
Almatevsk [construction] Engineering	Mitsui, Mitsubishi, Toyo
Yaroslavl [catalytic reformer] Tecnik	Mitsui, Thyssen Rheinstahl
Tuapse [upgrading]	Sumitomo
Perm (Permnefteorgintez)	En and Son
"EPEK," (Groznefteorgsintez, Bashneftekhim, Ufa Refinery, Moscow lubricants plant	Mineral Rohestoff Handel*

Storage, Terminals, Ports

Floating oil storage (St Petersburg City Government)	Atlas consortium
St Petersburg oil products terminal (Neftenalivnoi Rayon, Zolotye Vorota)	Pactank Int'l, Paribas Petroleum
"Transkama" Nizhnekamsk oil terminal construction (Nizhnekamskneftekhim)	Transchemical Corp
Tuapse port expansion	Bula Resources

Gas

(Urengoygazprom)	Camco
Astrakhan gas processing complex (Astrakhangazprom)	Santa Maria, Mori-Europe Westros
Surgut [associated gas recovery]	European Gas Turbine GMBh

Azerbaijan

Azeri field (Azerineft, Lukoil)	Amoco BP/Statoil, Ramco Unocal, McDermott, Pennzoil, TPAO, Delta/Nimir

Field/Project Joint Venture	*Foreign Investor(s)*
Kapaz field (Kaspmorneftegaz)	Apache International
Dostlug field	BP/Statoil
Shahe-Deniz field (Socar)	BP
Mir Bashir, Kazanbulak, Acidere, and Naftalan fields	Petoil
Guneshli field (Kaspmorneftegaz) enhanced recovery	Pennzoil/Ramco
"MegaOil"	Vista/MegaOil
"Ansad," Neftechala and Khilli fields (Socar)	Attilla Dogan Petrosan
Mashal and Gryazevaya Sopka fields Caspian Sea (Socar)	Hallwood Caspian Petroleum
"Baku-Ponder Services," Guneshli, Artuom Island and other fields (Socar)	Ponder Industries
Kyursanga field (Azerbaijan government)	Texaco
Karadag and Korgoz fields (Socar)	United BMB Group
Joint E&P	Unocal, Delta International
Onshore oil and gas infrastructure (Azerbaijantransdorstroy, Azerpromstroy)	Detla Hudson International
"Baku J.P. Kenny," engineering and construction expertise for on and offshore operations (Azerigas Gipromorneftegas)	J.P. Kenny

Armenia

Octemberian region [drilling] (Armenian government)	Armoil, DEP/EKY

Belarus

Nafan Refinery [construction]	Delfino, Fochi
NovoPolotsk Complex [upgrading]	
Mozyr refinery [upgrading]	Snamprogretti, Noringa
Nafton oil refinery and product marketing (Belnefteproduct)	Stephens East-West Consulting

Estonia

Oil products terminal at Muuga Harbor	Aspo Corp.

Georgia

Ninotsminda field	Makoil
"Georgia British Oil Co." oil and gas exploration	J.P. Kenny
Oil terminal at Supsa (Gruzneft)	Tramex International

Field/Project Joint Venture   *Foreign Investor(s)*

Kazakhstan
Oil

"Tenghizchevroil" Korolevskoye field*	Chevron (Parker Drilling)
Tenge field (Mangystaumunaigaz)	Anglo-Dutch
Arman field (Mangystaumunaigaz/Zharkyn)	Oryx Energy
Mertryi Kultuk block	Oryx Energy
South Zheltbay field	BMB
Volga and Temir fields	ELF

Aktyubinsk Province

Atyrau region, Dunga field	Oman Oil
Buzachi field	Hyundai
Buzachi field (Mangistaumanaigas)	Double River Oil & Gas
Uralskaya Oblast (Uralskgeo)	Easternoil Services,
Gandalf Explorers Inc.	
Oil and Gas Exploration	Turkiye Petroleri
Prorva gas field separation/processing plant	BSI Industries
Develop Kyzl-Kiya, Aryskum, Maybulak fields,	Canadian Occidential,
Explore South Turgai basin (Yuzhkazneftegaz,	Hurricane Hydrocarbons
Yuzhkazgeologiya)	
"Turan Petroleum," Djezkazgan region	Hurricane Hydrocarbons
	Wega D. Geophysical Ltd
South Central Kazakhstan	Hurricane Hydrocarbons
(South Kazakhstan oil and gas)	
Karakuduk field	Chaparrel Resources
Karazhanbas field (Karazhanbastermneft)	K. Hill International
Caspian Sea geophysical/seismic survey	Mobil, Shell, BP, British Gas,
(Kazakhstankaspiishelf)	Agip, Statoil, Total
Mangystau region well workovers	Bonus Petroleum
(Mangystauneftegaz)	
Kumkol field and offshore exploration	Petronas
(Kazaskhstanneftegas)	
Kukkol Field	Sumitomo, Preussag
Djezkazgan refinery construction	Enico
Atyrau refinery [reconstruction]	Hydrocarbon Engineering,
	Ronar Services, Nichimen
	Marubeni, Nissho-Iwai,
	Itochu, JGU, Chiyoda,
	Ferrostaal
Atyrau refinery construction	Mitsui, Mitsubishi, Toyo
	Engineering
Modernization of three refineries	Indian oil Corp, Engineers India
"Zhetybayquest," eastern shore Caspian Sea	Quest Petroleum
(Mangystaumunaigas)	

Field/Project Joint Venture	*Foreign Investor(s)*
Baiganinsky block III development	Repsol, Enterprise Oil
"Kazakh-Turk Petroleum (KTP)" Develop Yelemez, Bekpolat, Janathan, Liktibay, East Saztube, East Akyar, Darinskaya fields	TPAO
Refinery construction (Kazakhgas)	Tropak Systems
Operate fields and rehabilitation	United Biresmis, Muhedisler Burosu
"Kazgermunai," Akshabulak oil field development	Veba Oil, Erdgas Gommern
Oil field development, Atyrau region	Vegyepszer

Gas

Karachaganak field	British Gas/Agip
"Kazakhfragaz"	Gaz de France

Kyrgyzstan

Refinery construction and well workovers	Aztec Gas & Oil, US Exploration
Exclusive exploration rights for oil	Grynberg

Latvia

Reconstruction of Incuklans gas storage facility (Latvia Gas)	Enron

Lithuania

Klaipeda terminal modernization	Lancaster Distral Steel Co
Klaipeda terminal modernization	Tebodin
Butinge oil terminal	Agip
Gargdzie oilfield (Lithuanian Government)	Dansk Olie & Naturgas
"Genciai Nafta," Genciai, Nasodis and Kretinga oilfields	Svenska Petroleum

Turkmenistan

Yashlar (oil)	Bridas
"Keimir," Keimir and Ak-Patlauk fields (Balkanneftkhimprom)	Bridas
Shatlyk/Sovietabad (gas)	TPL
W. Turkmenistan oil/gas fields (Balkanneftekhimprom)	Oil Capital, Lapis Holdings
Burun field (Balkanneftkhimprom)	Occidental
Zhdanov and Lam fields, Southern Caspian Sea	Sundowner Offshore Services, Oil Drilling and Exploration, Lamarg Energy Assets
Koturdepinskii oil and gas field	Eastpac International
Oil and gas exploration	Elf

Field/Project Joint Venture	*Foreign Investor(s)*
Turkmenabasi Refinery [upgrading and modernization]	Penta Group

Ukraine

"Krymtexasnaft" Aktash field and other fields (Krymgeologiya)	OTM International, Hyteexplor
Ignatovskoye field	JKX Oil and Gas
"Crimean Petroleum Co" Delphin offshore region (Chernomorneftegaz)	J.P. Kenny
"Poltava Petroleum Co." Rudenkovskoye and Novo-Nikolaevskoye oil and gas fields (Poltava Gazprom, Poltava Neftegazgeologiya)	J.P. Kenny
Shebelinka refinery [additional construction] (Ukrgazprom)	Basic Systems Inc
Construct propane/Butane plant at the Yabonevskoye field (Goskomneftegas)	Chem Design
"Oukfragaz" (gas transmission and distribution)	Gaz de France
Odessa oil terminal	SBM

Uzbekistan

Mingbulak field (Uzbekneft)	Stan Cornelius
Kokdumalak field condensate recovery (Uzbekneftegas)	Dresser Industries M.W. Kellogg/Nissho Iwai
Oil and gas exploration	Elf
Karaktai field	Renong BHD
Oil refinery construction	Elf, Marubeni, Sinopec
Bukhara refinery construction (Uzbekneftegaz)	Marubeni, Chiyoda
Fergana refinery construction	Mitsui

Sources: *U.S. Energy Ventures in the Former Soviet Union and Eastern Europe, Foreign Energy Ventures in the Former Soviet Union and Eastern Europe*, US Department of Energy, Office of Oil and Natural Gas Policy, January 1995. "Joint Ventures in Russia," *Eastern Bloc Energy*, February 1995, pp. 2–5. Also: Russian Petroleum Investor, Nefte Compass, East-West Investment and Joint Ventures News (UN), International Letter (Gaz de France).

CHAPTER FOUR

The Perspectives of the Different Players

Since the breakup of the USSR, Western perspectives on Russia (and to some extent on other CIS countries) have been dominated by macroeconomic and macropolitical questions. This is hardly surprising. Potential investors are not encouraged to place large sums of money at risk against a backdrop of major and frequent changes in government, collapsing industrial production, hyper-inflation and a reform programme which has still to show real results with regard to stabilization and restructuring.

Western corporate perspectives

The difficulty of separating the macroeconomic and political problems from the oil and gas-specific issues looms large for foreign investors, as they try to sift through the risk factors involved in potential projects. In practice, the major economic and political questions impinge on every transaction. A short-list of the most important issues would consider the following variables:

— political stability at national, regional and local levels;
— central/regional/local political relationships;
— economic restructuring (marketization) and price reform;
— implementation and stability of legal and fiscal frameworks (including property rights, liability, taxation and repatriation of profits);
— guarantees concerning the transit of fuels across intra-CIS boundaries;
— low domestic prices and nonpayment problems, combined with noncon-vertibitility of currencies.

POLITICAL, ECONOMIC, AND LEGAL INSTABILITY. It is easier to be specific on the critical issues for a particular project than for projects in general. For example, some projects may be relatively insensitive to political change at the centre, but highly dependent on political stability in a given oblast or city. In general, the fragmentation of political authority in Russia is leading foreign investors to stress the increasing importance of the oblast, relative to tthe central authorities in Moscow.

Some projects are highly dependent on transit of oil and gas, and therefore on the maintenance of good relations between states. For others this may not be a significant issue. There is always a danger that the big uncertainties may also distract attention from the more mundane, bureaucratic day-to-day problems that can threaten a venture. Petty bureaucrats on the CIS side who feel alienated from—or even hostile to—new foreign-investment projects may have the power to block or sink a project.[1]

It is hard for a company to define the conditions under which it would consider Russia a suitable place for large-scale (multiples of $100m) investments, and even harder to envisage any likelihood of those conditions being realized within a five-to-ten-year period. Yet there is a risk in assuming that we can identify an era of future stability, when political change and economic reform will somehow have been completed, and stable legal and fiscal frameworks will be in place. It is perfectly understandable that investors should seek stability and predictability. But the CIS states are at a turning point in their political and economic history, and it is extremely unwise to imagine that the future can be foreseen in anything other than broad terms. It would clearly be easier for investors to wait until restructuring had stabilized the economy, with market-related prices and full currency convertibility. But those who intend to wait until this situation arrives will be doing business elsewhere for most of the next decade. Thus in answer to the recurrent question "would it be more sensible to wait for a few years, rather than investing today," we can only say that it is difficult to see how investors will know substantially more about the longer-term (twenty-year) future in several years' time than they do now. Those in positions of authority—centrally, regionally and locally—are likely to change—but this is not necessarily crucial. The era of Communist party stability, with its authoritarian political system and centrally planned system in which conditions and personnel changed very little over long periods of time,

---

1. For example the problems of White Nights in seeking agreed exemptions to the export tariff. "Russian Red Tape Gives Philbro Nightmares," *Nefte Compass*, vol. 2, no. 9 (5 March 1993), pp. 1–2.

has passed. But with its passing, the opportunities are becoming relatively greater. Those who invest now *may* be taking greater risks. They may also give themselves a much better chance of success.

The legal and fiscal dimensions of instability also loom large. In early 1995, foreign investors were still waiting for an oil and gas law and legislation on production sharing. Even supposing these are passed, there is no guarantee that foreign investors will find them satisfactory. Further changes will undoubtedly be made to the fiscal regime governing joint venture production and exports. A common position of potential investors is that nothing can be achieved until a stable legal and fiscal framework has been established, and has been working for a period of time. Such a view is understandable but irrelevant to operations over the next few years. Just as with political and economic stability, so with law and taxation: Russia is at the beginning of the process of establishing legal and fiscal frameworks, and these will undergo many changes over the next decade.[2] Any company which is intending to invest significant sums of money will have to do so in the full knowledge that major changes are likely. In the initial stages of this process, the legal basis of foreign business activity and the possibility of protecting the profits from investments will come constantly into question. Indeed, as William Butler stresses in his paper in this volume, in the minds of many investors legal uncertainties are more critical than political uncertainties.

REGIONAL DIMENSIONS: RUSSIA VERSUS THE OTHER FORMER REPUBLICS. In the immediate aftermath of the breakup of the Union, there was a school of thought which argued that Russia would be unstable for the next two decades, and that this was a reason to favour investments in Central Asia and the Caucasus—particularly in Kazakhstan and Azerbaijan, which seemed more likely to maintain authoritarian rule for the foreseeable future. This line of reasoning was based on the assumption that if the president of a country can be persuaded to approve a contract, then authoritarian rule will ensure that it is implemented.

The period 1992–95 has demonstrated the danger of confusing judgments about future political stability with current perceptions of the ease of doing business and "getting things done." It may be unwise for investors to take political risk positions on the basis of simplistic judgements as to whether, over

2. There is an enormous literature on Russian petroleum law and taxation which grows exponentially as the regime changes. For a summary see Peter Cameron, Investing in Russian Oil and Gas: the Legal Factor," in *Petroleum Review*, March 1993, pp. 120–21; Complexity in Russia," *Financial Times Energy Economist*, February 1993, pp. 21–25.

the life of their projects, Azerbaijan and Central Asian states will be intrinsically more politically stable than Russia. It may be tempting to assume that Kazakhstan and Azerbaijan are culturally homogeneous states with a high "natural" degree of cohesiveness, and that Russia is likely to be broken apart by ethnic groups seeking independence. Such claims require careful scrutiny. On closer examination, the Caucasus region enjoys neither ethnic homogeneity nor political stability.[3] The size and importance to the economy of the Russian population in Kazakhstan is also a significant issue.[4] This author has come across very few companies which have carried out detailed political analysis of any former Soviet republics other than Russia.

Those who have judged opportunities in Azerbaijan and Kazakhstan to be more attractive than opportunities in Russia have been encouraged by the relative lack of bureaucracy and the ease of access to key decisionmakers. This compares very favorably with the wearisome and labour-intensive process of dealing with three layers of Russian bureaucracy—central, regional and local—which means that firms need to work with key people at each level.

Moreover, from the perspective of proximity to world markets, there is an obvious advantage of being "on the edge" of the region, rather than near the centre (either of Russia or Central Asia) and therefore dependent on transit through potentially unstable regions of the country or through other states. Clearly Azerbaijan is particularly attractive in this respect, as is the Russian Far East (particularly Sakhalin). For the same reason, companies may also come to take opportunities in Ukraine more seriously. The transit aspects of oil and gas deliveries from Central Asia involving other CIS states (notably Russia) have become a vital factor requiring analysis, not just of political stability, but also of relations between producing states and transit countries (we return to the commercial aspects of transit below).

CULTURAL ATTITUDES. There is a tendency among foreign investors (and foreigners in general) to think that the Russians are not going to "make it" as capitalists; that they have neither the aptitude nor the application for efficient business operations. This kind of observation is often accompanied by assertions that, by contrast, Central Asians have a "trading mentality" which is

3. This text is being prepared in the aftermath of the Russian conflict in Chechnya, However, there are numerous other current and potential conflicts in the region, any one of which could be significantly destabilizing over a period of time. On the Caucasus, see Jonathan Aves, *Post-Soviet Transcaucasia*, RIIA, Post-Soviet Business Forum, 1993.

4. Anthony Hyman, "Moving out of Moscow's Orbit: the Outlook for Central Asia," *International Affairs*, no. 2, 1993, pp. 289–304.

much closer to the Western business ethic. Interestingly, those who hold this view often ascribe the state of affairs to the lack of any democratic or capitalist (including private property) ethic in Russian history. For Russia, this is a questionable historical observation—there have been periods in which business and private enterprise thrived in Russia—and it is certainly at least as valid for Central Asian countries, where neither democracy nor capitalism have any significant historical roots.

The issue here is surely not the extent to which a Western-style business ethic has manifested itself in the past, but rather whether it can be successfully fostered in a new political and economic environment. The emergence of an entrepreneurial class should not be ruled out—but nor should the possibility of authoritarian government with an anti-private enterprise ideology—in any part of the former Soviet Union.

CORPORATE ROLE AND PROJECT SELECTION. One of the most interesting and important questions for potential investors is the role that they wish to assume in a particular project. For small, particularly service-oriented, companies, the choice is driven by finance and expertise. For the large multinational oil companies, on the other hand, with major financial resources and wide expertise in all aspects of the industry, the choices are extensive. However, a wide variety of opportunities does not necessarily mean a selection of attractive projects, and we return to this issue in the context of host country perspectives.

At the outset of foreign involvement in Russia, there seemed to be clear-cut choices between different roles: equity investors in joint ventures; service companies involved in refurbishing and enhancing existing projects; marketing companies planning to sell products (possibly inside Russia but mainly to foreign buyers). As we saw in chapter 3, these roles have become decompartmentalized, particularly as far as JV equity investment and refurbishing/enhancement are concerned, but also in so far as the functions of service company and marketing company are being combined. Those involved in JVs are increasingly taking on the marketing of the resulting products in order to ensure that returns are maximized. Those involved in refurbishment, both in oil and gas, are also more and more taking a direct share in the additional product which results from their efforts.

There is a tendency for companies wishing to gain experience, while limiting their financial exposure, to start with relatively straightforward refurbishment/enhanced recovery projects in the expectation that, if successful, they may move on to large investments. Some companies have taken the view, however, that participation in refurbishing and enhancing existing operations may expose them to the risk of future liabilities (particularly in respect of environmental damage) arising from the earlier development of the field. Such companies have attempted to involve themselves only in new greenfield projects where they have complete management control of the development from the outset.

Finally, there has been little interest in downstream (distribution and marketing initiatives) because of the slowness of price reform and still distant prospect of currency convertibility. European gas companies, hopeful of moving surplus gas to their own markets, are active in this area, as are a very few companies in the Baltic states. The Finnish company Neste has opened some petrol stations in the St Petersburg area. In principle, the energy price liberalization of early 1995 should mean stronger incentives in this area, though it must be added that at April 1995 there was no expectation of any sharp increase in domestic Russian prices for oil and gas.

Host country perspectives

One of the greatest difficulties for foreign investors is that, even when they have overcome the hurdle of communicating verbally with their Russian and CIS partners, they find themselves speaking a different language. In particular, they have difficulty in making their interlocutors understand the aspirations of investors, and the need to outline a project which will command the support of top management. Problems, it is said, arise from the failure of Russian and CIS partners to understand the commercial concepts which underpin such projects—rates of return, time value of money, etc. While this is undoubtedly the case in very many instances, it is probably not a decisive impediment for most projects. Younger people are gaining more rapid promotion than in the Soviet era, and such people are likely to be more amenable to market-based commerce and quicker to learn its rules. They are likely, in time, to transform the present situation whereby, in far too many instances, too few employees know or care whether a firm is making any money. The main issue, therefore, is not whether Russian and CIS partners can be educated in foreign commercial practices—that will happen, but it will take time. The problem is rather that for the time being these partners have a different agenda, and/or a different set of attitudes, which the Western partner either has difficulty understanding, or believes should not be allowed to affect the project.

PROJECT OPPORTUNITIES. Host countries in the main believe that foreign participation is required only for tasks which cannot be accomplished by the

Russian-CIS domestic industry. Foreign partners often complain that they are not offered "good" projects—meaning straightforward exploration and production opportunities; that they are being asked either to pick up the pieces of some development which has run into difficulties as a result of poor implementation, or to develop an extremely difficult field which would be marginal under any circumstances. For the host country, this seems entirely logical.[5] Foreign participation should be concentrated where it is most needed and foreigners should not be allowed to profit from developments which can be handled with domestic resources.

The perception of whether foreign investment is needed is a key issue. One group of foreign investors—believing they had a close understanding with both central and local governments—carried out a feasibility study on the super-giant Shtokmanovskoye gas field in the Barents Sea. The Russian government subsequently awarded the development to a Russian consortium—Rosshelf.[6] This may be an understandable move on the part of a host government, but it causes considerable disillusionment in the ranks of foreign investors. Eventually, shortage of capital investment, technology and expertise may force the foreign investment option on host countries if projects are to progress—this is likely to apply particularly to a project such as the Shtokmanovskoye field. Indeed, shortage of capital may cause foreign participation to be reconsidered even for projects which, from the purely technological point of view, could be accomplished without foreign assistance.

THE NEED FOR FOREIGN TECHNOLOGY. There is a strong belief among many host country partners (but particularly Russians) that while they may need investment, they have little requirement for technology. With much of the Western media and academic literature encouraging foreign companies to view the Russian oil and gas industries as a "disaster area," it comes as something of a surprise to many potential foreign investors to attend conference presentations (particularly by Russian representatives) in which the view is advanced that foreign companies have little to contribute to technological know-how. Foreign investors tend to view this as unwarranted arrogance. Russians, on the

5. Mark Moody-Stuart, "Foreign Investment in Russia: Obstacles and Opportunities," *The Russian Oil Industry: Foreign Investment Opportunities*, 2d Annual Russian Oil Conference, 11-12 February 1992. Proceedings available from the Royal Institute of International Affairs, London.

6. Many factors contributed to this decision, including strong pressure by the military-industrial complex in the region, and the fact that Gazprom was not included in the original consortium. The Rosshelf consortium includes Gazprom. *SWB*, Part 1, Former Soviet Union, SU/W0258, A11/12, 12 November 1992. See also the chapters by Julian Cooper and David Humphreys in this volume.

other hand, tend to believe that foreign companies are insisting on the use of foreign equipment and technology simply in order to increase their profits at the expense of Russian companies. They are fiercely proud of what they have achieved in the oil and gas industries, and resent being viewed as technologically backward. It is indeed true that in certain areas the Russian gas industry is the world leader, for example in laying and welding large-diameter pipe under Arctic conditions. The critical foreign contribution is the pipe and equipment, but Gazprom has been accustomed to arranging large-scale equipment purchases with minimal foreign involvement on Russian territory.

During the Soviet period, the prevailing view was that where the presence of foreign partners was absolutely essential (i.e., for installation and training), they were to be tolerated for the minimum necessary period and excluded as quickly as possible. This view is no longer prevalent and, as we have seen, the host countries are now looking for a long-term presence and a long-term commitment from foreign investors. At the same time, in the words of former deputy prime minister Fyodorov: "In many cases there is still opposition to foreign investment, to really allowing the free flow of capital and the free action of nonresidents and resident foreign companies. People fear that half the country will be bought by foreigners and everything will be in foreign hands, and they do not understand that efficiency and the legal framework in any country ... can only work on a proper international scale where foreign capital creates jobs and efficiency."[7]

LOCAL AND INFRASTRUCTURAL INVESTMENTS. Almost all Russian and CIS partners require would-be foreign investors to commit themselves to investing—sometimes on a large scale—in local infrastructure. For the Russian partner this is entirely logical: a feature of the Soviet period was the development of oil and gas with a casual disregard for the needs of both workers and the local communities which were affected by the development. There are dozens of accounts of development being carried out in Arctic conditions with workers in trailer-caravans lacking even the most basic amenities. Equally common are accounts of Siberian and other developments where, because infrastructure budgets were devoted to production work, towns and cities lacked schools, hospitals, shopping and entertainment facilities. Hence communities and workers are determined that foreign investors should be required to make a substantial contribution toward these facilities—in effect to fill the gap left by the Soviet authorities.

7. Part of Fyodorov's statement to *Russian Oil Industry*.

This causes considerable problems for foreign investors, many of whom are prepared to be "good corporate citizens" but are wary of writing what amount to blank cheques for provision of social infrastructure. It must be said that foreign companies are likely to be more receptive to requests for this type of contribution once they are assured of a cash flow from the project. They are unlikely to be prepared to view infrastructure investment as an "entry fee" to a project.

Establishing limited liability for infrastructure investment in the eyes of host country partners is part and parcel of the issue of "who is in charge" of the development, a problem which has worsened with the fragmentation of power and authority among central, regional and local political and industrial groupings. The typical statement from each of these parties is that "I am in charge—you need to deal with me". To a certain extent this is true, in that each of the parties can erect significant obstacles to the development process. The obstacles at the local level are most likely to be in the form of demands connected with infrastructural and social development, as well as environmental protection.

PRESSURE TO MOVE DOWNSTREAM. There is a strong feeling (reflecting Marxist theory, in which all the present partners were educated) that poor countries sell primary resources and are exploited by rich countries which are able to control the lion's share of the profits by processing and marketing these resources—hence the increasing interest in becoming involved in a downstream marketing joint venture between Gazprom and the German company Wintershall to market natural gas in Germany (and some East European countries).[8] Table 4-1 shows the results of Gazprom's aspirations to take shares in the marketing of gas in all countries to which they export. While most of the related joint ventures have had less immediate effect than the collaboration with Wintershall, the portents for the future are clear.[9]

Attitudes toward foreign investors cannot be generalized, and are evolving all the time, but CIS partners can be expected to be extremely sensitive to any suggestion that

— foreign partners should be allocated either projects or acreage that the domestic industry believes itself to be capable of developing independently;

8. An account of the Wintershall/GAZPROM partnership and its origins can be found in Jonathan P. Stern, *Third Party Access in European Gas Industries: Regulation-Driven or Market-Led?* (RIIA, 1992), pp. 88-91.

9. Jonathan P. Stern, *The Russian Natural Gas 'Bubble': Impact on European Markets*, Royal Institute of International Affairs, 1995.

Table 4-1. *Gazprom's Joint Ventures and Trading Houses*[a]

Country	Joint venture partner	Joint venture name	Percent Gazprom share
Austria	OMV	GVH (Gaz und Varenhandelshaus MbH)	n.a.
Finland	Neste	Gasum	25
France	France	Fragaz	n.a.
Germany	BASF[b]	WINGAS	35
	WIEH	50	
	Zarubezhgaz	n.a.	
	Daimler Benz	DITGAS	n.a.
	Ferrostahl	Metaprom	n.a.
Greece	DEPA	Prometheus Gas	n.a.
Hungary	MOL/Mineralimpex/DKG East	Panrusgas	50+
Italy	SNAM	Promgaz	n.a.
Poland	POGC	Gaztrading	n.a.
	POGC	Europol Gaz	48
Slovenia	Petrol	Tagdem	n.a.
USA	Bechtel	Northgas	51

a. Trading Houses have also been set up in: Bulgaria and Turkey.
b. Wintershall

— they are necessarily technologically inferior to foreign partners;

— the foreign partner is only there to make "a quick buck" and then disappear;

— and therefore by implication the foreign partner is resistant to investment in social infrastructure, which, for the Russians, is a "natural" extension of resource development.

This is not to suggest that the host country perspective is necessarily "correct" (although it is certainly not automatically wrong), but rather that foreign investors need to be sensitive to these perspectives. Russian and CIS partners may, in turn, need to accept that foreign investment on a large scale will not be forthcoming unless more incentives are offered. In particular, a demonstrable foreign investment "success" (involving significant and well publicized-profits) might be useful for the host countries, by encouraging others. The reality is that domestic political sensitivity toward the foreign investment community may preclude such a potentially useful "demonstration" project being implemented, particularly because, in the words of a Western banker: "What it boils down to is that Russians can't understand why foreigners should make a profit from taking Russian minerals out of the ground." [10]

Thus many foreign companies find it easier to do business outside Russia,

10. Leyla Boulton, "Move to Speed up Energy Sector Aid Already in Pipeline," *Financial Times*, 6 April 1993.

in republics where, irrespective of the state of democratic and market-reform credentials, there is a recognition that foreign technology is essential and a greater acceptance of the concept of profitability.

Regional perspectives and the "Energy Charter"

One of the priorities for foreign investors is to be able to export their share of the products of their investments to world markets. In many cases this may depend on the willingness of third countries—principally former Soviet republics—to allow transit through their territories. The principal countries involved in the transit of fuels from Russia are Ukraine, Belarus, the Caucasian countries (mainly Azerbaijan) and the Baltic countries (notably Latvia and Lithuania). Oil and gas exports from Central Asia (Turkmenistan and Kazakhstan) to Europe need to pass either through Russia and Ukraine, or through the Caucasus.

TRANSIT ISSUES. While oil transit is an issue, the potential for transporting oil by road, rail, pipeline or ship gives considerable flexibility to would-be exporters. There are also substantial opportunities for swapping oil between different potential markets. One important recent event was the formation of a consortium involving the governments of Kazakhstan, Russia, Azerbaijan and Oman on a possible oil pipeline from the Tenghiz region to an export outlet.[11] The government consortium has announced plans for a pipeline to the Russian port of Novorossiisk on the Black Sea.[12] Given the inability of the parties to agree an equity relationship with the major foreign investor, it is uncertain whether this pipeline can be financed and, if it can, whether an agreement between the pipeline consortium and the foreign investor can be reached. There are other initiatives aimed at creating a Mediterranean export outlet. However, the extent to which these have survived the post-1991 experience of interruptions of oil and gas pipelines in the Caucasus by warring factions is uncertain.[13] One route proposed by Turkey and Azerbaijan in early 1993 runs from Baku directly into Iran and thence to Turkey.[14]

---

11. John Leslie, "A Bird in the Hand," and John Roberts, "No Silk Route for Central Asian Exports," *Financial Times Energy Economist*, August 1992, pp. 12–15; November 1992, pp. 5–9.

12. *SWB*, SU/W0254 A/6, 30 October 1992.

13. For background information see Aves, *Post-Soviet Transcaucasia.*, pp. 33, 40. For specific details of these events, see "Georgian Oil Cut-off by North Ossetia: Armenia also Affected," *SWB*, SU/W0233 A/11-12, 5 June 1992; "Report on Armenian Emergency after Destruction of Pipeline," *SWB.*, SU/1597 C1/1, 27 January 1993.

14. John Murray Brown, "Turkey and Azerbaijan Sign Oil Pipeline Accord," *Financial Times*, 10 March 1993.

While former Soviet republics might ideally wish to avoid Russian territory in devising export routes for their oil and gas, this has generally proved impractical. The most, and in the majority of cases the only, economically viable routes for both oil and gas exports to world markets are through Russian territory. This is particularly true for gas from Kazakhstan and Turkmenistan. But the transit issue is more acute in the case of natural gas than in the case of oil, because the absolute requirement for pipeline transportation (as opposed to the options of rail or ship in the case of oil) greatly reduces delivery flexibility and increases dependence on transit countries. These issues have been graphically illustrated by the recent difficulties experienced in relations between Russia and Ukraine, and between those two countries and Turkmenistan (see Box 4-1). The complex problems created in Ukraine's relationship with Russia and Turkmenistan by that country's dual role as a transit region through which the bulk of those countries' gas must flow on its way to export markets, and simultaneously a major purchaser of their gas, have yet to be settled.

The community of interest between the three countries is clear: Ukraine needs to purchase Russian and Turkmen gas; Turkmenistan needs markets for its gas and transit routes through both Russia and Ukraine to Europe; Russia finds the import of Turkmen gas useful (although possibly not essential in the future) and badly needs an uninterrupted flow through Ukraine to safeguard an important source of hard-currency earnings. Thus everybody can threaten to cut off everybody else's gas, but nobody will benefit from such action. Bradshaw's conclusion on post-Soviet interdependence is particularly applicable to the natural gas industry: "It is clear that the Soviet legacy presents them with a series of problems that are best dealt with by cooperative action ... the economic transition requires collective action and the management of interdependence. At present, political factors dominate and the state-centred self-interest of the geopolitical transition serves to undermine the collective action necessary to bring about a successful geoeconomic transition." [15]

The country with the fewest options is Turkmenistan, and its refusal to join the CIS Intergovernmental Council on Oil and Gas (see chapter 2) is unwise. From the viewpoint of 1995, its grand plans for gas pipelines moving east and west appeared to be a very long way from commercial viability.

A solution to these problems might be based on an agreement on a wider regional framework for transit of oil and natural gas,[16] since transit issues

15. Michael Bradshaw, *The Economic Effects of Soviet Dissolution* (RIIA: Post-Soviet Business Forum, 1993), p. 50.

16. Deborah Hargreaves, "Uniform CIS Pipeline Rules Urged," *Financial Times*, 9 March 1993

Box 4-1. *Commercial gas disputes in the post-Soviet period*

Turkmenistan-Russia
Turkmenistan exports gas to former republics in Central Asia and the Caucasus, but its two most important customers are Russia and Ukraine. As the map shows, all Turkmen gas has to transit through other republics (including Russia) to reach Ukraine. Russia consumes some Turkmen gas from pipelines which go to Ukraine, and some in the Urals from an extension line through Kazakhstan. Immediately following the breakup of the USSR there were demands from Turkmenistan that Russia should pay in hard currency at "world prices" for gas deliveries, and predictable refusals from the Russians. This situation was exacerbated by the Turkmen withdrawal from Gazprom (all other republic Gazprom organizations are continuing to coordinate their activities). By 1995 the situation appeared to have improved, with the Turkmens apparently beginning to realize that for the marketing of their gas outside Central Asia, they are—in the short to medium-term at least—totally in the hands of the Russians. An important test will be whether the sales and transit contracts for 1995 are honoured.

Turkmenistan-Ukraine
In 1992, Turkmenistan's resentment against what it perceived as exploitative behavior on the part of other former republics came to a head when it cut off gas deliveries to Ukraine, having failed to agree an acceptable price increase. After a seven-month disruption, deliveries were finally restored in October 1992, following agreement on prices and transit fees, but further protracted disruptions took place in 1993 and 1994. The complex mix of rouble and quasi-hard currency prices (in terms of which both governments assess the goods to be bartered) is likely to give rise to continuing disputes in the future, unless the Russians are able to act as "regulator" of the relationship.

Russia-Ukraine
Since virtually all Russian oil and gas exports to Europe need to transit Ukraine, and since the latter is also a major buyer of Russian gas, a highly complex commercial situation has developed between the two countries in respect of this trade. The fundamental issue is the relationship between the price that Russia charges for its gas and the transit tariff that the Ukraine charges for Russian exports to Europe. In October 1992, Russia's Gazprom —retaliating for alleged nonpayment of gas which had been delivered—cut back deliveries to Ukraine. The latter reacted, predictably, by exceeding its offtake of Russian gas, thereby curtailing deliveries to European customers. This led to accusations (by the Ukrainians) of nondelivery and counter-accusations (by the Russians) of nonpayment, followed by threats to stop deliveries (by Russia) and counter-threats to cut off exports to Europe (by Ukraine). Despite the fact that these are essentially commercial issues, their political importance can be judged by the fact that in every case the final agreements were clinched at prime ministerial level.

---

range wider than the former Soviet republics. The pattern of movement of fuels from Russia and other CIS countries through Central and Eastern Europe to the western part of the continent forms an important part of the calculation for a foreign investor, especially as far as natural gas trade is concerned.

THE ENERGY CHARTER Conceived by Dutch Prime Minister Ruud Lubbers at the European Council meeting in June 1990, the European Energy Charter is an attempt to accelerate the development of energy resources in the former USSR and Eastern Europe. This development could both provide a major opportunity for East-West industrial cooperation and act as a driving force for recovery in the East.[17] Misinterpreted initially—principally by American and Japanese governments—as a West European attempt to monopolize CIS oil and gas resources, the term "European" was subsequently dropped from the title of the Charter. The political declaration of the Charter was completed at the December 1991 conference in the Hague and the Charter was signed by some 50 countries in December 1994.[18] The Treaty aims at establishing:

> A legal framework in order to promote long term co-operation in the energy field, based on the complementarities and mutual benefits, in accordance with the objectives and the principles of the Charter. (Article 2)

Substantive chapters of the Charter Treaty are concerned with:

— commerce: including trade in nuclear materials, competition rules, transfer of technology, free access to capital, and free transit
— promotion and protection of investment: with distinctions between existing and new investments, rules of conduct as regards compensation for losses and expropriation
— issues of a generic nature: transparency of legislation and decisionmaking, state sovereignty, environmental impact
— dispute settlement: taking into account GATT rules
— transitional arrangements: 24 countries registered transitional arrangements with phase-outs of various durations, but not extending beyond 1 July 2001.

It remains to be seen whether the Charter will become an effective tool in facilitating and resolving the problems which have been identified in trade with, and investment in, the countries of the former Soviet Union. A key provision of the Treaty is that of "free transit," and the interpretation and enforceability of transit where a country may believe it commercially attractive to block the passage of oil and gas through its territory may be an early test of the strength

17. Clive Jones, "The European Energy Charter," *Energy Focus*, vol. 10, no. 1 (April 1993), pp. 14–17.
18. Notably the United States, Canada, and Norway did not feel able to sign the Charter Treaty, although they may subsequently decide to do so. See Julia Doré and Robert de Bauw, *The Energy Charter,* Royal Institute of International Affairs, 1995.

of theTreaty. In general, commercial companies have moved from being hostile to the Treaty (on the grounds that it would add to regulatory processes and complicate commercial contracts) to being cautiously supportive, if skeptical that it will genuinely assist their business.

CHAPTER FIVE

The Changing Foreign Investment Agenda: Short- and Longer-Term Trends

It is hard to think of a previous occasion where such an immense and potentially promising set of oil and gas provinces—denied to foreign investors for many decades—has been suddenly opened up. To some extent, the immensity of the terrain and the diversity of the opportunities present problems in themselves.

Roughly five years have elapsed since foreign companies were first presented with the opportunity of investing in the former Soviet oil industries. A great deal of that time has been spent on focusing on opportunities, complexities and problems in various regions and sectors. Add to these issues the volumes of capital needed to unlock resources and the risk and uncertainty of the environment in which such investments must be made, and the relatively slow progress being made is wholly understandable.

Every change in government and adminstration at any level, every change in fiscal conditions, every announcement made by a Russian decisionmaker (no matter how ill-informed) gives rise to nervousness—both for operating personnel and for senior management who need to approve investment budgets.

There is, in fact, a danger of overreacting to daily events and believing that there is a simple relationship between the progress of democracy and economic reform on the one hand, and the prospects for foreign investment on the other. A return to authoritarian, centralized government—while politically unattractive—could improve the foreign investment climate. It would probably mean a return to Soviet-type patterns of foreign investment, with a few large players, but investing on a much increased scale. In such a situation, it would be interesting to see whether those currently involved in projects would have an advantage over those investors who had decided to wait.

Corporate attitudes

This author has identified two general corporate attitudes toward investment in former Soviet oil and gas industries:

— "This is not for us. The risks are too great and the pay-off too uncertain."
— "We're going to be in the oil business for the next fifty years; Russia and the CIS probably represent the biggest opportunity during that period. Therefore we have to have at least a presence there."

Those who take the second view tend, however, to add the rider: "But we're not going to bet the company on a multibillion dollar project at this point in time." The first rush of enthusiasm during 1988–90 has been tempered by the realization that by the second year of the post-Soviet era, conditions had become even more difficult and uncertain. They have not improved significantly since. In the short term, investors are looking to retain a presence, while minimizing their financial exposure. This has led many companies to shift their focus of interest

—to smaller projects;
— away from exploration and production, toward refurbishment;
— away from immediate capital investment and toward study and cooperation projects.

The contribution of foreign investment

Oil produced with foreign participation accounted for less than 12 million tons, or 4 percent, of total Russian production in 1994, as noted in chapter 3. These volumes are likely to rise slowly but surely. Nevertheless, at the present rate of development it it would be surprising if production from foreign investments were to exceed 50 million tons per year (1 million barrels a day) before 2000. Moreover, this outcome is more likely to result from a large number of ventures producing small quantities of oil, than from any single very large production ventures. In 1993, the largest level of annual output from a joint venture was 2.3 million tons; most were in the range of 0.1-0.5 million tons. Nevertheless, given the political and commercial circumstances, even the present level of production should be seen as a major achievement on the part of the parties involved.

However, there are great dangers of mutual disillusion setting in on both sides, with

— Russians believing that foreign investors are simply not serious;
— foreign investors believing that Russians are incapable of getting their political and economic act together.

The situation is not helped by the seemingly endless stream of high-level missions, conferences and government-to-government agreements, apparently promising major and immediate investments but seemingly yielding very little of short-term substance. At a more humble level, in the words of the Russian prime minister, "One gets the impression of enormous foreign interest from the fact that all the hotels in our oil regions are literally thronged with foreign businessmen. But these are mostly ordinary middlemen, hacks who also make the rounds of Moscow offices."[1]

Foreign investment has not made a significant difference to Russian oil output in the period up to 1995. If the decline is to be halted, this will be achieved largely by domestic efforts. The situation in gas is rather different, in that output decline as such is not a key issue. Significant foreign investment in gas pipeline infrastructure should certainly improve the security of deliveries about which European importers are becoming increasingly concerned. If the capacity of existing oil and gas infrastructure could be maximized through refurbishment, then this would help to minimize the problems caused by inevitable delays in the development of new fields and the construction of new infrastructure.

Once again, however, we are talking about marginal, if not insignificant, impact.

One conclusion of this paper must therefore be that, while the importance of foreign investment ought not to be underestimated, we should question the notion—advanced by both Western and CIS commentators—that such investment can somehow save the Russian and CIS oil and gas industries from potential disaster. The same can be said about Western technology.

1. "Russian Official Sees an End to Oil Production Slide," *Oil and Gas Journal*, 19 October 1992, pp. 31-3.

It is certainly counterproductive to oversell the undoubted virtues of advanced technology to these industries. There is no sign that foreign investors are able to make such technology available on a scale which will drastically affect the short-term fortunes of the oil or gas sectors. These conclusions are not intended to deride or minimize the efforts which are being made; they simply caution against excessive optimism and the inevitable disenchantment which will follow in its wake.

Longer-term trends

This author's guess is that, although we will witness a large number of small ventures in Russia and other CIS states,

- there will be only a very small number of multibillion-dollar investments over the next decade;
- these are at least as likely, and possibly more likely, to involve natural gas as oil;
- the gas projects are likely to involve European companies as principal partners;
- if political conditions in Russia and other CIS countries worsen, there will be a re-emergence of patterns of conflict over trade familiar from the Soviet era.

It may, furthermore, be wise to ask hard questions about the economic logic of creating new, ever-longer and politically problematic oil and gas supply lines from Russia and Central Asia to Europe. There are at least two reasons for this. The political stability of the region which we knew as the Soviet Union has been shattered. Political uncertainty will be a feature of the next decade and in certain regions this will periodically spill over into instability and military hostility.

Second, if the former Soviet and East European states can achieve convertible-currency status, despite the political legacy of the Soviet period, Western Europe may no longer be regarded as the most desirable destination for oil and gas. The regional oil and gas trade patterns which were established during the Soviet period were not entirely illogical for many former Soviet republics and East European countries. Whatever the political appeal of diversifying sources of supply, it will be difficult and costly for many importing countries to establish the necessary alternative infrastructure. This observation applies especially to natural gas supplies, and particularly to countries with few geographical advantages in respect of alternative suppliers. The future may demonstrate that, with a new commercial basis for CIS oil and gas exports, profitability can be maximized by minimizing transportation costs. Foreign investors should keep an open mind on these matters.

Part 2

MINING AND METALS IN THE CIS: BETWEEN AUTARKY AND INTEGRATION

David Humphreys

The CIS ranks among the world's largest producers of nonferrous and precious metals. Although metals production has fallen over the past five years as a result of general economic dislocation and the poor quality of capital in the industry, it has fallen less than industrial production generally in the CIS. This has had the relative importance of the sector and of releasing substantial quantities of metal for export. The breakdown of interrepublic trade and the growth of regional marketing centers which has accompanied demands for political devolution have meant that the trade in metals has increased in a rapid and uncontrolled fashion. In certain cases, notably that of aluminum, this has severely disrupted Western markets. Such trade does not, however, imply genuine integration with the Western market system in so far as inputs into metals production in the region are not based on market values and the statistical information which should be supplied as an obligation of market participation has not been forthcoming.

Notwithstanding the current problems of the CIS metals sector, there are strong grounds for arguing that it should be made a priority of future economic development in the CIS. It is already the largest export sector after oil

79

and gas and can be developed more rapidly than any internationally competitive manufacturing capability. However, even maintaining production at no more than current levels, at standards which are environmentally acceptable, will require a massive infusion of capital. A number of Western mining and metal companies have expressed an interest in participating in the foreign investment, the Russian authorities have in practice shown themselves to be ambivalent. They continue to evince a clear preference for keeping the best deposits for domestic developers, and are suspicious of the motives of foreign companies. The risk-reward structure that Western investors have to live with is poorly understood and the project terms offered them often display a distinct lack of realism. There are also practical problems arising from disputes over the jurisdiction of resources between the center and the regions.

The establishment of an enforceable legal and fiscal regime that will permit Western mining companies to commit substantial investments depends on the attainment of political stability. At the same time, the minerals sector, as one of the few of any international value in the post-Soviet economies, is itself a pawn in the political struggles, and its status will not be fully clarified as long as those struggles continue. In the meantime, Western companies will have to live with a high degree of uncertainty and will remain vulnerable to corrupt practices. Much of the practical interest is likely to be directed to the new Central Asian states, where the matter of authority over resources is clearer. International organizations could promote the redevelopment of the CIS metals sector and expedite the process of integration into the market system through a selective program of regional assistance.

CHAPTER ONE

Introduction to Part Two

The mining and metals industries of the CIS countries have embarked on a process of transition from an approach based on national self-sufficiency, or "autarky," toward a fuller integration into world markets. The short answers to the questions "how far down the road they have progressed?" and "what remains to be done?" are, respectively, "not far" and "a great deal."

The longer answers, effectively the subject of this paper, are infinitely more complex. They turn on an appreciation of developments in the broader political domain, on the struggle between the various factions in the capitals, and between the capitals and the regions. They also turn on developments in the CIS economies at large, the speed and success of the privatization process, progress with currency stabilization, provisions on capital movements and liberalization of energy prices. It would be difficult for anyone to comment on every one of these matters with authority.

All such problems notwithstanding, there is still something to be said for a minerals specialist with global experience seeking to clarify what is going on in this key sector. For it is increasingly important to view the CIS countries' minerals sectors in their world context, something that has not generally been done, nor, arguably, been very necessary, in the past.

As table 1-1 shows, the CIS republics collectively are major world producers of nonfuel minerals, ranking first in nickel and palladium, second in aluminum and platinum, third in copper and iron ore, and fourth in gold. They are also major exporters to the rest of the world, something which has in the past three years given rise to increasing concern among Western producers, notably of aluminum and nickel. As a group, nonfuel minerals represent the second most important export item after oil and gas.

As a region that covers over one-sixth of the earth's surface but still ac-

81

Table 1-1. *CIS Production and Exports of Metals, 1993*
Thousand tonnes

Metal		Production	World ranking	Percent of world	Exports (to West)	World ranking
Aluminum	- mine[a]	7,260	5	6	...	...
	- metal	3,134	2	16	1,820	1
Copper	- mine	833	3	9	...	...
	- metal	948	4	8	365	4
Gold	- mine[b]	244	4	11	260	2
Iron ore	- mine[ac]	154	3	16	4	11
Lead	- mine	195	5	7	...	...
	- metal	317	5	6	51	11
Nickel	- metal	182	1	23	145	1
PGMs[d]	- platinum[be]	21	2	16	21	2
	- palladium[be]	72	1	56	72	1
Zinc	- mine	452	6	7	...	...
	- metal	502	4	7	149	6

Sources: Kontsem Aluminiy; European Aluminum Association; Brook Hunt and Associates; World Bureau of Metal Statistics, *World Metal Statistics*; Gold Fields Mineral Services, *Gold 1994*; UNCTAD, *Iron Ore Statistics, 1994*; Commodities Research Unit; Johnson Matthey, *Platinum 1994*; International Lead and Zinc Study Group, *Lead and Zinc Statistics*; RTZ.
a. Gross weight.
b. Tonnes.
c. Million tonnes.
d. Platinum group metals.
e. Production assumed equal to exports.

counts for less than a sixth of its metals production, the CIS has a potential as a future producer that cannot be ignored. Beyond that, the fact is that the CIS countries have only a limited range of options as to how they will pay their way in the world in coming years. With the populous countries of the Far East on one border and the resurgent economies of Eastern Europe on the other, the CIS states will struggle to advance themselves as international manufacturers. In the short to medium term, minerals may represent one of the most promising sectors on which to base a redevelopment strategy.

There are, of course, substantial contrasts between different parts of the CIS. While much of the attention has understandably focused on the Russian Federation, several mineral-rich Central Asian CIS republics have adopted an approach markedly different from Moscow's. Generalizations about the CIS therefore tend to have limited validity. On the other hand, many of the formal and informal linkages between the mining and metals sectors in the various parts of the CIS still exist, and the nature of the transportation system means that trade data are often still not separated out by country. In addition, most of the production data which exist apply to the area as a whole.

The structure of the paper is as follows. Chapter 2 deals with the legacy of communism. This is essential to an understanding of the attitudes of the present and the main features of the approach that is now emerging. Chapter 3 looks at the current conditions and organization of the CIS mining and metals industries. Chapter 4 examines the external trade of the CIS countries and its impact on world markets. Chapter 5 moves on to an assessment of the regime facing foreign companies interested in investment in this sector in Russia. A more summary assessment is made for the Central Asian republics. Chapter 6 tackles some of the issues that need to be addressed by, respectively, CIS governments, foreign investors and international organizations, if the process of integration is to be expedited. Chapter 7 offers some concluding thoughts.

CHAPTER TWO

The Legacy of Communism

Soviet Marxism gave primacy to politics in the allocation of economic resources. Economics was henceforth to be the servant of the public will, not its master. The public will was embodied in the State Plan, and the role of mining and metals production, apart from the direct provision of social employment, was to furnish the raw materials required for the fulfillment of the Plan's objectives.

The ability of the political authorities to shape the economy was held to be contingent on the possession of a high measure of independence from interference by countries outside the Soviet sphere. Trade was permitted only to the extent that it was essential to fill gaps in the Plan's input requirements—this largely meant technology products and (in the later Soviet period) grain—while selected commodities produced in the Soviet sphere were allocated the function of earning the foreign exchange necessary to pay for these goods.[1] Among the more important products assigned this export role were several nonfuel mineral commodities, notably gold, platinum group metals, diamonds and nickel. Foreign investment, denounced by Lenin as an instrument of imperialism even more than trade, was seen as compromising the communist world's capacity for political self-determination. The result was an essentially isolationist approach to economic development in general, and to mineral procurement in particular. Although the more extreme form of this principle gave way to a more relaxed interpretation in the 1960s,[2] the notion that dependence on trade should be strictly limited continued right through to perestroika, and

1. William Nelson Turpin, *Soviet Foreign Trade: Purpose and Performance* (Lexington Books, 1977).
2. R. G. Jensen, T. Shabad, and A. W. Wright, "The Implications of Soviet Raw Materials for the World Economy," in Jensen, Shabad, and Wright (eds), *Soviet Natural Resources in the World Economy* (University of Chicago Press, 1983).

the value of trade relative to GDP remained at very low levels in comparison with most Western economies.

Within the confines of the Soviet sphere, mineral raw materials played a wholly different role—that of systematically breeding dependence between various countries and regions. The strategy of developing the dependence of Eastern Europe on Soviet raw materials has been well documented, as has the dependence of the smaller Soviet republics on Russian oil and gas.[3] Often in the name of a regional policy intended to promote greater equality through the dispersal of economic activity, the Soviet Union developed a complex web of material dependencies amongst the republics; ores mined in the Soviet Far East, for example, were shipped to Kazakhstan for smelting, and hauled on to European Russia for fabrication. Metallurgical ores and products are estimated to have accounted for some 30 percent of all bulk transportation under the Soviet system.

From these basic characteristics of Soviet communism flowed a series of institutional arrangements and, perhaps even more importantly, a complex of attitudes and ideas, which are still very much in evidence.

First, procurement of mineral materials is still commonly perceived as a physical problem rather than an economic one. If, as was the case for so long, the economy is viewed as a vast input-output table, then what matters is volume flows. To produce so many refrigerators requires so many meters of copper tubing, requires so many tonnes of copper metal. Prices and money enter the system only as aspects of accounting, not of allocation.

Given such a premise, it is unsurprising to find that mineral production is still regarded essentially as a scientific matter. Mines and processing plants are generally managed by engineers and technologists, whose job it is to maximize throughput on the basis of whatever capital or ore bodies are assigned to them, and whose interest in and awareness of what ultimately happens to their products are minimal. The feedback from the market to the plant that is typical in the West is still largely absent. Although managers are often highly professional, and delighted to talk technicalities, attempts to extract information on the economics of their operations are frequently rebuffed with the response that these are not matters for scientists. Their job is to deliver tonnage.

The ability to deliver tonnage in mining hinges on mineral ore grades, and these inevitably decline with time. Although the term "economic" is used in the CIS countries to distinguish material which will be recovered from that which will not, the term has little in common with that used to define cut-off

3. Michael Bradshaw, *The Economic Effects of Soviet Dissolution,* Post-Soviet Business Forum (RIIA, 1993).

grades in the West. Consistent with the broader perspectives of state planning and with an underlying theory of value which placed particular emphasis on labor inputs, economics is still widely considered in the CIS countries to incorporate such objectives as the provision of employment and the limitation of import dependence. Cut-off grades are therefore as much a matter of technical possibility as of financial calculation. There are small underground lead-zinc mines in central and southeastern Kazakhstan producing under conditions and at grades (1–5 percent lead and zinc combined in the total volume of ore) which elsewhere would be unthinkable, while on the Kola Peninsula, in Western Siberia and in Azerbaijan, aluminum is produced from nonbauxite materials at a cost perhaps two to three times that of producing it from the bauxite ores used universally in the West. Sometimes it seems that mines are worked until every last lump of mineralized rock has been removed and that to do otherwise would be considered wasteful.

For similar reasons, all estimates of mineral reserves have to be treated with profound skepticism. The criteria on which such estimates were devised, in so far as they can be grasped at all by a Western economist, are simply not relevant to the market economy context, and comparisons with the reserves of other countries are meaningless. Dr. Vitaly Borisovich of the Moscow Geological and Prospecting Institute claimed in 1991 that there were some 9,000 mineral deposits in the CIS countries awaiting development, while at the same time noting that the exploration work on many of these had been carried out 20–30 years previously.[4] In the same paper it is claimed that the CIS is the world leader in proven reserves of iron, nickel, cobalt, tin, tungsten and titanium, and reserve life expectations—as shown in table 2-1—are in several instances given as over 100 years. Elsewhere, similar claims have been made for CIS world leadership in terms of reserves of copper, manganese, molybdenum, lead and zinc.[5] Such claims rest uncomfortably with the facts that a number of the metals listed have been subject to declining production trends in recent years, and that some have been traditional import items, as is the case, for example, with tin, tungsten and molybdenum. The emphasis in all this on physical availability rather than cost of recovery encourages the suspicion that, viewed in market terms, Soviet reserves were hugely overestimated. This overestimation has in turn generated the widespread belief in the region that it is prodigiously rich in minerals—indeed uniquely endowed—a point to which the paper returns later.

4. Vitaly Borisovich, "Mining in the USSR and Conditions for Foreign Investment," paper presented to the Metal Mining Agency of Japan Forum in London, 9 October 1993.

5. A. I. Krivtsov, "Geology, Resources and Products of Metallic Ores in the USSR" (origin of paper uncertain, c. 1990).

Table 2-1. *CIS Metal Reserves, 1991*

Metal	Years of current production
Bauxite	178
Cobalt	62
Copper	85
Lead	104
Molybdenum	163
Nickel	59
Tin	57
Titanium	535
Tungsten	106
Zinc	103

Source: See text.

A second vestige of communism evident in the mining and metals industries of the CIS today is secrecy. Information is power in a bureaucratic system, and those with power do not relinquish it lightly. Requests for production information at plant level or in Moscow are commonly met with embarrassment and dissimulation. Those without the information may well not be prepared to admit it in so far as it reflects adversely on their status. Those with it may be reluctant to release it because they suspect it may be of commercial value, even if it is not evident exactly what this might be. Although a chink in this veil of secrecy became evident with the release of information on aluminum production at a conference at St. Petersburg organized by Concern Aluminiy in September 1992, apparently without incurring the wrath of the authorities, this remains the exception rather than the rule. The 1956 decree that classified statistics on the production of nonferrous metals and many nonmetallic minerals as state secrets remains in force, in Russia at least, and although there is talk of revoking it, so far nothing has been done. The statistical services of the other republics are as yet relatively undeveloped at best, and in practice production figures are as problematic here as for Russia. Restrictions apply also to the release of information on mineral deposits. Information is released on an apparently arbitrary and discretionary basis, data declared secret one day mysteriously becoming available the next.

Gold provides a good illustration of the sort of problems to which this semisecrecy. Although production figures for Russia are still technically secret, Goskomstat, the State Statistics Committee, revealed in May 1993 that production in 1992 was 129.5 tonnes, 12 tonnes down on 1991. Later in the same month, the chairman of the Russian State Committee on Precious Metals and Stones, Yevgeny Bychkov, who should have been in a position to know, stated that Russian output in 1992 had in fact been 146 tonnes, 7 percent less than in 1991. Subsequently, the head of the State Geological Committee countered that production had in fact increased in 1992 over 1991, and stood at 170 tonnes in the latter year. The US Bureau of Mines, meanwhile, has estimated production in 1992 at 192 tonnes—but still down on 1991.[6] Part of the explanation for these discrepancies is almost certainly that the *artels*, or cooperatives, which now produce around half Russia's gold, have not been reporting their output. On balance, it seems probable that production was actually nearer the upper end of the range. However, it is on a declining trend, principally as a result of growing production and staffing problems in the inhospitable Magadan region in the Far East.[7]

A no less important dimension of the tradition of secrecy is the profound lack of awareness in the CIS countries of mining activities elsewhere. Many plant managers have only the vaguest notion of activities in other parts of the CIS, far less outside it. The kind of information flows which oil the wheels of the Western industry—the trade press, international conferences, stock market analyses, consultants' reports—simply do not exist in the CIS countries, and large Western mining companies visiting the region have had to get used to the fact that many senior people they meet have never heard of them, and that their successes elsewhere count for little. It is a situation which deprives the policymakers of the CIS countries of a comparative framework within which to view their industry, its efficiency and environmental friendliness, as well as leaving them vulnerable to less than scrupulous operators. It is also a situation in which prejudices can flourish, not least prejudices about the extent of the CIS countries' mineral wealth and the rent that can be generated from its exploitation.

A final point concerns the geographical structure of the industry. The attempt to use the mining and metals industries to knit together the various outlying parts of the Soviet Union has resulted in an industry in which the location of producers and the linkages between them seem often to make little sense in market terms. Materials have historically been hauled considerable distances without transport costs being imputed to production. Although such linkages weakened with the death of the Soviet Union, the lack of alternative markets, the existence of dedicated transport facilities, and the (initial) dependence on a common payments system meant that they did not disappear overnight. Metals industry managers seeking to expand their dealings with the

6. Reports in *Metal Bulletin*, 3 June 1993 and 10 May 1993, and *Mining Magazine*, July 1993.

7. Natalia Zubareva, "New Developments in the Gold Mining Industry of the Russian Federation," paper presented to the Western Gold Show, San Francisco, November 1992.

outside world have found that the inward orientation of the Soviet empire has created a transport system in which the options for foreign trade are strictly limited. The metals trade press regularly carries stories of shipments from CIS countries being delayed at ports, or of feed shortages at metallurgical plants arising from rail transport difficulties.

CHAPTER THREE

The Current Condition of the Industry

The opening of the door on the CIS mining and metals industries has produced a number of surprises for Western observers. The growth of the aluminum smelting industry in Siberia had been consistently underestimated through the 1970s and 1980s, with the result that by 1990 the most authoritative Western estimates of CIS production, those of the US Bureau of Mines and of Metallgesellschaft of Germany, stood at around one million tonnes below what turns out to have been the actual annual level. Annual production of nickel had been underestimated by some 100,000 tonnes, partly, it seems, because Western analysts could not envisage what possible use could have been made of the higher tonnage. (The answer lay in the widespread use of nickel to upgrade poor-quality steels and in the underdeveloped nature of the market for stainless scrap, a source of around half of all the nickel units consumed in the West.) Copper production was similarly underestimated. At the same time, the production of lead and zinc appears to have been consistently overestimated.

Given the relative size of the Russian Federation, it is less surprising to find confirmation that it dominates CIS production, in some cases—for example, platinum group metals and cobalt—being the sole producer (see table 3-1). Outside Russia, the most important CIS republic as far as nonferrous metals are concerned is Kazakhstan, which has copper mines in the vicinity of Dzhezkazgan and Balkhash and a large number of small polymetallic copper-lead-zinc mines. It is also the CIS's principal producer of chrome ore—from the Donskoye complex. Uzbekistan is an important producer of gold, most of this from the huge Muruntau operation, while the Ukraine is a major producer of iron ore and manganese ore. The mining industry of Armenia, which ac-

Table 3-1. *Distribution of Metals Production among CIS Countries*
Percent, 1990 estimates

Metal	Russia	Ukraine	Kazakhstan	Uzbekistan	Other (principal producer)	
Aluminum mine	70	7	15	...	8	(Azerbaijan)
Aluminum metal	83	2	...	...	15	(Tajikistan)
Cobalt mine	100	...	...	...	...	
Copper mine	58	...	32	8	2	(Armenia)
Copper metal	60	...	32	8	...	
Chrome ore	4	...	96	...	...	
Gold mine	67	...	5	25	3	(Armenia)
Iron ore	45	45	10	...		
Lead mine	20	...	63	15	2	(Georgia)
Lead metal	10	...	90	...	...	
Nickel mine	99	1	...	...	...	
Nickel metal	99	1	...	...	...	
Manganese ore	...	75	5	...	20	(Georgia)
Molybdenum mine	58	...	5	5	32	(Armenia)
PGMs	100	...	...	...	...	
Silver mine	43	...	49	5	3	(Armenia)
Tin mine	100	...	...	...	...	
Zinc mine	38	...	55	6	1	(Georgia)
Zinc metal	33	2	46	19	...	

Source: Author's estimates.

counted for a large part of the CIS's molybdenum supplies, is believed to have been shut down on account of the political problems of the region, and by severe energy shortages.

The condition of the mining industry, though inevitably highly variable from place to place, has generally been revealed as extremely poor. Ore grades are low by world standards, and waste generation commensurately high. Managements may be technically competent, but they are constrained by the quality of the capital available to them, the product of decades of underinvestment. Trucks are small by Western standards. There appears to be nothing larger than 100 tonnes. Large open-pit operations in the West frequently use trucks of 200 tonnes capacity and above. There are constant complaints about the nonavailability of spares for drills and other mobile equipment, a matter not helped by the fact that much heavy mining equipment was produced in Belarus, supplies from which have been affected by the general deterioration in interrepublican trade relations. Borisovich, in the paper already cited, talks of losses from mining and beneficiation running as high as 35–40 percent for lead, zinc and aluminum and 25 percent for copper and manganese.

The severe climate of many mining regions, and the determination to extract every last lump of mineralized rock as an alternative to incurring the capital expense of opening a higher-grade mine elsewhere, has led to miners having to operate in extremely difficult conditions. Winter temperatures of -30C and below in some mining areas create major problems for processing (which generally requires large quantities of water), and make alluvial mining such as that carried out in the Magadan Oblast impossible. In the Urals, poor-quality bauxite is being recovered at depths of 1,000 meters from mines suffering severe problems of water and rock mechanics as well as resource exhaustion. In the West, nearly all bauxite is recovered from open pits, most of the European underground mines of the type common in the Urals having been closed down. As an example from copper, the two mines feeding the copper smelter at Balkhash in Kazakhstan would, by most Western definitions, be considered unviable. The one at Kounrad has an average grade of 0.3 percent copper, and is having to remove 6 tonnes of overlying rock to recover one of ore. The one at Sayak grades 0.6 percent, but there is no concentrator on site, and the crude ore has to be hauled 200 km for processing.

Where mines adjacent to smelters are finally shut down because the ore can no longer be treated, the problem of ore quality is often simply replaced by that of having to transport mine product vast distances. The four copper smelters in the Urals, for example, which have seen a number of their local feed sources dry up in recent years, have been bringing in concentrates over thousands of kilometers from Mongolia, Uzbekistan and the Caucasus. Worse, since copper concentrates in the CIS countries generally tend to have metal values only around half those in the West (15–20 percent as opposed to 28–34 percent metal content), a considerable amount of earth is also being carried around. Commercial transportation tariffs would clearly kill much of this activity.

The problem at the metallurgical plants is partly one of feed, and partly one of capital. Most are currently operating well below their nominal capacities. Falling mine output, disruptions to interrepublican trade and a straightforward lack of money have left smelters scrabbling for concentrates. Many plants are extremely old, some dating back to before the Second World War, and are in desperate need of replacement. Calculations by the German aluminum company VAW suggest that the cost of retrofitting CIS aluminum smelters could run to $9 billion.[1] With energy available at a fraction of the world price, many

---

1. Horst D. Peters, "The Future of the Russian Aluminium Industry," paper presented to *Metal Bulletin*'s International Aluminium Conference, Oslo, September 1992.

are extremely energy-inefficient by Western standards. Even where good equipment exists, as for example in Norilsk, which possesses an Outokumpu flash smelting furnace, lack of foreign exchange to buy parts has inhibited proper maintenance. Ironically, Soviet technologists developed one of the most advanced lead-smelting processes in the world (Kivcet), but lack of capital has prevented its adoption except at one lead plant, that at Ust-Kamenogorsk in Kazakhstan.

For many of the same reasons, environmental standards are generally extremely low. Sulfur capture at copper smelters varies between 35 percent and 75 percent, as against the 98 percent or so achieved by many Western smelters, while it is simply nonexistent at two lead smelters in Russia (Dalpolymetal and Electrozinc). Norilsk Nikel, in the Far North, where the lack of any local market for sulfuric acid inhibits further sulfur recovery, is most probably the largest source of airborne sulfur in the world. In the aluminum industry, all bar three of the fourteen smelters in the CIS region use outdated Söderberg technology, with inadequate gas scrubbing systems. Their fluoride and dust emissions are between eight and ten times the level permitted in the EU.[2] Not surprisingly, these sorts of conditions have at some plants been a continuing source of labor unrest. An extract from an internal report by a colleague on his return from a visit to a metallurgical operation in the former Soviet Union during the second half of 1992 sums up the problems.

> As visitors we were not provided with any safety equipment. The workers rarely wear hard hats, safety boots or goggles. The walkways were made of wooden planking, and individual planks were frequently missing, as were ladder rungs. The smelter in particular was extremely dangerous with vessels of molten material passing over the heads of the workers. Scrap and slag littered the smelter floor. The corrugated iron roof had rusted through, and was partly open to the sky. Fragments of metal were hanging from the roof ready to fall on the heads of the hatless workers below. The smelter was originally built in the 1930s. We were not allowed to photograph it for obvious reasons.

Such reports, which have become commonplace over the past few years, at first encouraged the belief among their authors that things could not go on like this much longer, and that production levels must fall. Although not wholly wrong, such judgments seem in retrospect seriously to have underestimated the resilience of post-Soviet managers and their capacity for improvisation.

2. H. O. Bohner, "Aluminium Smelters in the Former USSR,." paper prepared at the request of the European Aluminium Association, June 1993.

The vagaries of the planning system meant that their job was never a straight-forward one under the old dispensation, and a certain amount of imagination was always a requirement of the job. Plants have always tended to keep large maintenance staffs to fabricate the components necessary to keep them running. Moreover, since obtaining greater access to the West, several metallurgical operations, notably in Kazakhstan and the Urals, have been able to toll-smelt Western concentrates, and thereby to maintain production levels.

Thus, while it is certainly the case that nonferrous metal production in the CIS region has fallen since the late 1980s—the peak was in 1988—it has fallen less than industrial production generally (see table 3-2). Indeed, the incentive for producers to withhold production for private sale means that it has probably fallen less than official statements would suggest. Between 1990 and 1992, while industrial production in the CIS fell some 30 percent, aluminum production fell by only 9 percent, copper and gold production by 12 percent, and zinc output by 16 percent. As a result, the relative importance of the sector to the economy of the region increased. The nonferrous metals sector was estimated in 1993 to be contributing about 6 percent of Russia's GDP but to be on track to grow to 10 percent.[3] Indeed, nonferrous metals must be considered, along with financial services, the nearest thing that country has to a buoyant sector, wages in the industry standing at around twice the national average. In so far as the nonferrous metals sector, with all its problems, is probably one of the most competitive internationally, this has a certain undeniable logic.

The administration of metals production has undergone several reorganizations since 1988, when the dismemberment of the monolithic Soviet Ministry of NonFerrous Metallurgy first began. Since the start of 1993, responsibility for nonferrous metals production in Russia (together with that for the iron and steel industry) has rested with the State Committee for Metallurgy, a body described as "a corporate body of the federal executive power."[4] The Committee presides over some 920 production units and includes all base metal production save that coming from the Norilsk Nikel Combine.

The precise relationship between the Committee and the individual enterprises it administers is unclear. The official line is that enterprises are free to pursue their own purchasing and sales activities. The reality is that the state re-

3 Vladimir Popov, "Russian Macroeconomic Performance and Implications for Mineral Production," paper presented at a CRS workshop on *Post-Soviet Minerals: Production and Policy, and Implications for Western Producers*, Ottawa, 17 May 1993.

4. L. Shevelev, "Russian Ferrous Metallurgy During Transition Period to the Market Economy," paper presented to AMM/PaineWebber conference, Steel Market Strategies VIII, New York, June 1993.

Table 3-2. *CIS Metal Production Trends, 1988–93*

Thousand tonnes

Metal		1988	1989	1990	1991	1992	1993
Aluminum	- mine[a]	9,248	8,993	9,246	7,870	7,614	7,260
	- metal	3,450	3,420	3,523	3,250	3,199	3,134
Copper	- mine	1,148	1,160	1,067	1,051	971	833
	- metal	1,435	1,392	1,252	1,154	1,103	984
Gold	- mine[b]	280	285	270	252	237	244
Iron Ore	- mine[ac]	248	241	236	199	175	154
Lead	- mine	270	260	240	230	215	195
	- metal	478	470	460	397	360	317
Nickel	- metal	320	320	316	297	246	182
PGMs	- platinum[bd]	14	17	22	34	23	21
	- palladium[bd]	55	51	58	67	65	72
Zinc	- mine	670	650	610	580	506	452
	- metal	705	684	644	575	540	502

Sources: See table 1-1.
a. Gross weight.
b. Tonnes.
c. Million tonnes.
d. Production assumed equal to exports.

mains the owner of many of the enterprises and controls most aspects of their existence. State subsidies determine costs of energy and transportation, state factories account for a substantial part of sales, while the state's failure to apply the bankruptcy law which entered into force in March 1993 ensures that it is rare for anyone to have to go into liquidation. If the levers of the state no longer work as well as they once did, they certainly still exist.

No mines have yet been privatized, but a number of metallurgical enterprises—for example, the aluminum smelters at Bratsk, Novokuznetsk and Krasnoyarsk—have been converted into joint-stock companies. However, this has effectively meant putting them into the hands of employees and regional authorities, and has rather the hallmarks of Yugoslav-style collectivism than of privatization as it would be recognized in the West. It is difficult to see how it could be otherwise. The poor state of the industry, the environmental liabilities it carries with it and its dependence on subsidies make most of the enterprises simply unsalable. Moreover, many enterprises have over the years acquired extensive social obligations—for schools, hospitals, housing and farms—which commercial investors are reluctant to assume. Recognition of this, combined with a growing acknowledgment of the strategic importance of the sector to the economy's future, makes it probable that most of the sector will remain under state control for some time to come. In the course of 1993 there was a perceptible retreat from ideas of mass privatization in the sector, not just in Russia, where the incumbent government of Viktor Chernomyrdin has been characterized by a markedly more etatist approach than the previous one of Yegor Gaidar, but also in Kazakhstan, where proposals for privatization of the mining and metals industry had to be deferred. In the latter case the Kazakh state may have perceived additional justification in the need to maintain control of sales so as to be able to service crucial barter deals with Russia for energy and transport. The cost of not servicing these debts was vividly demonstrated at the end of 1993, when Russia cut off cross-border power supplies to Kazakhstan, severely disrupting metal production.

In Russia, precious metals come under the jurisdiction of the State Committee for Precious Metals and Stones (Komdragmet), set up in 1991. Unlike the Committee on Metallurgy, which has certain operating responsibilities, Komdragmet is concerned essentially with strategic matters (e.g. the establishment of production quotas) and sales. Gold production is actually carried out by 56 companies formed into voluntary associations ("joint-stock companies") following the disbanding of Rossalmazzoloto in 1992, and a large number (200+) of small-scale *artels,* or cooperatives. The relationship between the central organization and producers is ill-defined, and a constant source of dispute and uncertainty. As a measure of its economic importance, Komdragmet became caught up in the power struggle between the president and parliament during the summer of 1993. The prime minister granted the Committee a degree of independence from the finance ministry in May. Then Yeltsin issued a decree in early June reaffirming finance ministry control. In July 1993, the Supreme Soviet countered with an assertion of its authority through its control of the Central Bank.[5] While this jousting has sometimes been presented as a debate over whether gold should be treated as an industrial product or as a monetary one, in reality it reflects the fact that, as one of the relatively few elements in the Russian economy with genuine international status, gold cannot be kept out of the political arena.

---

5. *East European Markets,* 6 August 1993.

CHAPTER FOUR

Trade with the West

Under communism, foreign trade was subordinated to the needs of the planning process. It was not, as it is in a free market system, a spontaneous response to differential factor endowments and product prices. Rather, it was an approach which sought "to use the Western market for tactical and strategic advantage, but without accepting any obligation to participate responsibly in the operations, the improvement, or the maintenance of that market."[1] Consistent with such an approach, trade with the outside world was a state monopoly, all such activity being channeled through the Ministry of Foreign Economic Relations and its foreign trade organizations.

Amongst metal exports (see table 4-1), gold held a special position as a product which could be used to settle balance-of-payments deficits. Releases tended to be highly erratic and, as such, were a constant source of speculative interest in the West. Although information on the sector is still patchy, with the release of information having a tendency to confuse as often as to clarify, the current view is that both production and stocks of gold in the Soviet Union were significantly overestimated. Western estimates of reserves of 2,000–3,000 tonnes, prevalent in 1990 and 1991, have given way to figures on around only a tenth of this scale.[2] As a producer, the CIS was dislodged from its number two position by the United States in 1990, and in 1992 it was pushed down to number four by Australia.

Other nonfuel mineral commodities which historically played an important role as foreign exchange earners were diamonds and ferroalloys. Effectively

1. Turpin, *Soviet Foreign Trade*.
2. An excellent review of this debate as it unfurled is to be found in Andrew Smith, *Precious Metals Outlook*, Union Bank of Switzerland, 31 January 1990, 30 September 1991 and 4 June 1992.

Table 4-1. *CIS Metal Exports to the West, 1988–93*

Thousand tonnes

Metal	1988	1989	1990	1991	1992	1993
Aluminum	234	290	364	713	1,000	1,820
Copper	76	115	261	262	300	365
Gold[a]	258	285	315	325	220	260
Iron ore[bc]	3	4	4	5	6	4
Lead	12	32	53	45	70	51
Nickel	70	85	85	115	120	145
Platinum[a]	14	17	22	34	23	21
Palladium[a]	55	51	58	67	65	72
Zinc	28	18	19	5	80	149

Sources: See table 1-1.
a. Tonnes.
b. Gross weight.
c. Million tonnes.

all diamonds in the region come from the autonomous republic of Yakutia (now Sakha) within Russia, an area first opened up to production in the 1950s. Although this development makes the CIS only the fourth largest diamond producer in the world in terms of total caratage, it has a higher proportion, maybe 25 percent, of world production of gem-quality stones. These stones have traditionally been marketed through the De Beers Central Selling Organization in London, an arrangement that was renewed for a further five-year period in 1990.

The ferroalloying agents, manganese and chromium, historically represented significant export items for the Soviet Union, though depleting ore bodies and increased off-take by East European countries meant that by the 1980s exports had fallen to very low levels. Simultaneously, exports of nickel had been growing rapidly.[3] The opening up of a new ore body near Norilsk on the Taymyr Peninsula and the addition of new smelting capacity established the Soviet Union as the world's largest producer of nickel. Although within the Arctic Circle, and unconnected with the rest of Russia by overland transportation, Norilsk was an ideal enclave in which to develop an export-oriented industry. It had access to the sea and possessed an ore body of undoubted international standing. Moreover, as a byproduct of the nickel came substantial quantities of platinum group metals, copper and cobalt, all of which have served as useful additional foreign exchange earners.

3. David Humphreys, "Trade in Ferroalloying Materials," in John E. Tilton (ed.), "East-West Mineral Trade," special issue of *Resources Policy*, vol. 12, no. 3 (September 1986).

Since 1990, a great deal has changed—and very little has changed. The collapse of domestic, and particularly military, demand in the CIS area has released a considerable amount of metal for export. This is most dramatically illustrated by the case of aluminum, where annual exports have boomed from around 290,000 tonnes in 1989 to over 1.8 million tonnes in 1993. Previously, much of this metal went to the Soviet aerospace sector. The same export expansion has occurred on a smaller scale for a variety of other base metals, including copper, nickel and zinc. No less important for world markets has been the abrupt cessation in the buying of metals of which the CIS has traditionally been a net importer, for example, tin and molybdenum.

Along with the changes in trade volumes has gone a radical change in the character of the trade. The pressure from the new republics and from regional authorities within them to retain more of the rent from the sale of their natural resources has led to tougher sales and procurement policies at republic level and increasing demands for political devolution—a process sometimes referred to as "sovereignization"—at intrarepublic level. To appease this tendency at intrarepublic level, many producing enterprises have been granted the right to market a proportion of their output directly. Even in cases where "state orders" (i.e., preemptive government procurement orders) are still imposed, they are frequently ignored.

The result of this has been twofold. First, it has tended to break down traditional internal supply links. Given the opportunity to earn hard currency for their products, many enterprises have directed their sales abroad rather than to traditional domestic customers. Kazakhstan's decision to sell more of its chrome ore and lead on world markets in 1993 left Russian ferroalloy producers and battery makers idle.[4] (The seven plants of Russia's battery consortium, Electrozariad, require some 185,000 tonnes of lead a year, and there have even been reports of them buying in the West.) Similarly, the increased facility to import Western concentrates for toll-smelting at Kazakhstan's lead and zinc plants has undermined traditional links with local, small-scale mines. The second consequence has been the gradual loss of government control of the export market. Although the Russian government has sought to offset devolutionary pressures with a series of central licensing arrangements and export taxes, these have tended simply to encourage the development of black market trade—or "back-door" trade, as it is somewhat euphemistically called. Domestic Russian prices of metals are still below world prices (see table 4-2), if

4. *Metal Bulletin*, 7 June 1993

Table 4-2. *Comparison of Prices in Moscow and London,[a] 1993, 1994*
U.S.$ per tonne

Metal	18 February 1993		23 September 1994	
	Moscow	London	Moscow	London
Aluminum	680	1,204	1,220	1,609
Copper	1,091	2,212	1,443	2,556
Lead	340	411	447	622
Nickel	2,594	6,208	4,736	6,450
Tin	3,131	5,785	4,675	5,410
Zinc	680	1,062	711	1,023

Sources: Metal Bulletin and Interfax.
a. Prices of Moscow Nonferrous Metals Exchange (converted from rubles at the prevailing exchange rate) and of London Metal Exchange.

not as dramatically so as was the case in 1991 and 1992, providing a business opportunity for those who can buy in rubles and sell in dollars. Indeed, back-door trade has been quite the best way to get rich quick in the CIS countries over the past few years and doubtless some of the young Russians acquiring prime London properties are among the beneficiaries.

On one level, such an outcome is entirely consistent with market princi-ples. Because of the value-subtracting nature of much of CIS manufacturing, it makes eminently good sense to sell the raw material rather than the lower-value product made from it. *The Economist* has mischievously suggested that Russia could double its GDP by selling all its raw materials rather than doing anything to them.[5] The problem, if it needs spelling out, is that such a strategy would lead to the almost immediate cessation of virtually all industrial activity and a politically intolerable level of unemployment. The government has un-derstandably been trying to steer a way between the extremes of negative value added and deindustrialization. It does not want to discourage the trade because of its foreign exchange needs, but at the same time it wants to make sure the benefit of this trade goes into its own coffers rather than into private bank accounts in Switzerland, and it wants to keep its factories running to avoid social unrest.

The sense in which it can be said that nothing much has changed in relation to the CIS countries' external trade is in terms of official attitudes. Foreign trade continues effectively to be used as a practical convenience, rather than engaged in as an ideological expression of a commitment to market values. Although it may well be that CIS countries' exports are in some cases interna-

5 . "Russia's Value Gap," *The Economist*, 24 October 1992.

tionally competitive, it is equally clear that in other cases they are not. The fact is that with factor inputs—labor, transportation, capital and energy—being priced on a basis other than the market, it is not immediately obvious which is which. The essential driving force for the commodity export trade is still, as it was previously, the requirement for hard currency, and the fact that there is really nothing else available to sell that the world will buy.

The continuity in attitudes is evident in the reaction of Russian officials to charges that they have been dumping their metals in the West. Such charges have been met by a mixture of puzzlement and aggrieved self-righteousness. The implicit reproach is that "the West has been complaining all along that we do not participate in international markets. Now we are doing so, that is apparently wrong too." Alternatively, Western observers simply do not understand the desperate requirement for foreign exchange—which may be a fairer point, though not one that gives much comfort to Western metals producers. For free trade to work properly, prices do, of course, need to reflect market-based opportunity costs. It is, however, perhaps not too surprising that such a fact is not immediately intelligible to those schooled under communism.

The second element that betrays a less than total conversion to the free trade system is the continuing suppression of data on imports and exports. Properly functioning markets require good information, to permit rational decisionmaking by producers and consumers alike. The provision of such information is an aspect of taking responsibility for the operation and maintenance of the market system, as discussed at the beginning of this chapter. Although the CIS states have released odd bits of information on trade, as on production, and shown willing by joining various metals study groups, they have promised more than they have delivered. There is perhaps a misconception that the absence of planning necessarily implies the existence of a market. It does not, certainly not while the attitudes and preconceptions of planning persist. The market has its own institutional requirements and obligations, and these are still not met and honored in the CIS countries.

The case of aluminum provides a good illustration of some of these problems. The Soviet Union exported to the West some 100,000–200,000 tonnes a year through most of the 1980s. Then CIS sales—largely Russian—mushroomed dramatically in the early 1990s. The figure given in table 4-1 above of 1.8 million tonnes in 1993 conveys the order of magnitude of the increase, though the truth is that no one is certain of the exact figure. Some numbers have been released by the Russian authorities, but not in a sufficiently detailed form to permit their validation. In any case, by their nature, they almost certainly exclude unofficial sales. Although a great deal of information can be obtained by the examination of importing countries' trade accounts, these do not provide comprehensive coverage, and do not include deliveries to the London Metal Exchange, which has been a major recipient of metal. For present purposes, the figure of 1.8 million tonnes looks reasonably robust for 1993, while the figure for 1994 is likely to be nearer 2 million tonnes. Sales of this order have enabled the CIS to surge ahead of Brazil, Australia and even Canada as an exporter. The speed of the buildup of CIS aluminum exports, and its coincidence with a recession in the industry, has inevitably sparked a fierce response from Western producers.

As the closest market to the CIS, and an area containing a number of the world's higher-cost smelters, Europe has tended to feel the impact of CIS countries' sales most acutely. While simultaneously making some production cutbacks, the industry, through its representative body, Eurométaux, lodged a complaint with the European Commission in December 1992, with a view to having quotas imposed on CIS sales in the EU area. The case was partly based on a consideration of tonnage, but also on the heavy discounting that had allegedly been taking place, particularly for off-grade metal. Although evidently reluctant to take up the matter at a time when it was doing all it could to encourage the CIS states to trade their way into the Western system, and to conclude partnership and cooperation agreements with some of them, the European Commission agreed to mount its own investigation. Having satisfied itself that injury had indeed taken place, the Commission announced in August 1993 that, until November of that year, while it was trying to negotiate a settlement with the Russian authorities, aluminum imports from the CIS for domestic EU consumption would be limited to 60,000 tonnes. In justifying its stance, the European Commission noted that "aluminum produced in the CIS states enjoys the advantage of artificially low energy prices, and environmental standards that are far less strict than in western countries."[6]

The Russian response to this was to point out, with some justification, that the imposition by the EU of controls on purchases of aluminum, as an internationally tradable commodity, would do nothing to increase prices. It might in any case reasonably be asked how the objective of promoting freer trade was served by the suggestion that countries with lower environmental standards ought not to be allowed to trade with the EU, or how the process of marketization in the CIS countries would be assisted by the reimposition of tougher central controls. Symbolically, however, the quota was important as a sign of the growing frustration in the West over the slow pace of marketization in the CIS

6. *The Financial Times*, 10 August 1993.

states, and marked the end of the honeymoon period in trade relations which began with the destruction of the Berlin Wall. In January 1994, a multilateral solution to the problem of aluminum oversupply was forged. Under the terms of a Memorandum of Understanding signed in Brussels, representatives of Australia, Canada, the EU, Norway, the United States and the Russian Federation agreed that, in the event of Western producers voluntarily making production cuts of the order of 1.5 million tonnes, and in return for a major package of technical assistance from the Western signatories, Russia would institute a staged production cutback of 0.5 million tonnes. The MoU was to have a maximum life of two years.

CHAPTER FIVE

The Rhetoric and the Reality of the Foreign Investment Dimension

The limitations of generalization in relation to CIS mining and metals are nowhere more evident than in the area of foreign investment. Considerable variations exist in perspectives on, and responses to, the idea of foreign investment, both between CIS states and within them. Thus far, the Central Asian republics, notably Kazakhstan, Uzbekistan and Kyrgyzstan, have shown themselves most flexible, and, having a number of attractive opportunities in gold, have tended to attract a major part of the investment interest. The Russian Federation's approach, by contrast, has been more cautious and ambiguous, though in general more positive at the periphery than at the center. However, it is still the biggest and most interesting game and, as such, the principal focus of this chapter.

The Russian law on foreign investment, approved by the Supreme Soviet in July 1991, accords foreign investors the right to participate in joint ventures with nationals, to create wholly owned subsidiaries, to buy existing enterprises and "to acquire rights to use land and to engage in other natural resources."[1] While obviously representing a revolution in principle, such a law does not of course guarantee that in the privatization process there will be many enterprises offered in their entirety to foreigners, or that the conditions of investment will be such that foreign investors would want to put their

1. James P. Dorian and Vitaly T. Borisovich, "Energy and Minerals in the Former Soviet Republics," *Resources Policy*, vol. 18, no. 3 (September 1992), pp. 205–09.

money in anyway (see contribution by William Butler in this volume). A September 1993 decree for the first time established the unequivocal right to private ownership of land. But foreigners remain for the time being excluded from these provisions. Proposals to allow foreigners to buy land for green field development purposes were under discussion in early 1995. But even if these are passed, it is unlikely that they will apply to minerals extraction.

Of equal importance to potential investors in mining and metals in Russia is the mineral resources law, "On the Subsoil," which was approved by the Supreme Soviet in February 1992 and enacted by presidential decree the following April. Consistent with Article 11 of the old Constitution of the Russian Federation, this stipulates that subsoil resources are owned "by the nations residing on respective territories." This wording is highly ambiguous, leaving it unclear whether the republic, territory *(krai)*, province *(oblast)* or subordinate autonomous district is the relevant territorial unit. The intention is clearly to devolve jurisdiction over resources (and certainly this is how it has been interpreted by the provinces themselves), but at the same time the law appears to reserve certain strategic functions—for example, the establishment of national schedules for exploitation—to the federal authorities.[2]

The new constitution of 1993 states that "ownership of land and other natural resources may reside in private, state, municipal or other hands." (Article 9). This seems to imply some liberalization, but the formulation is so open ended as to defy precise interpretation. Pointing in the other direction, Article 36 of the new constitution specifies that "conditions and schedules for land use are determined by federal law," implying a continued strategic role for the state.

This ambiguity of general provisions has been carried over into the rules governing the implementation of the subsoil law. These were laid down in a second law, "Regulation for Licensing Procedures with Respect to the Use of the Subsoil," which was approved in July 1992. This spelled out, in general terms, the different types of licenses (for exploration, exploitation and waste recovery), what they should include, how they should be allocated (by tenders and auctions) and what should be the structure of payments. While it makes clear that the licensing procedure will be administered by the State Committee for Geology (Roskomnedra), the actual issue of licenses is left as a matter to be agreed jointly between the central authorities and the representatives of the relevant territory. Local authorities have the right to impose additional licensing conditions, e.g. in relation to road construction or other social projects.

2. Vladimir Kozhkar, "Legal Mechanism of the Use of Subsoil in the Russian Federation," *Russian Business Monitor*, no. 1 (1993), pp. 29–35.

A law containing detailed provisions for mining concessions in the gold and precious metals sectors was approved by the Supreme Soviet at the end of July 1993. With a view to resolving clashes between the claims of the center and those of the territories, this proposes that central and regional authorities collaborate each year in the preparation of a list of mining concessions, which should specify those concessions that will be subject to federal licensing, those that will be subject to local or regional licensing, and those for which the two levels will share jurisdiction. (In practice, Roskomnedra seems to have been operating on the principle that gold deposits with reserves greater than 100 tonnes are "national assets." while those with less can be handled locally.) It reaffirms the principle of open tendering for concessions, but qualifies this by limiting foreign participation to 50 percent.[3]

A practical example of the sort of problems which uncertainty over jurisdiction between the central and regional authorities—and indeed between different branches of the central government—can create, is supplied by the case of Sukhoi Log, a hard rock gold deposit near Bodaibo in the Irkutsk region of Siberia, reputed to contain reserves of more than 2,000 tonnes of gold and to be the largest unexploited gold deposit in Russia. In April 1992, Star Technology Systems, an offshoot of an Australian mining company, Central Mining, concluded an agreement to acquire 31 percent of the Lenzoloto joint-stock company (successor to the state body of the same name) which held the Sukhoi Log concession, even as other companies were discussing access to the deposit in Moscow. There was an immediate objection from the Committee for Precious Metals and Stones and the Committee for Geology on the grounds that Lenzoloto did not have the authority to concede rights over the deposit. The Committee sought to rule that the concession would have to be put out to tender. Although the Star deal was formally approved by the Committee for Management of State Property in March 1993, Roskomnedra continued to insist that it did not comply with licensing requirements, and to withhold geological information necessary for the deposit's development. In August, a conciliatory commission was set up by the central and local authorities with a view to resolving their differences, and it was not until December 1994 that Star's license was finally confirmed.[4]

A second problem for foreign investors is a predisposition on the part of the Russian authorities to give preference in awarding concessions to domestic

3. *East European Markets*, Moscow Bulletin, 6 August 1993.

4. Reports in *Mining Journal*, 17 April 1992; *Financial Times*, 18 November 1992, 25 March 1993 and 24 August 1993; *Eastern European Markets*, Moscow Bulletin, 13 November 1992 and 16 April 1993; *Metals Week*, 19 December 1994.

enterprises, a predisposition that has become more marked since Viktor Chernomyrdin became Prime Minister—his experience as head of Gazprom presumably having convinced him that Russia can go it alone on these matters. The most celebrated example of this tendency is in the energy sector—the decision in November 1992 to award a license for the development of a large gas deposit in the Barents Sea to an all-Russian consortium, Rosshelf, thereby displacing a Western consortium of Conoco, Norsk Hydro and Neste which had already spent tens of millions of dollars working on the project under an agreement concluded with the Soviet government in 1989.[5]

The same forces are at work in nonfuel sectors too. During the tender for the Udokan copper deposit, a major deposit situated east of Lake Baikal in Chita Oblast estimated to contain some 20 million tonnes of copper, it was made clear to those participating that preference would be given to investors with a domestic orientation and prepared to give emphasis to social considerations. After six of the eight companies qualifying for the tender had withdrawn, the license was awarded in January 1993 to the Chita-based Udokan Mining Company, a consortium comprised of: (35 percent) a group of Russian investors, the Arter Group, including several industrial combines; (20 percent) the administration of Chita province; and (45 percent) the Chita Minerals Company, a US-registered investor involving the Quaker Coal Company and Hong Kong businessman Eddie Wong. Part of the rationale for the award was reportedly that Wong had secured a sales agreement with the Chinese trader CNIEC for a major portion of the output from the mine. However, a debate subsequently developed, heavily fueled by domestic industrial interests (including the ore-starved smelters of the Urals), as to whether the export of the mine's product was consistent with the terms of the license. As a result, the project partners were required to investigate the feasibility of processing the concentrates domestically instead. In February 1994, Chita Minerals Company withdrew from the project. Although the remaining partners continued with a feasibility study for a scaled-down operation, the Moscow authorities were said to be contemplating a new tender.[6]

Nor did Sukhoi Log escape nationalist pressures. One of the devices employed by Komdragmet and Roskomnedra during 1993 to try to block Star's participation in the project was to prepare a draft decree designed to exclude foreign company involvement in the development of the deposit, and to organize a tender exclusively for Russian companies. Yevgeny Bychkov, head of

5. *Wall Street Journal*, 26 November 1992; and *The Economist* 13 March 1993.
6. *Metal Bulletin*, 21 January, 9 September and 16 September 1993; *Mining Journal*, 5 February, 28 May 1993, 19 November 1993 and 11 February 1994: and *Metals Week*, 8 March 1993.

Komdragmet, was quoted as saying, "We have dozens of other gold deposits which can be exploited by foreign companies. But this one must be exploited by ourselves."[7] Although the decree was subsequently abandoned, Bychkov continued to insist for some time that the matter remained open.[8] The underlying message, however, was clear and was consistent with the evidence furnished by various other tenders that have taken place. Foreign investment was sought principally in projects too low-grade or too technically difficult for local operators.

Such ambiguities mean that potential foreign investors in Russia face a very high degree of uncertainty. Those with an eye too firmly on the geological potential of the region, or who have been listening too much to those with a vested interest in promoting inward investment (and they are many), can all too readily overlook this basic fact. Moreover, the overt enthusiasm displayed by Western oil and gas companies for the region has not done any favors for their more cautious brethren in mining and metals. If the latter industry seems to be dragging its feet, and to be reluctant to take the sort of risks that are evidently acceptable to oil and gas companies, then it does so only in recognition of the fact that the economics of the two industries are wholly different, as many oil companies that bought into mining in the 1970s found to their cost. Oil and gas companies generally have to commit a higher proportion of their cash flow to exploration to secure their reserves than do mining companies, but at the same time expect higher margins from production. In addition, known occurrences of oil and gas are more heavily concentrated in the CIS region than is the case with most hard minerals, and there is thus more to play for. Western oil companies have not had a massive new opportunity of this kind since the discovery of Prudhoe Bay in 1967. Mining companies have more options. Russia's legislation on mineral resource development, which has largely been drafted with oil and gas in mind, gives scant recognition to these substantive differences.

Underlying Russia's response to foreign investors in the mining and metals industry are several widespread preconceptions.

The first, which has already been touched on, is that Russia is prodigiously rich in mineral terms and that it is, in this respect, a special case. The preconception is of long standing, but has been sustained in recent years by the lack of awareness in Russia of opportunities and developments in other parts of the world. Opening the first School of Mines in St. Petersburg in 1719, Peter the

7. *Financial Times*, 1 April 1993.
8. *Metal Bulletin*, 3 June 1993.

Great stated: "Our Russian state, in distinction to many other foreign countries, is blessed with all necessary metals and minerals."[9] Two hundred and fifty-five years later, Party Secretary Brezhnev echoed the theme with the claim that "the natural resources of our country allow us to look to the future without trepidation. To cut a long story short, our country is a country with uncounted riches and *inexhaustible* opportunities."[10] Nor have Western commentators been free of this preconception. At roughly the same time as Brezhnev made his remarks, Alexander Sutulov wrote: "The amazing fact about Soviet mineral resources is that in many cases they are in considerably higher abundance than the relative importance of the Soviet territory."[11] Cold Warriors, such as Daniel Fine, also found it convenient in the early 1980s to play up the Soviet Union's mineral wealth as a means of promoting their case that it was bent on cornering the world's strategic mineral resources.[12]

The point is not to dispute Russia's undoubted mineral potential, but only to stress that these preconceptions are essentially ideological. Despite the desperate state of much of its existing mining industry, Russia almost certainly has extensive unexploited mineral resources, though how many of these are actually "reserves" as the term is used in a market context—that is, amenable to commercial recovery at current prices and using existing technologies—remains to be proven. There is a vast quantity of technical information on CIS geology—after all, there were over 700,000 people involved in Soviet geological exploration—but, as already noted, the resource data that exist have been compiled on a wholly different set of criteria from that employed in the West. Moreover, computers have not been used in reserve estimation. It is, however, evident that deposits of many metals in Russia west of the Urals are seriously depleted. It is equally clear that major hurdles will have to be overcome before those to the east, in Siberia, and to the south, in the Central Asian republics, can be made viable at international prices for energy and transportation. Sadly, Russia is not a special case. It is in competition for investment with a number of other minerally prospective parts of the world, many of them with attitudes more amenable to foreign investment than those which currently prevail in Russia. Mineral potential is an absolute requirement of mining investment, but

9. Quoted in Alexander Sutulov, *Mineral Resources and the Economy of the USSR* (McGraw-Hill, 1973).

10. Quoted in Marshall I..Goldman, "The Changing Role of Raw-Material Exports and Soviet Foreign Trade," in Jensen, Shabad and Wright (eds), *Soviet Natural Resources*.

11. Sutulov, *Mineral Resources and the Economy of the USSR.*

12. Daniel I. Fine, "Mineral Resource, Dependency Crisis: The Soviet Union and the United States," in J. A. Miller, D. I. Fine and R. D. McMichael (eds), *The Resource War in Three-D: Dependency, Diplomacy, Defense* (Pittsburgh, 1980).

by itself is insufficient. Companies have to be able to give something back to their shareholders.

The second preconception concerns the motives of foreign investors. Consistent with the communist view that what matters with minerals is their physical availability rather than their commercial viability, there appears still to be a widespread view that what Western companies are principally after is material supplies. The view is perhaps sustained by a vestigial suspicion that the West has squandered all its resources, and by the ubiquity in the CIS countries of Western traders trying to secure metal. From such a perspective it is logical that policymakers should determine that if the West wants Russia's resources then it should be made to pay dearly for them. As one old-guard official at the Russian Vnesheconombank revealingly remarked during a meeting with Western analysts, "Russia is minerally a very rich country, having X trillion rubles' worth of reserves. [The number is unimportant but was astronomically big. That given by Borisovich for the same year (see footnote note 4, page 86) was 18 trillion rubles for proven reserves and 135 trillion rubles for total reserves.] Why should we allow foreigners to come here and take them away?"[13]

The tax provisions proposed by the Russian government for the minerals sector seem to reflect the belief that mining Russia's minerals could be highly advantageous to Western companies and an associated fear of underselling them. Western companies are, after all, capitalists and expressions of interest may too readily be taken as greed. There is also a mistaken belief that the conditions of the hard minerals business are analogous to those for oil and gas. As noted above, they are not. Oil and gas may, like mining, involve recovering things from the earth and substantial capital investment, but margins in the former are greater and paybacks quicker. Bidders for a 52 percent share in the Julietta gold mine in the Magadan Oblast, on which offers were invited during 1993, were told to expect to pay 20.4 percent state tax on gross revenues (10 percent of this a mineral resources tax and the balance a contribution to financing exploration and road construction) plus a 32 percent tax on profits—conditions sufficiently onerous to scare off any possible interest from foreign investors. Significantly, discussions on tax matters frequently reveal a terminological difficulty over the difference between profits and revenues.

Another aspect of this ambivalence toward foreign investment is a fundamental uncertainty as to whether foreign investment is necessary anyway. Russians know they have the natural resources, and, unlike many developing

13. Visit by author, 14 August 1991.

countries, clearly have the skills necessary to exploit these resources. While technological deficiency may justify inward investment in Russia's oil and gas sector, this is less evidently the case in the hard minerals sector. All that they really lack here is capital. However, in a country where the provision of capital has traditionally been a matter of political will, and the role of free capital markets is little understood, it is not at all clear to many why it should be necessary to resort to sources outside the country to meet this requirement. In giving precedence to domestic companies in the two projects mentioned above, there seemed to be no consideration given to the matter of capital availability. The Russian mining and metals industry needs a massive infusion of capital even to maintain existing operations, far less to expand them. But what they often seem to be looking for is capital without the capitalists.

On top of the problems of perception, there is the very practical problem of corruption. Much has been written on the subject, but Aleksandr Rutskoi summed it up neatly when he remarked that the Sicilian Mafia would soon be sending its members to Russia for training. In the political confusion that has characterized the past few years, corruption has increased everywhere, though it is perhaps most evident at the center. There is a particular problem with the gerontocracy, for whom time is running out and who see a major pay-off as the only way in which they will be able to retire in comfort. In the absence of case law on business for the legal system to apply, there is no effective appeal against these practices. It is a worry for companies looking to invest in Russia that anything that looks like being successful will inevitably become the target of unwanted attention.

Some of what has been said here applies also in the Central Asian CIS republics, although in general governments in this region have been quicker to appreciate the value of foreign investment and what needs to be done to attract it. They have, after all, always been importers of capital. Kazakhstan is currently offering foreign companies tax holidays for the first five years and taxation at 50 percent of the normal rate for the second. Although these concessions do not cover extractive activities generally, they do cover the treatment of wastes from such activities and the mining of arsenical gold ores. In addition, there is in these republics a better understanding of the need for a project to earn hard currency, to obtain full world prices for its products, to repatriate profits, to have assurances of fiscal stability and not be forced to convert to local currency unnecessarily. In part, this reflects the fact that the thinking on natural resource development is not so heavily oriented toward oil and gas as it is in Russia. There are, of course, problems here for business, but they are of a rather different nature. One problem is the simple remoteness of the region

Table 5-1. *Foreign Investment Interest in Central Asian Gold Projects*

Investor	Project	Type	Reserve	Production	Cost
Newmont	Muruntau, Uzbekistan	Dump leach	8.7 m.oz	310,000 oz/y	$150m
Goldbelt, Pegasus Gold	Leninogorsk, Kazakhstan	Dump leach	2.8 m.oz	100,000 oz/y	$37m
Minproc, Chilewich, Public	Bakyrchik, Kazakhstan	Buy in/dump leach	8.0 m.oz+	40,000 oz/y (additional)	$25m
Lonhro	Amantaytau, Uzbekistan	Hard rock/bacterial leach?	6.6 m.oz+	350,000 oz/y	$100m

Source: Press reports.

and its lack of developed infrastructure. Until access is opened to the south, any bulk materials recovered from this area will have to be hauled considerable distances overland—Russian land mostly—to be brought to market. The second problem is a political one. Although investors find that the unitary political structures and the possibility of dealing directly with the political leadership of these countries make for a more efficient and less bureaucratic form of decisionmaking, the dependence of the outcome of such decisionmaking on individual personalities could equally come to represent a serious drawback.

Most interest in this part of the world has focused on gold projects, since these offer a portable product and relatively quick paybacks. Heap-leaching projects have been particularly popular. Since this technology was not previously available in the CIS region, there are considerable accumulations of oxide wastes from gold-mining operations well suited to heap-leaching. The technology has the additional benefit of involving limited capital requirements. As a reworking of materials already mined, such projects do not involve mineral rights issues. The US Company Newmont Mining has been working with local joint venture partners, the Uzbek State Committee for Geology and the Navoi Combinate, on a project to rework the ore dumps at the large Muruntau gold mine in Uzbekistan (see table 5-1). The European Bank of Reconstruction and Development(EBRD) agreed to back the $150 million project, and production was scheduled to start in the first half of 1995.[14] Goldbelt Resources of Canada has conducted a feasibility study for a similar project at gold dumps near Leninogorsk, and has agreed in principle an alliance with Pegasus Gold to assist with development finance.[15] In August 1993, in

14. *Mining Journal*, 19 November 1993.
15. *Mining Journal*, 17 September 1993.

the first case of its kind, Bakyrchik Gold, a joint venture comprising the US subsidiary of Minproc Holdings of Australia and US commodity trader Chilewich International, made an £8.2 million offering on the London Stock Exchange to help fund the purchase of a 40 percent share in the existing Bakyrchik mine in northeastern Kazakhstan (the other 60 percent is held by the Kazakhstan government), and to finance an expansion of the operation from around 80,000 oz/year to 120,000 oz/year.[16] The gold produced by the venture will be sold to the government for hard currency and there are said to be no limits on repatriation. This Stage I development is intended to prove the technology to be used in a 230,000 oz/year Stage II expansion, due to be implemented in 1995.

16. *Financial Times*, 2 August 1993; and *Metal Bulletin*, 9 August 1993.

CHAPTER SIX

Issues for the Promotion of Integration

The CIS states have taken some tentative steps away from the autarkic principles which have governed the organization and objectives of the mining and metals industries throughout most of this century. However, they are still very far from being integrated into the Western market system. As stressed at the outset, how far the process of integration advances, and at what pace, are matters that will be determined in the broader political arena. As such, they are beyond the scope of this paper. With that rather fundamental proviso in mind, this chapter seeks to highlight some of the more sector-specific issues that need to be addressed if the process of integration is to be furthered.

Issues for the CIS

Markets are there to be used by producers and consumers alike, but their use carries with it corresponding obligations. One of these obligations is to supply information on levels of trade, and on the development of domestic production and consumption. Such information is the lifeblood of a properly functioning market. Without it, prices cannot reasonably be expected to do the job of honestly reflecting the balance of supply and demand, and of providing appropriate signals to decisionmakers in the market about purchases, sales and investment.

Another obligation that rests upon market participants is to acknowledge that their actions have consequences for world prices. In an oversupplied market, it is simply unreasonable to continue to unload production and ignore the adverse impact on prices for all producers. As long as the CIS was a marginal element in the world market for metals—a price-taker rather than a price-maker—such an attitude, while unhelpful, was defensible. With the CIS now a supplier of 22 percent of the Western world's nickel and 12 percent of its aluminum, it is not. The solution to the problem lies in a combination of privatization on the one hand, and the market pricing of factor inputs on the other. While genuine privatization may take some time to achieve, there have been some positive moves on the latter issue. Energy and transport prices have risen dramatically, partly as a result of pressures from the IMF. Transport costs between the Siberian aluminum smelters and Murmansk are reported to have increased from a rate equivalent to $10/tonne in 1992 to $45/tonne in October 1993. General trends in transport tariffs suggest that they may have increased further since then. While it is acknowledged that too rapid an adjustment to world factor prices risks destroying the entire industry, these developments should assist the movement of domestic product prices toward world prices, and accordingly reduce incentives to export—as well as opportunities for corruption. They may also force marginal producers out of production, if not through bankruptcy then simply through lack of liquidity.

As regards inward investment, there is the need for a better understanding of the fact that, in view of the long-term nature of the business, investors in mining and metals need a stable legal and fiscal regime, or at least a realistic prospect of such a regime in the not too distant future. They cannot live with a situation in which organizational responsibilities are constantly changing and in which regulations are no sooner proposed than they are overridden by a further set, as was the case during the 1992–23 "war of laws." Still less can they live with a situation in which the rules are changed after agreement on the terms of a deal have been reached, as happened to the White Nights oil venture (where taxation on the project, which involves Philbro and Anglo-Suisse, was radically increased after the investment had been committed), and also to De Beers's marketing arrangements for diamonds (where Sakha was accorded the right to market 20 percent of its diamond output two years after De Beers had been awarded an exclusive five-year contract). Moreover, there needs to be some acknowledgment in the design of regulations for the mining and metals businesses of the fundamental difference between the economics of this sector and the economics of oil and gas. In practice, this means lower tax and royalty rates for metals.

Coupled with this requirement for a more stable and attractive investment regime is the need for officials in the CIS countries responsible for dealings with Western companies to inform themselves better about how Western markets work, and who the players are. The first phase of liberalization saw a huge influx of Western traders, stake claimers, equipment salesmen, consultants and other intermediaries. It is quite evident that many CIS industrialists, being unfamiliar with the essence of these various functions (many of which have no analogue in the CIS countries), have become frustrated with the short-term horizons their exercise involves. Better information would permit a more constructive use of these groups, and establish a better position from which to gauge, in the investment context, who are the long-term players, and which of them have the resources to be serious partners in resource development. It would also provide a better handle on the sort of incentives structure likely to win the interest of foreign investors in a competitive global market. The provision of the 1993 Russian Precious Metals and Precious Stones Law that keeps maximum foreign ownership participation below 50 percent, and the fact that the granting of exploration licenses gives explorers no rights over anything they find, for example, are hardly designed to stimulate investor interest.

In organizational terms, the key question is where the dividing line of responsibility for mineral administration will eventually fall, as between the center and the regions, and as between the various institutions at the center. Regrettably, this issue has not been resolved by the promulgation of a new constitution, and until it is there is perhaps little that foreign investors can do other than talk to everyone who seems to have some place in the decisionmaking process. Since such people are numerous—everyone wants to be in on the act—this is an extremely costly and time-consuming process. What companies really need is a clear indication of who has the authority to grant access to any particular deposit. The current compromise of sharing this responsibility between the center and the region is extremely difficult to administer, and leaves companies vulnerable to exploitation for political ends and to double taxation. Although there is widespread acknowledgment of the need to amend the 1992 Subsoil Act to clarify this and other matters, the nature of the changes necessary is a matter of fierce dispute between the parliament, which has close ties with the regions where mining interests are strongest, and the administration, which favors a more centralized approach based on the perspectives of the oil and gas sectors.[1]

Equally necessary is clarification of the functions of the central bureaucracy. The conflicting jurisdictions of the Committee for Geology and the Committee for the Management of State Property have already been noted in connection with Sukhoi Log. Furthermore, as a vestige of universal state control, some organizations have distinctly ambiguous roles, being responsible

1. *East European Markets*, Moscow Bulletin, 22 July 1994.

for the execution of policy, and at the same time operators within the sector they are administering. Thus in discussing licensing arrangements with one of the state committees in Moscow, a company could effectively be dealing with a possible competitor. The same applies with environmental matters. The Ministry of the Environment not only determines the form in which environmental impact assessments should be presented, but also seeks to benefit by offering a consulting service for preparing such assessments. These overlapping functions offer considerable scope for conflicts of interest and leave foreign investors unduly exposed.

Issues for foreign investors

The appropriate strategy for a mining or metals company toward the CIS countries will depend on its own perception of the risks and rewards involved, and of its own particular strengths and objectives. Since few such companies employ political analysts—and even if they did it is questionable whether it would make much difference—the assessment of risk is often somewhat crude, and mixed in with more than a leavening of visceral sentiment. For those unprepared to make the leap of faith, or whose finances do not permit them to contemplate high-risk venturing, there is a strong case for staying out and waiting and seeing.

For those prepared to take the plunge, there are many possible strategies. For technology and equipment companies, there is huge scope for investment in the upgrading of existing facilities, the pay-off to come perhaps in an equity share of the recipient operation, or else in metal. A number of technology companies in the metals business, for example, Outokumpu and Kumera of Finland, Lurgi of Germany and Kaiser of the US, are pursuing just such an approach. For small exploration companies there is plenty of scope for seeking to identify workable deposits from among those on offer, and to acquire rights over them, with a view to taking a stake in the developing company or else selling out to a major.

Larger companies contemplating investments running to hundreds of millions of dollars, still without the kind of constitutional and legal guarantees that such companies would normally look for from a host country, are bound to tread cautiously, albeit at the same time seeking to establish their credentials as serious potential investors (a more difficult job than it may sound, given how little many officials in the CIS countries know about the industry beyond their borders).

Pending the establishment of an appropriate investment regime, there is still much that can be done by such companies in terms of identifying projects that are of a sufficient size and quality to be in principle exploitable, and many companies are doing just that. Given the secrecy that has surrounded this part of the world for most of the century, the vast scale of the region and the sometimes haphazard way in which information is released, such a process of identification is no small task, nor is it cheap. However, it is a necessary precondition of any investment. Without a suitable ore deposit or other investment opportunity, the investment regime is academic.

The range of opportunities is as yet relatively limited. Few companies are likely to be interested in the outright acquisition of existing facilities, even if they were to be offered them (which, as argued above, is unlikely), not least because of the problems posed by current work practices, expectations about the social role of producers and inherited environmental liabilities. Minority equity holdings will hold even less appeal. At the other extreme, there seems little immediate prospect of companies being permitted to pursue greenfield exploration as an investment option either. Most of the opportunities available in the CIS countries up to now have been late-stage exploration projects—that is, deposits which have been delineated but not yet developed—and part-developed projects. In the first wave of interest by foreign companies, it was evident that an attempt was being made to palm off on foreign companies deposits that were considered too low-grade or technologically too difficult for development by domestic operators. Although more attractive deposits have since surfaced, it is possible that some good prospects are still being held back. Amongst the projects being promoted, there is a high proportion of gold deposits, gold projects having the attraction, from both the host country's and the company's point of view, of requiring little infrastructure and providing a portable and fungible product.

Beyond improving their understanding of the mineral potential of the CIS countries, the larger companies must seek to develop long-term relationships with nationals. Given the uncertainty over who exactly are going to be the key players under a future mining regime, the issue is, again, not a simple one. It is probable that confidence building at the regional level, where personnel have a tendency to change less, will eventually prove to be of overriding importance. But for the present substantial powers remain in the capitals, and relationships need to be developed there too. Whatever the regime that ultimately emerges, the development of strong personal links will, for cultural reasons, be important in Russia, and also in Kazakhstan and Uzbekistan.

Companies that give the impression of being long-term players should stand a better chance of influencing the design of legislative arrangements than those looking to make fast money. For this reason, a case could perhaps be made for a company going into a project smaller than it would normally contemplate, both as a demonstration of good faith and to provide a base from which to learn more systematically about how the CIS countries are developing and how to do business there. It would then be possible to come at a larger project better informed and with the status of an insider. Indeed, projects might be designed on a modular basis. The US Company Cyprus Minerals, for example, has taken a third share in a gold project at Kubaka in the Magadan Oblast, perhaps illustrating this logic.[2] Other possibilities for companies include a major effort at educating local officials and industrialists in the nature of operations outside the country, the establishment of training opportunities for local middle management, and the development of technical joint ventures.

Although, as Jonathan Stern has observed in his paper on oil and gas,[3] uncertainty will remain substantial on the post-Soviet scene for a long while to come, industry always has to live with uncertainties of one sort or another. The question is rather about the degree of risk and the devices that are available to limit it. It is also about the scale of potential benefits. Those who decide to wait and see run the risk that, by the time they have determined that it is safe to go back into the water, many of the best opportunities may have gone. Moreover, where the technical and commercial risks of a project are seen as being of an acceptable order, there exist several sophisticated ways of laying off political risk, e.g. through the use of nonrecourse financing, the spreading of risk among lenders in several different countries, and the involvement of international institutions, as was done on the Escondida project in Chile.[4] For British investors it is also perhaps worth pointing out that this is not quite such exotic territory as at first it may seem. Prior to the October Revolution, British companies were involved in the development of nonferrous metals production in the Urals, Caucasus, the Altai and Kazakhstan, and owned smelters at Karabash and Alaverdi. Even after the revolution, between 1921 and 1928, a British company, Lena Goldfields, operated the gold mines along the Lena River in the region now administered by Lenzoloto.

2. *Interfax Mining Report*, 13-20 August 1993.

3. Jonathan Stern, *Oil and Gas in the Former Soviet Union*, Post-Soviet Business Forum (RIIA, 1993).

4. D. W. Loughridge, "Escondida: A Project Financing for the 1990s," Proceedings of a Symposium, *Raising Capital in the 1990s: Options for the Extractive Industries*, American Institute of Mining Engineers, New York, 1990.

Issues for international organizations

International organizations have thus far shown relatively little interest in the mining and metals industries of the CIS. This is understandable to the extent that their primary focus has been on generic matters that affect the whole economy—currency stabilization, financial services, food distribution and so on. Greater recognition must be given to mining and metals, however, on the grounds that it is one of the very few sectors in which the CIS economies are at least partially competitive internationally, and on which future growth might be built. There are, after all, as has been argued throughout, only a limited number of options.

International organizations have rightly stressed the critical importance of free trade as a means of facilitating the CIS countries' fuller integration into the market economy and rewarding the process of democratization. Western markets must be kept open to CIS countries' exports just as consumers in these countries must be encouraged to import where this is feasible, always of course emphasizing the rules governing the conduct of such trade, including the publication of appropriate statistics. However, in encouraging exports, international organizations have to acknowledge the fact that the CIS states have little to sell other than their mineral products. The general burden of adjustment is therefore tending to fall disproportionately on one sector. One way of responding to this—the way the EU chose in the case of aluminum—is to seek to force the CIS countries to exercise greater self-restraint in their trade behavior by blocking out their products. Unfortunately, this tends to run counter to the marketization process, and to perpetuate East-West confrontational perspectives. A more constructive approach might be to ensure that the sectors being adversely affected are compensated for the broader responsibility they are being asked to assume, by according them priority status in the aid provisions being directed to the CIS.

Europe clearly has a particular role to play in this regard. While it may have been affected most acutely, as a result of its proximity, by the unrestrained exporting of metals by the CIS countries over the past three years, by the same token it is also the region which stands to benefit most from the opening up of the region in the longer term. Europe is, after all, the world's largest consuming area for minerals and metals, and the CIS is on its doorstep. Indeed, the CIS region should be seen as potentially an integral part of the European supply picture, *not* something outside it, far less a threat to it. European-based companies are well qualified and well placed to assist with the development of the CIS countries' mineral resources, and both they and the

European consumer would benefit from some institutional encouragement.

There are a number of means by which this might be done. One would be through the designation of the mining and metals sectors in the CIS states as priority sectors in the EU technical assistance program, TACIS. Alternatives might be support for structural developments which could benefit the sector— for example, assistance for the upgrading of transportation and social infrastructure in minerally prospective areas—or for the mitigation of the environmental impacts of current production. No less useful would be restructuring programs for the winding down of nonviable operations. A regionally based approach would have the advantage of being more tightly focused, and of being consistent with the emerging political reality of devolution.

Aluminum companies in Europe and the United States have proposed imaginative and detailed schemes for the temporary closure of Russian smelting capacity while plants undergo modernization and cleanup, which would give the market a break from overproduction and improve the technical and environmental standards of Russian capital in the longer term. Such schemes, however, require government support and so far this has not been forthcoming. On a more modest scale, opportunities exist for intergovernmental support in the provision of financing for the business training of middle management, for study visits to operations outside the CIS countries, and for the staging of seminars as a means of promoting industry-to-industry dialogue and a common conceptual basis for that dialogue. There are also opportunities for the promotion and funding of joint R&D ventures in the sector, and for assistance in the promotion of local consumption. The Brussels-based federations, Eurométaux and Euromines, have been active in trying to promote a direct dialogue with the industry in Russia, and in seeking to win financial support for various initiatives of this sort from the European Commission.

The most direct means of assisting the process of integration is through the provision of investment finance, and through political risk insurance for mining and metal projects within the region. The EBRD is already active in several gold projects in the CIS, and has indicated that it is prepared to consider further opportunities in the mining and metals sector.[5] In addition to this sort of commercial finance, there may also be justification for highly focused soft finance. Unfortunately, the EBRD, unlike the World Bank, does not have a special loans facility for the funding of feasibility studies. In the event that some soft finance does eventually become available, there are strong reasons for resisting the common tendency to spread it thinly as a means of giving

5. Speech by Masato Miyachi of the EBRD, reported in *Metal Bulletin*, 3 June 1993.

everyone something, and rather for directing larger amounts to specific ventures which would act as showcases of what state-of-the-art technology and work practices can achieve. Such showcases are likely to provide a more persuasive justification for the reform process than any amount of discussion or speechifying.[6] This is a big game with a lot at stake. Small amounts are unlikely to alter the evaluation of political risk.

6. Speech by Constantine S. Nicandros to RIIA on *Russian Oil, Western Investment: Putting the Puzzle Together*, 1 July 1993; published in *The World Today*, RIIA, October 1993, pp. 186–89.

CHAPTER SEVEN

Conclusion

Much remains to be done to achieve the integration of the CIS countries' mining and metals industries into the world market. Those industries have not yet been subject to a full program of marketization. Indeed, as other writers have emphasized, the current condition of the CIS economies is the product less of deliberate reform than simply of the collapse of the old system.[1] Many of the attitudes and behavioral patterns of the earlier system persist—a sort of central planning without the central plan. A large part of production capacity is still in state hands, if not under detailed state control, and there is still a strong predisposition toward self-sufficiency. Devolution of authority to the regions and a greater preparedness to sell in the West may give the illusion of working with the market, but the structure of input prices of producing industries is still largely artificial, while the valuation of production is distorted by the condition of local currencies and secrecy continues to impede the flow of business information.

It is clear that, in Russia at least, the metals sector is considered too strategically important for the national economy, and the social costs of its disintegration too high, for the matter to be left entirely to the regions and the enterprises. It was perhaps significant that when, in a major policy statement in June 1994, Prime Minister Chernomyrdin stated that "we cannot sanction mass closure of our exhausted plants, since that would usher in an unsupportable rise in unemployment," he chose to illustrate the problem by reference to remote mining communities.[2] The same perspective was evident in the Russ-

1. Anders Åslund, *Systematic Change and Stabilization*, Post-Soviet Business Forum, (RIIA, 1993).
2. "No exits on the road to market," *Financial Times*, 16 May 1994.

ian government's approval, at the end of 1993, of what can best be described as a Brezhnevian modernization plan for the metals industry for 1993–2000. Under this plan, to be administered by the Committee for Metallurgy, it was proposed to modernize 140 major metallurgical plants and to commission some 20 million tonnes of nonferrous mining capacity. The plan, it was stated, would cost the equivalent of $30 billion.[3]

In view of the complete inability of the Russian government to fund such grandiose schemes, they are little more than exercises in wishful thinking. It is, in that context, all the more striking that attitudes toward the foreign investors who might be able to contribute to the process of modernization remain distinctly ambivalent. If there are those in government who are prepared publicly to acknowledge the role that foreign capital might play, there are others whose attitudes show a marked continuity with those of the old order. Illusions persist about the mineral wealth of the region and the rent that can be extracted from it, while suspicions remain about the motives of foreigners. There is a recognition of the need for investment, but at the same time a desire to remain in control of the assets. There is an evident fear of being taken advantage of while in a weak position. There is little appreciation of the achievements of the industry beyond the borders of the old Soviet Union, or of the risk-reward structure to which Western multinationals are subject to. Attitudes are more positive in the regions, where the benefits of foreign investment can be more readily appreciated, but the degree of independence from central interference that the regions can expect over the longer term remains an imponderable. Unfortunately, the resolution of this problem is all the harder to the extent that mineral resources are themselves a key counter in the struggle between the center and the regions, not to mention the struggle between the various institutions and factions at the center.

Meanwhile, the fabric of the industry itself continues to decay. If the metallurgical industry is still generally serviceable, it is dirty and inefficient and in desperate need of a major capital infusion. More serious is its shortage of feed, a problem that was at least partially disguised by the import of surplus concentrates from the West during 1992 and 1993. The mines, still in state hands and most of them unsalable, are suffering the effects of years of neglect. Existing operations are running out of ore, and the development work necessary to bring in replacement reserves has simply not been carried out. On top of this are the problems arising from increased transportation costs between mines and smelters and the escalating problems of intercompany payments—a func-

3. *Metal Bulletin*, 30 June 1994; and *Mining Journal*, 1 July 1994.

tion of mounting corporate indebtedness and of the introduction of new currencies by each of the CIS states. Except perhaps for the aluminum industry, where much of the smelter feed is imported and where Western traders have been playing an important part in providing liquidity, it is difficult to see how metal production in the CIS region can do anything other than continue to decline over the next few years. As for the level of exports, this depends crucially on the future course of domestic metals consumption. From the perspective of early 1995, it would appear that metals consumption is likely to stabilize before production, and that exports will accordingly fall.

Despite the all too evident problems, there are nevertheless strong reasons for believing that mining and metals are sectors that Russia and the other metal-rich countries of the CIS should be targeting for investment. Mining and metals continue to earn significant, and much-needed, revenues, revenues that it will not be easy to replace. They are sectors in which these countries have at least some measure of international competitiveness, in which the technological lag relative to the West is not too wide, and which generate products that are readily marketable (an important consideration for a country with no history of marketing). Not too many other sectors offer this combination of characteristics. At the same time, investment in the sector would serve the important political objective of fostering social cohesion in some of the outlying regions, and of limiting the profound environmental damage that the sector continues to perpetrate.

The task of redeveloping the mining and metals industries of the CIS countries will clearly be greatly assisted by the active participation of foreign investors. However, for this to occur, foreign companies will need to be convinced that rewards for their shareholders are a real possibility, and that the regime under which they will be required to operate offers sufficient stability and guarantees to enable them to realize these rewards in practice. The companies will, in turn, need to be able to convince their bankers. At present, prospects are poor on both counts. Of course, there is nothing that says any country has to accept foreign investors on its soil; but then again there is nothing that says foreign investors have to invest where conditions do not warrant investment. The choice that the CIS states make on this matter will determine what sort of force they are to be in the world mining and metals industry in the first half of the twenty-first century.

Part 3

THE CONVERSION OF
THE FORMER SOVIET
DEFENSE INDUSTRY

Julian Cooper

The former Soviet Union possessed a defense industry of formidable size. The newly independent states, in particular Russia and Ukraine, are now faced with major problems of restructuring the parts of this inheritance located on their territories. The procurement of new weapons has been cut sharply, confronting producers with urgent problems of reorientation to civil work. Efforts to restructure are unfolding in a context of economic transformation and political uncertainty. At the same time, Russia and some of the other states are attempting to elaborate new military doctrines and to decide what kind of defense industries, and on what scale, will be required in the new conditions. This security concern is beginning to change the terms of debate on conversion. Meanwhile, restructuring is under way, and challenging new business opportunities are being discovered by Western companies.

CHAPTER ONE

Introduction to Part Three

At the heart of the former Soviet economy was a defense industry of quite extraordinary scale. Its priority development over several decades distorted the development of the entire economy and ultimately contributed to the decline and eventual collapse of that economy. The Russian Federation and the other successor states of the USSR, but in particular Russia and Ukraine, now face formidable problems of economic restructuring. The military sector has to be scaled down substantially, preferably in such a way that its skills, technologies and production capacities can be harnessed to the broader task of economic renewal. This would be a difficult enough challenge for stable societies with mature economies: in Russia and the other countries of the former Soviet Union the partial reorientation of military-industrial complexes is being undertaken at a time of fundamental economic and political transformation.

The Soviet defense industry was dominated by a group of powerful industrial ministries constituting what became known as the "defense complex."[1] These ministries, eight in number at the time of the break up of the USSR, controlled most of the factories responsible for the manufacture of weapons and other military hardware. However, materials, equipment and components were also supplied by enterprises of other, nominally civilian, ministries. Most factories of the defense complex also had some civilian involvement, producing a wide range of consumer items, including the bulk of all Soviet-built electronic and electrical household goods, and industrial, transport and agricultural equipment.

Subordinate to the ministries of the defense complex were approximately 1,100 production associations and enterprises and 920 research and develop-

1. For a more detailed account of the former Soviet defense industry see Cooper (1991).

129

ment (R&D) organizations, employing a total of more than 9 million people.[2] But this elite group of industrial ministries also maintained an extraordinary range of nonindustrial facilities, including construction organizations, farms, hospitals, rest homes, and holiday camps for children. The recreational facilities were often located in the most attractive regions of the USSR, including the Crimea, the Caucasus and the Baltic republics. Taking account of those engaged in such nonindustrial activities, total employment in the defense complex was probably as much as 12 million.

A striking feature of the Soviet defense complex was the large scale of its enterprises and research organizations. According to data on the defense industry of the Russian Federation, three categories of enterprises can be distinguished. The core of the industry was represented by those enterprises (half of the total number) for which military production was the basic activity. On average, at the beginning of 1992, such enterprises employed approximately 10,000 workers. Of the remaining enterprises, half were categorized as "mixed," undertaking both military and civil work. These enterprises were generally somewhat smaller, employing 8,000 workers on average. The remaining enterprises were essentially civilian in character and much smaller in size, with average employment of 2,000 workers.[3]

The small, specialized subcontracting firms typical of market economies were almost entirely absent: it is notable that of Russian enterprises undergoing conversion during the first nine months of 1992, only 2 percent employed less than 500 workers.[4] The same bias toward giant establishments was also characteristic of the research and design organizations of the defense complex, which typically employed some 2,000 people each.

The Soviet defense industry operated under a highly centralized system of planning and management which ensured that it had first claim on the high-quality resources available in the economy. In order to maintain relatively low prices for end-product weapons, these quality inputs were often supplied to enterprises at centrally fixed prices which did not reflect the true resource costs involved in their production. Vital to the ability of the defense industry to develop and build technically advanced armaments was the existence of a relatively stable labor force of above-average skills. Privileged rates of pay played a role in attracting and keeping skilled personnel, but quite as important was the maintenance by enterprises and R&D organizations of what by

2. *Voprosy Ekonomiki*, 1992, no. 8, p. 96.

3. *Voprosy Ekonomiki i Konversii*, 1992, special issue, pp. 70–71.

4. *Russia—1992: Economic Situation*, Center of Economic Analysis and Forecasting, Moscow, November 1992, p. 109.

Soviet standards were relatively good housing, welfare and social facilities. In this respect the Novosibirsk Aviation Production Association is typical. For decades this enterprise has been a leading producer of combat aircraft, including, most recently, the Su-24. Its "empire" includes 270 housing blocks, 20 nurseries, polyclinics, a rest home, a "Palace of Culture" and a sports stadium.[5] These facilities were usually built on the basis of funding provided from ministerial sources or from retained profits, while their running expenses were regarded as an overhead item in the cost of production. Given the distorted price and cost structures and the multiplicity of channels for concealed subsidization, neither Moscow-based officials nor enterprise managers had any real understanding of the true resource costs involved in producing weapons for the Soviet armed forces.

There is no dispute that the defense complex was the strongest part of the former Soviet economy, able to produce military and space technology to world standards. Use was made of imported equipment, but not to the same extent as in some branches of the civil economy. Much of the advanced production equipment used by the military sector was built by enterprises within the defense complex. Wide use was made of individual and small-scale production technologies employing highly skilled workers possessing craft skills. Where volume methods were more appropriate, considerable ingenuity was shown in adapting production processes to secure quality production with relatively unskilled labor. In some industries, notably those relating to electronics and conventional munitions, a high proportion of female labor was employed. Often deprived of access to the latest technologies employed in the West, Soviet designers and engineers showed great skill in finding alternative solutions. Creative software development, for example, helped to make good deficiencies in computer hardware.

The military economy was not restricted to the defense complex. Almost all industries were to some extent involved in military production, including consumer branches. Some of the best enterprises in the textile industry, for example, were employed in the manufacture of uniforms and parachutes. Each service of the armed forces also had its own network of repair plants and R&D organizations, engaged not only in the servicing of armaments, but also to some extent in the development and modernization of military equipment. Many civilians were employed in this "second" defense industry under the Ministry of Defense. But the demands of the military had an even more pervasive impact on the Soviet economy. The USSR maintained an extraordinarily

5. *Ekonomika i Organizatsiya Promyshlennogo Proizvodstva*, 1992, no. 2, pp. 148–51.

comprehensive system of mobilization preparation: measures designed to facilitate a rapid conversion of the economy to a war footing in the event of need. Not only did enterprises of the defense industry maintain reserve production capacities and substantial stocks of strategic materials, but some parts of the civil economy were also expected to have mobilization plans. Based on worst-case assessments of the mobilization planning of the United States and other NATO countries, this elaborate system raised production costs and also helped to sustain a "dual-use" culture to the detriment of the civil economy. Thus many civil organizations had no choice but to use military-standard trucks, farms were supplied with heavy-duty crawler tractors built by enterprises able to switch to the production of tracked military vehicles—and civil transport aircraft, and their engines, showed the influence of military requirements. Dualism was also apparent in the nuclear, space and telecommunications industries.

It was recognition that the Soviet economy was militarily overburdened that led Gorbachev to take action at the end of 1988 to reduce budget expenditure on the armed forces. There is little doubt that at the time when the decision was taken Gorbachev had exaggerated expectations. Perhaps misled by the Western peace movement's rhetoric of "conversion" and the "peace dividend," and still retaining a residual faith in the ability of planning to bring quick results, he launched a drive for a partial conversion of the defense industry to civilian purposes. Between 1988 and 1991 reductions in military procurement and military R&D turned out to be larger than originally planned: 29 percent for the former (plan 19.5 percent) and 22 percent for the latter (plan 15 percent).[6] As for conversion, there were plans and programs in abundance; but at the same time the planning system itself was suffering progressive disintegration: thus the governments of the post-Soviet states had only modest practical achievements on which to build.

In the former USSR the extent of the militarization of the economy, the activities, and in many cases even the identities, of individual enterprises and R&D organizations, and everything connected with mobilization planning, were all concealed from ordinary Soviet citizens and, to a lesser extent, from interested Western agencies, by a truly extraordinary regime of secrecy. Millions of people inhabited an archipelago of "closed" towns denied any open acknowledgment, appearing on no maps. The ubiquitous "first departments" of the KGB policed this system—with what in retrospect must be acknowledged as considerable success. Secrecy and restrictions remain, but in Russia

6. *Voprosy Ekonomiki i Konversii*, 1992, special issue, pp. 16, 18.

at least it is now much easier to obtain information on the defense industry, to visit its facilities and to meet its personnel, although it is still difficult to obtain reliable statistical data.

Partly for informational reasons, but largely because the Russian Federation inherited most of the former Soviet defense industry, this study focuses on the biggest of the successor states, with some references to Ukraine and other newly independent countries.

CHAPTER TWO

The Defense Industry
in Disunion

The break up of the USSR and the collapse of the communist regime had immediate, profound consequences for the defense industry. The newly independent states found themselves in possession of elements of a military-industrial complex previously structured according to a Union-wide division of labor determined by the central authorities in Moscow.[1] The Russian Federation alone inherited something resembling a coherent defense industry. On its territory were located approximately 70 percent of the enterprises of the former Soviet defense complex, responsible for three-quarters of former Soviet military output, and 74 percent of military R&D facilities, which had performed almost 90 percent of all military R&D in the Soviet Union.[2] The Russian defense complex in 1992 consisted of approximately 1,200 associations and enterprises employing 5.5 million industrial production personnel, plus some 700 research institutes and design organizations employing more than one million people. In recent years this military-related R&D base has absorbed approximately 70 percent of all state budget expenditure on science in Russia; at the same time it has implemented up to half of all centrally funded civil R&D.[3]

Of the other successor states, only Ukraine possesses major facilities on any scale for the manufacture of end-product weapons, including strategic

1. See Cooper (1993a) for a more detailed account of the defense industry inheritance in each of the newly independent states.

2. *Moscow News*, 1992, no. 7.

3. *Voprosy Ekonomiki i Konversii*, 1992, no. 4, p. 17.

missiles, tanks and naval surface vessels. But these enterprises are heavily dependent on Russia and other states for supplies of basic systems and components. For this reason Ukraine cannot be said to have a defense industry; rather it has a random set of enterprises and R&D establishments which had an economic rationale only within the former Union division of labor. At independence, total employment in the defense complex of Ukraine amounted to approximately 1.2 million, with 344 enterprises. However, there was a high level of concentration; 54 enterprises accounted for 80 percent of military production.[4]

The absurdities of the former Soviet division of labor are illustrated by Kazakhstan: a major specialty of the military sector of this almost land-locked republic is the manufacture of naval armament. Belarus, with only four percent of the enterprises of the former Soviet defense complex on its territory, has important facilities for electronics-related military production, but little end-product weapons assembly. Of the other independent states, Georgia is an exception in so far as it builds combat aircraft—the Su-25 is assembled at a plant in the capital, Tbilisi. But this activity is almost totally dependent on Russian supplies.

One immediate outcome of the disintegration of the Union was the break-up of the industry's highly centralized administrative structures. The Union ministries disappeared. In Russia, some of the ministerial structures were transformed into semicommercial concerns and corporations, often headed by former deputy ministers, now designated presidents. By mid-1992 one "union" (of the aviation industry), thirty concerns and four corporations had replaced the former ministries of the defense industry of Russia.[5] Some ministerial personnel chose to leave to form new commercial structures, the most notable being the Military-Industrial Investment Company, the general director of which, Vitaly Doguzhiev, is a former minister of the USSR missile-space industry. Other parts of the Union ministries, together with elements of the former Military-Industrial Commission, were converted into defense departments of a new Ministry of Industry. This ministry proved to be too large and unmanageable. Later on in 1992 it was disbanded and replaced by a set of committees—a State Committee for Industrial Policy and four sectoral committees, including one for the defense branches of industry. In September 1993 this defense industry committee was upgraded to a State Committee and at the end of 1994 Goskomoboronprom, as it is generally known, was granted

4. *Inzhenernaya Gazeta*, 1992, no. 129–30.
5. *Voprosy Ekonomiki i Konversii*, 1992, no. 4, p. 107.

ministerial status, allowing its chairman, Viktor Glukhikh, to become a full member of the government.[6] Goskomoboronprom, employing approximately 1,200 people, coordinates policy for the defense complex and is closely involved with the Ministry of Defense in the placement of military orders. Its internal departmental structure reproduces the old branch ministerial segmentation.

In the former Soviet Union the most powerful of all the industrial ministries was that for the nuclear weapons industry. It is a matter of no surprise that it has managed to save most of its administrative structures from the wreck of the Soviet system. It has now been transformed into the Ministry of Atomic Energy of the Russian Federation. The enterprises and R&D organizations of this ministry, responsible for both the military and civil nuclear industries, employ more than one million people.

A striking feature of the new administrative arrangements for the Russian defense industry is the extent to which the former leading personnel of the Union industry are still in responsible positions. It is clear that the old network of personnel contacts has been retained largely intact. The major difference now is the absence of the Communist Party. Without the backing of the Party, the central management bodies of the defense sector find their authority seriously weakened. At the same time, the demise of the Party has deprived the Moscow center of an important channel of information about defense industry developments in the localities.

Within the defense industry of Russia new, nonstate commercial structures have emerged, although not to the same extent as in some civil sectors. There are presently at least eight major commercial banks within the defense complex, and by the autumn of 1992 there were also some 3,000 cooperatives, 300 small enterprises and 170 joint ventures in it as well.[7] By the end of 1992 the privatization of defense sector enterprises was well under way (see below), although the process was not without controversy.

Certain regions and cities of Russia have exceptionally high concentrations of military-industrial facilities. In research and development the city of Moscow with its surrounding region is predominant, accounting for a very large proportion of R&D in the aviation, missile, radio, electronics and nuclear industries. Shipbuilding research and design is very heavily concentrated in St Petersburg. Major centers of end-product weapons production include the republics of Udmurtiya and Tatarstan, and the cities and regions of Ekater-

6. *Sobranie Zakonodatel'stva Rossiiskoi Federatsii*, 1994, no. 32, Presidential order no. 2146 (3 December, 1994).
7. *Inzhenernaya gazeta*, 1992, no. 126–27.

inburg, Chelyabinsk, Samara, Tula, Nizhny Novgorod, St Petersburg, Perm, Novosibirsk and Omsk. The Sverdlovsk (Ekaterinburg) region alone has half a million people employed in the defense complex.[8] In the Far East, Vladivostok, Khabarovsk and Komsomolsk-na-Amure are important centers of naval shipbuilding.

There is another specific feature of the geography of the Russian defense industry that further complicates its transformation—the existence of closed towns with economies completely dominated by specific types of military research or production. The existence of the ten closed towns of the nuclear weapons industry is now well known, but in addition there are at least seventy specialized military sector towns, including sixteen in the Moscow region. Military production usually accounts for 80-95 percent of their industrial output.[9] Examples include Zelenograd (electronics), Zhukovsky (aviation), Podlipki (Kaliningrad) (missile-space industry), Fryazino (electronics), Vladimir-30 (lasers), Zarechny (Sverdlovsk region) (nuclear industry), Krasnoyarsk-35 (missile industry) and, in the shipbuilding industry, Bolshoi Kamen (Far East), Murmansk-60, and Severodvinsk (nuclear submarines). The size of these monoindustrial towns varies, from a population of 30,000 or less (Zarechny) to more than 250,000 (Severodvinsk).

Whereas Russia could create new administrative structures for the defense sector on the basis of former Union organizations, this option was not open to Ukraine and the other successor states. Here, ministries, associations and concerns had to be created from scratch, and staffed in the main by personnel with no previous ministerial experience. In principle this created opportunities for breaking away from traditional Union practices, but in general familiar models were chosen. Oversight of defense sector facilities in Ukraine is exercised by the Ministry for Machine Building, the Military-Industrial Complex and Conversion. However, the facilities formerly subordinate to particular Union ministries as a rule have formed associations and concerns reproducing the former branch segmentation, missing an opportunity to recast the defense industry inheritance in a more radical manner. Similar developments have been observable in Kazakhstan and Belarus.

---

8. *Krasnaya Zvezda*, 6 February 1993.
9. *Inzhenernaya Gazeta*, 1992, no.126–27; *Moscow News*, 1993, no. 8, p. 4.

CHAPTER THREE

The Defense Industry in Transition

Faced with the necessity of stabilizing an economy in severe macroeconomic disequilibrium, the new Russian government under Boris Yeltsin and Yegor Gaidar which came to power following the disintegration of the USSR decided to cut state expenditure on the armed forces. The item to suffer most was expenditure on weapons procurement, which was reduced by 68 percent in 1992. However, it was decided that military R&D would receive some protection, the reduction in budget expenditure amounting to a planned 16 percent.[1] Overall, military expenditure in constant 1991 prices fell from 80.9 billion rubles in 1991 to 65.5 billion rubles in 1992, reducing the military's share of GNP from 8.5 to 5.2 percent.[2]

These cuts were associated with very substantial reductions in the volume of procurement of individual categories of weapons. Whereas in 1988 the Soviet armed forces received 2,800 tanks, in 1992 the Russian army purchased a mere 20 units![3] In 1992 the Air Force could not afford to buy any MiG-29s or Su-27s, and during that year no new naval ships were laid down at Russian shipyards.[4] It was expected (no hard information on the outcome has come to hand) that in 1993 orders for military aircraft and helicopters would be less than 15 percent of the 1991 level.[5]

1. G. Khizha, cited in *RFE/RL Research Report*, vol. 1, no. 33 (21 August 1993).
2. *Krasnaya Zvezda*, 10 February 1993.
3. *Megapolis Express*, 1993, no. 4, 27 January 1993, p. 12.
4. *Rabochaya tribuna*, 26 March 1993 (supplement) and 18 December 1992.
5. *Krasnaya Zvezda*, 3 March 1993.

If armaments production had declined to the extent of the fall in procurement, the plight of the Russian defense industry would have been much more serious than it turned out to be. In reality, the fall in military output was cushioned to some degree by production for export, and also by enterprise stockpiling in expectation of a change of policy.

The year 1992 began with unrealistic hopes for arms exports. Output was planned on the basis that export sales would amount to $6 billion; in the event sales reached a mere $2 billion, which led to the accumulation at factories of substantial stocks of unsold military equipment, including more than 200 combat aircraft and 1,000 tanks.[6] Reduced levels of output were associated with some moves to rationalize the production base. Tank building, for example, formerly undertaken by four plants in Russia, was concentrated at only two facilities, at Nizhny Tagil in the Urals and Omsk in Siberia. Similarly, the building of nuclear submarines is being concentrated at the largest facility, Severodvinsk.

In 1992 the output of the defense complex (excluding the nuclear industry) fell by almost 20 percent. Military production was reduced by 50 percent, while in real terms the industry's civil output maintained its 1991 level.[7] The collapse of military production led to a sharp change in the proportions of the different categories of output within the defense complex: the civilian share increased from 58 percent in 1991 to 76 percent in 1992.[8] According to Khizha, the former deputy prime minister, the military output of the defense complex in 1992 was only one-quarter of the level of 1988.[9]

Reduced levels of budgetary funding created serious problems for the R&D system of the defense industry. Levels of budgetary support were cut much more sharply for civil R&D than for military. In addition, with the disappearance of the industrial ministries and the collapse of profitability, nonbudget funding of R&D was reduced to an extremely modest level. These developments led to a paradoxical outcome: in relative terms the Russian industrial R&D system became even more heavily militarized than before. But funding levels were nevertheless inadequate to maintain the military R&D system, which began to suffer a severe hemorrhaging of manpower.

Price liberalization at the beginning of 1992 had a profound impact on the defense industry. Accustomed to receiving high-quality materials and compo-

6. *Izvestiya*, 23 February 1993; *Kommersant*, 1993, no. 7; *Rossiiskaya Gazeta*, 17 February 1993.

7. *Krasnaya Zvezda*, 28 January 1995.

8. *Voprosy Ekonomiki i Konversii*, 1992, no. 4, p. 4; *Krasnaya Zvezda*, 3 March 1993.

9. *Rossiiskie Vesti*, 24 October 1992.

nents at artificially low prices, the industry suddenly experienced dramatic price increases. The monopoly power of some suppliers was probably a factor, but in general it is likely that prices moved to reflect more accurately the true resource costs involved. However, the Ministry of Defense, constrained by the provisions of the state budget, was often unable to raise the prices of end-product weapons, with the inevitable result that enterprises became unprofitable and in many cases fell into severe financial difficulty. To make matters worse, the break-up of the USSR disrupted traditional supply relations, especially with Ukraine. By the end of 1992 more than 20 enterprises of the defense complex had stopped work completely, 140 were on the verge of ceasing production, and 400 were operating with a reduced working week.[10] The Ministry of Defense was often late in making payments for weapons and other hardware: by the end of 1992 enterprises were owed about 20 billion rubles.[11]

These developments led to a dramatic decline in the pay of defense industry personnel. From being the elite of the industrial labor force, workers of the military sector suddenly found themselves pushed to the bottom of the pay hierarchy. This slippage began under Gorbachev, but accelerated precipitately in 1992. State orders for weapons to be procured by the Ministry of Defense in accordance with state budget allocations were based on a fixed monthly wage rate with no provision for indexing. In these circumstances it was inevitable that enterprises involved in military work would find their freedom of maneuver severely limited. By the end of 1992, the average monthly wage of workers in the defense complex was just 11,452 rubles, only 62 percent of the average for industry as a whole of 18,372 rubles. Even workers in light industry, traditionally one of the worst paid branches, were receiving 13,375 rubles at that time. Defense sector pay would have been even lower had it not been for substantial state subsidies and credits to maintain conditions of work.[12] By the end of 1994 the position was showing no improvement: for Goskomoboronprom, the average pay was 198,000 rubles (including a low of 138,100 rubles in electronics, and a high of 274,200 in shipbuilding), compared with 310,600 rubles for industry as a whole.[13] However, these average levels of pay conceal considerable variation between regions, and even between individual enterprises in the same region. Those successful in maintaining levels of activity and finding new domestic and export customers have been able to maintain high levels of earnings. In general, however, reduced profitability has made it

10. *Krasnaya Zvezda*, 13 March 1993.
11. *Krasnaya Zvezda*, 6 March 1993.
12. *Krasnaya Zvezda*, 13 March 1993.
13. *Krasnaya Zvezda*, 28 January 1995.

difficult for enterprises and R&D organizations to fund housing and social provision, vital for the maintenance of a stable, high-quality labor force.

On the basis of their experience in 1992, defense sector enterprise directors insisted that changes must be made for 1993. They demanded that the profitability of military contracts should be increased, that payments should be made promptly, and that enterprise working capital should be indexed to protect it from erosion by inflation.[14] In the event, their hopes were disappointed. Military output of the defense complex declined in 1993 to less than one-third of the 1991 level and, to make matters worse, civilian production also declined by 14 percent.[15] These trends were maintained in 1994: the total output of enterprises of Goskomoboronprom fell to less than 40 percent of the 1991 level, with military production at only 20 percent of the 1991 level and civilian, hit by a collapse in demand and foreign competition, at just 53 percent.[16]

Given the acute problems of the defense sector, it is not surprising that many workers are choosing to leave in search of employment elsewhere. Few employees appear to have been made redundant. Those leaving have tended to be younger, skilled personnel able to find work in the new nonstate sector. Recruitment of new young workers has been substantially reduced. Since 1991 some two million employees have left the defense industry, and the Ministry of Economics has forecast an additional reduction of approximately 500,000 in 1995.

For many of the closed and other "postbox" towns (so known because formerly identified only by a post office code number), conditions have deteriorated rapidly as military orders have fallen and the ministries previously responsible for funding the upkeep of the towns have disappeared. Zelenograd provides a good example. Formerly 90 percent of the town's production was for military purposes. In 1992 output fell by almost 55 percent, resulting in substantial hidden unemployment. Levels of pay fell to well below the average for Moscow (to which Zelenograd is administratively attached). Deprived of profits, enterprises and institutes have been unable to contribute to the maintenance of the town.[17] The residents of closed towns are often reluctant, however, to switch to an open status because they fear that their communities will start to suffer the problems of the wider society from which they have hitherto been protected. In Severodvinsk, for example, a survey of attitudes

14. *Krasnaya Zvezda*, 6 February 1993.

15. *Krasnaya Zvezda*, 28 January 1995.

16. Ibid.

17. *Rossiiskaya Gazeta*, 5 January 1993; see also *Rossiiskaya Gazeta*, 26 February 1993 (on the missile-space town of Kaliningrad).

undertaken by the management of a number of enterprises revealed that 60-70 percent of workers wanted the town closed again! It should be added that this view conflicted with that of others in the town, including the mayor, democratic public organizations and new commercial organizations.[18]

Interviewed in March 1993 by the newspaper of the National Salvation Front, *Den'*, Georgy Khizha, the Deputy Prime Minister for Industry, described the changes in the Russian military-industrial complex in 1992 as "in a certain sense a tragedy." Cleaners in a commercial bank, he observed bitterly, could now earn more than the skilled specialists of the defense industry. While he acknowledged that there was no alternative to a reduced level of military work, he expressed concern that the industry's general technological level was being gradually eroded.[19] As discussed below in Chapter 6, Khizha is not alone in his concern for the fate of Russia's defense industry.

18. *Nezavisimaya Gazeta*, 25 March 1993. It was later reported that the local authorities had decided to transform the town once again into a so-called closed administrative-territorial entity (BBC, *Summary of World Broadcasts*, SU/1687 C3/4, 13 May 1993).

19. *Den'*, no. 9, 7-13 March 1993.

CHAPTER FOUR

Conversion: Policy and Programs

In any economy, conversion of the defense industry is an extremely difficult undertaking. The relatively successful experience of postwar reconstruction in Western countries provides few lessons of value to Russia today. After the Second World War, it was relatively easy to reconvert factories temporarily diverted to military work, because of the existence of pent-up consumer demand and developed market institutions. Since then, there has been little experience of carrying out direct conversion on such a pattern in the West. At times of reduced military expenditure, defense contractors have opted for company rationalizations involving closures and redundancies. If they have chosen to enter new markets, they have tended to do so through diversification, establishing new operations or buying into existing companies. During the present post–Cold War downturn, some firms engaged in defense production have chosen to specialize even more narrowly on military work, seeking to ensure survival by concentrating on their greatest strengths in particular niches of the weapons market.

In the former Soviet Union conversion (*konversiya*) was generally understood in a very specific sense from the outset: capacities and personnel freed from military production at existing enterprises would be switched directly to civil work. Similarly, existing research and design facilities of the defense industry would become involved in the development of civilian technologies. It was not envisaged that existing establishments would be closed down or broken up, or that labor would be transferred out of the defense complex on a substantial scale.

Under Gorbachev, as we saw earlier, there were attempts to undertake the partial conversion of the Soviet defense industry as a centrally managed process. Considerable effort went into drawing up ministerial plans and programs, culminating in the elaboration of a draft Unionwide State Program for Conversion. This was never finally approved for implementation. In the absence of a national program, enterprises attempted to develop their own survival strategies, at times supported by regional or citywide collaborative efforts. Thus, while conversion planned from above was an almost total failure, some initiatives from below, at the enterprise level, did develop prior to the collapse of the USSR.[1]

With Russian independence, President Yeltsin was determined to pursue the policy of conversion with even greater vigor. In government circles, at least among more radical elements, there appears to have been an optimistic belief that an abrupt curtailment of military orders, coupled with price liberalization and measures to promote marketization, would jolt the defense industry into decisive action, in part by destroying any residual hopes that there would be a policy reversal.

At first responsibility for conversion was given to a State Committee for Conversion attached to the Presidential apparatus. Headed by a former military man turned entrepreneur, Mikhail Bazhanov, this committee achieved little and, amid rumors of an arms sales scandal, was disbanded in the spring of 1992. Since then there has been no single locus of responsibility for defense industry conversion; instead almost every agency of government has its own department or committee for conversion. As one Russian commentator observed wryly, "The number of leading and coordinating commissions and committees for the problem of conversion has come to be comparable with the number of enterprises being converted."[2]

In the former USSR one contentious issue had been the lack of a law codifying the rights of enterprises facing reduced military orders. To fill this legal vacuum, the Supreme Soviet of the Russian Federation adopted a Law on Conversion in March 1992. Conversion is defined as "the partial or complete reorientation from military to civilian needs ... of the liberated production capacities, scientific and technical potential, and human resources of defense and associated enterprises, associations and organizations."[3] The Law specifies that the state has to give an arms producer two years' notice of a reduction

---

1. See Cooper (1991), Cronberg (1992) and Malleret (1992).

2. *Krasnaya Zvezda*, 13 March 1993.

3. See Claudon and Wittneben (1993), pp. 116–25 for a translation of the March 1992 Law on Conversion.

in military orders. If this warning is not given, the state is obliged to compensate losses arising from conversion. There is also provision for various forms of social protection of the workforce. But the Law has remained on paper: resources are simply not available to fund its implementation.

The problem of funding has been a central policy issue. Given the acute budgetary crisis, the state has only a limited capacity to finance investment associated with conversion projects, or to provide support for enterprises and their personnel driven into financial difficulties by reduced military orders. One solution advocated with vigor by Mikhail Malei, one-time Presidential adviser on conversion and now head of the Security Council's Interdepartmental Commission for Scientific and Technical Issues of the Military-Industrial Complex, is the use of earnings from arms exports to finance conversion. Malei has argued for what he terms "economic conversion," based on generating finance within the defense industry itself, as opposed to "physical conversion." In his view conversion will cost $150 billion over a period of fifteen years. The proceeds from arms exports will be reinvested in civilian production and in the social infrastructure of the defense industry. Malei has consistently maintained that Russia has the potential to export arms to an annual value of 10-12 billion dollars. The failure to exploit that potential in 1992 led Malei to advocate arms sales at prices well below normal world levels: in his view such prices could be justified by Russia's low production costs.[4]

Malei's position has had its Russian critics. Academician Gennady Osipov, for example, has argued that, notwithstanding its apparent logic, economic conversion is doomed to failure. In his view it represents a technocratic approach, divorced from the real processes of development of the present-day international community. Other objections could be raised. Malei has not explained why Russian arms manufacturers should undertake conversion at all, if they are able to produce successfully for foreign markets. And if the earnings of successful exporters are to be allocated to those enterprises unable to sell abroad, what mechanism is to be used to redistribute the hard-currency proceeds? A redistributive policy is likely to be fiercely opposed by the successful enterprises. In practice arms exports have in any case collapsed, and there has been little scope for implementing Malei's strategy. In 1992 arms exports amounted to only 1.9 billion dollars and, notwithstanding vigorous efforts to promote sales and the creation of a new state export agency, Rosvooruzhenie, arms exports showed only a modest increase to 2.1 billion dollars in 1993.[5] Barter arrangements have played an increasingly important role

4. *Izvestiya*, 14 October 1992; *Moscow News*, 1993, no. 8, p. 4.
5. *Izvestiya*, 23 February 1993; *Segodnya*, 27 January 1994.

Box 4-1: *Conversion in Russia: Organizations and Personnel*

1) Presidential apparatus
   President's Adviser on Conversion: Mikhail Malei
   Security Council: chair—vacant (formerly Yury Skokov) (involved in issues of
       military-technical policy, industrial policy and conversion)
   State Technical Commission: chair—Yury Yashin (policy for the protection of in-
       formation, including that for the defense industry/conversion)
2) Council of Ministers—Government of the Russian Federation
   Department of the defense complex and conversion of the apparatus of the Council
       of Ministers: head—S Sidorov; first deputy head—Boris Tel'nov (coordi-
       nates actions of government departments and places state orders for
       weapons)
   Ministry of Defense: first deputy minister for military-technical questions—Andrei
       Kokoshin (also chair of the Committee for Military-Technical Policy) Ar-
       maments directorate, chief—Vyacheslav Mironov (also deputy chair of
       committee for military-technical policy)
   Ministry of Foreign Affairs: Directorate for Export Control and Conversion,
       head—Sergei Kortunov; Conversion department, head—G Zaitsev
   Deputy Prime Minister (for oversight of defense industry and conversion): vacant
       (formerly—George Khizha)
   Ministry of the Economy: deputy minister—Ivan Materov (including conversion)
   Department of the economics of the defense complex and conversion, head—
       Vladimir Salo: deputy—V Kotov
   State Committee for Industrial Policy: chair—Igor Shurchkov (has a
       conversion department)
   Committee for the Defense Branches of Industry: chair—Viktor Glukhikh; first
       deputy—Yury Glybin (responsible for conversion policy); deputy chairs—
       Anatoly Bratukhin; Boris Lapshov: Gennady Yanpolsky
   Under the Committee: Central Research Institute of Economics and Conversion of
       Military Production, director—Evgeny Kulichkov
   Committee for Machinebuilding: chairman—Anatoloy Orgurtsov; department of
       conversion, chair—A Dyatlov
   Ministry of Science and Technical Policy: minister—Boris Saltykov
   Department of Conversion and Export Control, head—Boris Urlov
   Interdepartmental Analytical Center: director—Aleksei Ponomarev (involved in as-
       sessment of conversion policy and projects)

---

in Russia's arms trade, with the result that in 1994 money earnings from arms
exports declined to 1.5 billion dollars.[6] However, some large orders obtained
in 1994, including a contract to supply MiG-29s to Malaysia, may lead to
higher export figures in 1995. There is a growing realization in Russia that it
will take time to win a significant share of the highly competitive post–Cold
War world arms market. It is also increasingly recognized that potential cus-

---

6. *Segodnya*, 18 February 1995.

Box 4-1: *continued*

3) Supreme Soviet of the Russian Federation
    Committee for Defense and Security: chair—Sergei Stepashin
    Committee for Industry and Energy: chair—Alvin Eremin; deputy chair—Vitaly
        Vitebsky (also leader of the group of deputies for the control of military-
        technical cooperation (arms exports); subcommittee for Conversion,
        chair—Yury Tarasyuk
4) Nonstate bodies
    Russian Union of Industrials and Entrepreneurs: president—Arkady Volsky; stand-
        ing committee for conversion, chair—Anatoly Kulakov
    League of Defense Enterprises of Russia: President—Aleksei Shulunov; vice-pres-
        ident—Vladimir Gladyshev; executive director: Vladimir Alferov
    Committee for Promotion of Conversion of the Chamber of Commerce and Indus-
        try: chair—Vladimir Gladyshev
    International Fund of Conversion: president—Mikhail Ananyan
    International Scientific and Production Concern "Konversiya": general director—
        Boris Korobochkin
    Center for Conversion of the Aerospace Complex: president—General Vladimir
        Tsar'kov
    Military-Industrial Investment Company: chair of board—Sergei Petrov; general
        director—Vitaly Doguzhiev

tomers are being deterred by Russia's domestic instability: a stable long-term customer–supplier relationship is essential for deals involving expensive, technically complex weapon systems. The commitment to expanding arms sales was underlined by the creation in December 1994 of a new State Committee for Military-Technical Policy, subordinated to the Presidential apparatus and charged with determining policy for exports and for the integration of arms production for export sales with the development of the defense industry for domestic needs and also conversion.[7]

Because of the failure to raise much finance for conversion from arms sales or from Western investors and international agencies, the Russian government has been seeking to elaborate conversion programs that can be financed from domestic budgetary sources and credits. Programs have been drawn up by the Committee for the Defense Branches of Industry and the Ministry of the Economy (the former State Planning Committee, Gosplan) as part of the draft federal program for restructuring the economy. Thirteen state programs have been prepared: twelve for the defense complex and one for the Ministry of Atomic Energy. The programs are as follows:

7. *Sobranie Zakonodatel'stvo Rossiiskoi Federatsii*, 1995, no.1, Presidential order no. 2251 (30 December, 1994).

1. The development of civil aviation (1992–2000)
2. The rebirth of the Russian merchant fleet (1992–95)
3. Equipment for the fuel and energy complex (1992–94)
4. Machinery and equipment for house building and road construction (1992–94)
5. Machinery and equipment for the forest products industry (1992–94)
6. Equipment for the processing branches of the agroindustrial complex (1992–95)
7. Technological equipment for light industry (1993–97)
8. Equipment for trade and public catering (1993–98)
9. High quality durable consumer goods (1992–94)
10. Communications and informatics (1992–93)
11. Program "conversion and ecology" (1992–93)
12. Medical equipment (1992–95)
13. Program of conversion of enterprises of the Ministry of Atomic Energy (1993–2000)

These programs will require substantial funding. Preliminary estimates indicate a total requirement of 554 billion rubles (in the prices of the fourth quarter of 1992), including 216 billion rubles from the state budget, 250 billion rubles in the form of preferential credits, 42 billion rubles from the extra-budgetary Fund for Support of Conversion, and 46 billion rubles from other sources. In addition, R&D costs of 117 billion rubles will have to be covered, plus subsidies of 94 billion rubles.[8] This ambitious set of conversion programs is to be supplemented by two further national programs—for the development of the Russian electronics industry and the civil space program. It is highly unlikely that funding will be found for all these programs: in 1993 and 1994 only three programs were funded—for civil aviation, shipbuilding and civil space research.

In the Soviet period the nuclear industry had one of the most comprehensive conversion programs, and there is considerable continuity between that program and the present Russian program. It is envisaged that by 1995 the volume of military production in the sector will have declined by 58 percent in comparison to the 1988 level. The principles shaping the program are the need to preserve the existing potential of the industry, an orientation to dual-use technologies "ensuring accelerated reconversion," and reliance, to a substantial degree, on the ministry's own internal sources of financing. The program

8. *Voprosy Ekonomiki i Konversii*, 1992, no. 4, pp. 18–20.

includes the development of microelectronics, computers and automation, fiber optics, advanced materials, medical equipment, food industry equipment, lasers, telecommunications, fifth-generation television sets, filtration systems, and clean rooms. The nuclear industry will also expand its existing gold production capacity.[9] Given that the Russian civil nuclear power program is undergoing a partial revival, and that Western finance should be available to some of the research personnel of the nuclear weapons industry through the newly established International Science and Technology Center, the prospects for the nuclear industry are probably more favorable than for other sectors of the defense industry.

Notwithstanding the failure of earlier attempts to plan conversion, there is still a belief in Russian government circles in the potential of national programs. However, a number of basic difficulties remain. First, the programs have been drawn up from above, taking account of the supply possibilities of existing enterprises, but taking little account of potential market demand. Second, the administrative structures formerly on hand to secure the fulfillment of programs of this type have to a large extent disappeared. Third, the programs are heavily dependent on state grants, or state-provided soft loans, and there is little prospect of adequate funding being available during the next few years. Malei has hinted that the elaboration and approval of national conversion programs may, nevertheless, serve a public relations function: "This is to appease any fears that the military-industrial complex will get a new lease of life."[10]

More promising is the increasing attention being paid to regional initiatives. As the inability of central institutions to direct and fund conversion projects becomes ever more apparent, republican, regional and city authorities, in association with local defense enterprises and R&D organizations, have been developing their own programs. (See paper by Sergei Manezhev in this volume.) These often provide for collaboration between organizations formerly of different ministerial affiliations. This must be regarded as a very positive development, helping to erode the vertical administrative logic characteristic of the former Soviet economy. Furthermore, the regional programs now being developed often involve organizations of the emergent nonstate sector, and have an orientation to local demand. As such they have the potential to promote the broader process of marketization. Regions with conversion programs now include such major centers of armaments production as the North-West-

9. *Moscow News*, 1992, no. 5, p. 5; speech of V. F. Konovalov, First Deputy Minister of Atomic Energy, at Symposium "Investing in Conversion," Birmingham, May 1993.

10. *Moscow News*, 1993, no. 8, p. 4.

ern economic region and the *oblasti* of Sverdlovsk, Omsk, Novosibirsk, Tula, Kaluga, Penza, Irkutsk and Nizhny Novgorod. Republican programs are being developed in Dagestan, Buryatiya, Tatarstan and Udmurtiya, the last of which is the most heavily militarized of all the constituent republics of the Russian Federation.

Policy for the former closed cities and the specialized science towns of the defense industry is gradually evolving. The towns are beginning to coordinate their efforts and form associations and unions to lobby for the creation of special zones of economic development, or science-technology parks. Again, there is a growing realization that the government in Moscow cannot provide all the solutions to the acute problems now arising from this extraordinary legacy of the Soviet period.

In general, policy for conversion in Russia has gradually acquired greater realism, but there has been a reluctance to envisage more radical solutions involving a more fundamental dismantling of the defense industry in the context of overall economic restructuring. As we shall explain in Chapter 6, more radical options are difficult to consider while basic issues relating to the future of military production remain unresolved. The same applies in Ukraine, where similar policy issues have arisen and where there have also been efforts to draw up conversion programs. A complicating factor here has been a lack of clarity on the nature of the defense industry that Ukraine requires, or can afford to develop. The Ukrainian government has drawn up a ten-year conversion program, the realization of which will require expenditure of $2 billion and 650 billion karbovanets, the new local currency. This national program includes 520 subprograms for the production of civilian goods.[11] As in the case of Russia, it is difficult to see how the state will be able to contribute much funding to the realization of these programs.

11. *Izvestiya*, 5 May 1993.

CHAPTER FIVE

Conversion in Practice

Faced with reduced military orders and little prospect of a substantial reversal of policy, many enterprises and research organizations of the Russian defense industry are endeavoring to increase their civilian involvement. In some branches the technical difficulties of redeploying resources are less acute, and it has proved possible to organize new production lines with relative ease. This applies in particular to the aviation, shipbuilding and telecommunications industries. In other branches—the ground forces equipment industry, for example—reorientation has proved to be extremely difficult.

At the enterprise level there are multiple problems. There is uncertainty about military orders, which are often reduced without notice, leading to the accumulation of stocks of half-completed hardware, components and materials. Production capacities freed from military work may be frozen on the grounds that they might be needed for a future revival of defense work. Workers and technical personnel may lack the skills for new civil activities, but there may be no resources for retraining. A major problem is lack of knowledge of the market potential of new civilian products. In many cases an enterprise decides to organize the production of a particular type of civilian good not because a market opportunity has been identified, but because it can be manufactured with a minimum restructuring of existing capacities and without the need for large-scale investment. *In general, supply-determined conversion has predominated;* demand-led conversion has been rare, and only began to develop as domestic demand collapsed in many sectors of the market in 1993–94. This pattern can be illustrated by the example of microwave ovens. Many plants of the radio and electronics industries have decided to organize manufacture of microwaves because of their relative simplicity from a production point of view. If present plans are realized, substantial overproduction would appear to be unavoidable. Sometimes defense plants have had an exaggerated view of their own capabilities, and have found to their cost that civil production may require a higher level of technology than military.[1]

In the past enterprises of the defense industry, like those in the rest of the economy, were little concerned with the economics of production. In principle a profit had to be earned, but enterprise managers had only a limited appreciation of the true costs of production and little control over the pricing of their products. They also knew that the penalties of failure were unlikely to be severe: in the last resort subsidies would be provided. Given this experience, it is not surprising that many conversion projects lack proper economic substantiation. Business plans are now being drawn up in a more systematic manner, but it is difficult to make reliable projections of future earnings and profits when inflation continues at monthly rates of up to 25 percent, and serious price distortions remain. Conversion projects apparently profitable today may turn out to be unprofitable tomorrow, just as some of the traditional civilian production lines of the defense industry have now become economically unviable. However, enterprise directors cannot delay action until stable conditions materialize. Initiatives taken now may turn out to be unprofitable, but at least experience of the market will be gained. In present conditions there is probably no alternative to a trial-and-error approach, which accepts that conversion is a complex, and costly, learning process.

Lack of customer purchasing power is a severe problem, hitting both traditional civil production and the new conversion production lines of the defense industry. In some cases customers are simply unable to pay for ordered goods. There is an obvious need for a wide range of modern equipment, but the potential customers lack the requisite purchasing power and banks are reluctant to provide long-term credit. This problem is hindering the development of such products as agricultural equipment for small farms, transport equipment, and medical technology for the health service. Demand for many types of traditional consumer goods produced by the defense industry has fallen. The new rich of the emergent private sector have a taste for, and money to buy, luxury goods, but prefer to import from the West. Some conversion, on the other hand, is taking the form of import substitution, replacing supplies from former Soviet republics. Thus the Voronezh Mechanical Works, the basic product of which is rocket engines, is now manufacturing oil industry equipment previ-

---

1. This has been claimed for the defence industry of the Sverdlovsk region. See *Krasnaya Zvezda*, 6 February 1993.

ously obtained from Azerbaijan.[2] With its foreign currency earnings, the energy sector provides one of the few buoyant markets, and it is not surprising that many defense plants have chosen to build production equipment for the oil and gas industries.

The state of the conversion process in Russia was summarized in a survey by the State Committee for Statistics undertaken at the end of 1993. At the 716 enterprises surveyed, the share of military output had declined from 52 percent in 1990 to 31 percent in 1993. During 1993 employment at these enterprises fell by 12 percent.[3] Surveys of enterprises undergoing conversion during the period 1992–94 have shown that little more than half of the assets released from military work were subject to reprofiling to civilian purposes. There are two main reasons why capacities have not been converted: some assets are too specialized to be reprofiled; but more important has been the retention of capacities to meet possible future military orders.[4] We return to this issue in chapter 6.

To date there have been few genuine redundancies as a result of cutbacks in military production: enterprises have made strenuous efforts to retain their workers. Those who have left have done so mainly on a voluntary basis, or as a result of early retirement. New recruitment has been severely curtailed, leading to serious problems for the technical institutes which regularly supplied graduates to the military sector. The scale of the retraining effort has been modest, but is now expanding: in 1991 only 1.9 percent of the industrial personnel of the defense complex underwent retraining, and in 1992 6.3 percent.[5] However, a price has had to be paid for the limited scale of unemployment: the state has been obliged to provide subsidies and credits, fueling the inflationary pressure in the economy.

Military R&D is also undergoing conversion. Many of the problems being experienced by enterprises are also typical for institutes and design organizations. Approximately 350 such organizations are now involved in conversion, almost half of them in three branches—the aviation, shipbuilding and radio industries. Some of the leading research establishments of the defense sector are being converted into Federal Scientific Centers with continuing, if reduced, state support. Examples include the nuclear weapons research and design cen-

2. *Inzhenernaya Gazeta*, 1993, no. 2.

3. *Segodnya*, 25 March 1994; *Ekonomika i Zhizn'*, 1994, no.15 (supplement *Vash Partner*, p. 2).

4. This has been acknowledged by Yury Glybin, First Deputy Chairman of the Committee for the Defence Branches of Industry (*Inzhenernaya Gazeta*, 1992, no. 126–27).

5. *Voprosy Ekonomiki i Konversii*, 1992, no. 4, p. 4.

Box 5-1: *Examples of conversion in Russia*

Tula "Shtamp"—a munitions plant which has undergone almost complete conversion, now producing gas stoves and samovars.

Biisk "Sibpribormash"—has refused military orders (munitions-related); converting fully to agricultural machinery production; may build a mini-tractor as joint project with a Chinese enterprise.

Bryansk chemical plant—a major producer of explosives, undergoing substantial conversion; civil goods include industrial explosives, furniture, and large-scale production of eau-de-cologne.

Balakirev mechanical works (Vladimir region)—an artillery plant. Part of its capacity is being converted to the manufacture of small tractors.

Arzamas-16 and Chelyabinsk-70—the principal centers of nuclear weapons research and development; both now involved in fiber optics technology for the communications industry.

Sverdlovsk-45 (Nizhnyaya-Tura) "Elektrokhimpribor' plant" —one of the main centers for the assembly and dismantling of nuclear warheads, now engaged in production of equipment for the oil and gas industry, magnetrons for microwave ovens, vehicle parts, and dairy industry equipment.

Partizansk "Uragan" works (Primorskii krai)—formerly built turbines for the navy; complete conversion to equipment for the fishing fleet and on-shore fish-processing plants.

St. Petersburg "Baltiiskii zavod"—a major naval shipyard now completing its last military order (nuclear-powered missile-carrying heavy cruiser); building chemical tankers to a German order and to preparing to undertake servicing of ships for an Austrian company. Now a joint-stock company.

Irkutsk aviation works—was building the Su-27, now organizing production of the Be-200 amphibious plane and the Yak-112 4-seater general-purpose aircraft.

Kaluga engine-building association—major producer of gas turbine engines for military aircraft and tanks (T-80); converting to production of diesel engines for agricultural use. Also has a joint venture with a German company for manufacture of equipment for the footwear industry, and is involved in building equipment for the textile industry.

---

ters of Arzamas-16 and Chelyabinsk-70, the aviation industry's Central Aero-Hydrodynamics Institute (TsAGI) at Zhukovsky and the St Petersburg State Optical Institute.

Notwithstanding all the obstacles and difficulties, some conversion is taking place in the defense industries of Russia, Ukraine and other states of the former USSR. This conversion activity owes much to the initiative and energy of individual directors of factories and institutes. Many projects may turn out to be economically unsound, but valuable experience is being gained, helping to break down the traditional behavior patterns and attitudes of the elite sector of the former Soviet planned economy. However, there is also much exaggerated propaganda about progress in conversion. What one Russian journalist has termed the "exhibition conversion" syndrome is prevalent: the development of new civil goods for display purposes when no actual serial production has been organized.[6] Exaggeration and display do, of course, play their part in attracting foreign support for conversion, an issue addressed in chapter 7.

6. *Sankt Peterburgskie Vedomosti*, 24 February 1993.

CHAPTER SIX

Beyond *Konversiya:* The Armaments Industry in a Restructured Economy

Since the Russian Federation became an independent state there have been many changes in the environment of the defense industry and the context of conversion. Economic transformation has progressed, albeit in fits and starts, privatization has gained momentum, political change has strengthened the role in government of experienced industrialists, and the new Russian armed forces have begun to consolidate. The Commonwealth of Independent States, to the surprise of many at home and abroad, has not only survived, but is to an increasing extent providing a framework for the partial restoration of fractured economic links between its members, including links in the defense industry. These developments have in some degree changed the agenda for conversion in Russia.

The acute difficulties of the Russian defense industry in 1992 led to pressure for a revival of military production. For a time Yeltsin himself appeared to be backing such a course: at a meeting of the government in February 1993, following his return from a visit to India, he cast doubt on the wisdom of cutting back military production so sharply, suggesting that increased production for export was a possibility. His statements were echoed by Glukhikh in his report to the meeting, who argued for an increase in defense orders. However, the Prime Minister, Viktor Chernomyrdin, sharply criticized Glukhikh's report, and no action appears to have been taken.[1] Some work has been created through the pursuit of an import substitution policy, aimed at reducing dependence on deliveries of strategically sensitive products from former Union republics.[2] But since the spring of 1993 domestic procurement has fallen further, while arms exports have remained static. The unrelenting downward trend in the volume of military output has generated mounting concern as to the future of Russia's military industrial base, within both the defense industry itself and the armed forces. The question of *what kind of defense industry Russia needs* has come to the top of the policy agenda. This shift of emphasis has to some extent displaced conversion as the central policy concern.

It has been widely recognized in Russia that one of the major obstacles to developing a coherent policy for economic restructuring is lack of clarity about the country's security policy. Technical policy for the armed forces has remained uncertain, and until the summer of 1994 there was no agreement on a new policy for the mobilization capability of the Russian economy (see below). These uncertainties have made it difficult to obtain agreement on how much of the capacity of the defense industry inherited from the Soviet past will be required for armaments production in the future.

Since the autumn of 1992, work has been under way on clarifying the technical requirements of the Russian armed forces to the year 2000 and beyond. Actively involved in this process is a Council for Military-Technical Policy chaired by the civilian First Deputy Minister of Defense, Andrei Kokoshin. The Council includes leading scientists, designers, economists and enterprise directors in the defense industry.[3] General principles have been agreed by the Security Council. Russia's strategic deterrent capability will be maintained, and there will be priority for the development of high-precision munitions, and also of improved systems of communications, reconnaissance, early warning and combat control. Equipment for the development of mobile forces will be a priority.[4]

This clarification of military technical policy is closely linked to the determination of priorities for defense R&D. According to Kokoshin, there will more emphasis on the modernization of existing armaments, and on reducing the variety of weapons produced, with increased standardization between dif-

1. *Izvestiya*, 5 February 1993; BBC *Summary of World Broadcasts*, SU/1606 C1/3, 6 February 1993.
2. *Izvestiya*, 5 February 1993.
3. *Krasnaya Zvezda*, 11 March 1993.
4. *Krasnaya Zvezda*, 6 February 1993.

ferent systems. A major thrust of policy will be the development of dual-purpose technologies and systems having both civil and military applications. One of the goals of such a policy, Kokoshin has stated, is to enhance the mobilizational capacity of the economy. Pursuit of these priorities, it is claimed, should lead to a reduction in the number of military R&D establishments.[5] As a former academic specialist on the United States, Kokoshin is well aware of current thinking in the West on policies for military-civilian industrial integration, in particular the emphasis on dual-use technologies.[6] This also relates to two further policy concerns, namely mobilization policy and industrial strategy.

Until the very last days of the former USSR, policy for the mobilization of the economy in the event of war or other national emergency was never discussed in open publications. It was always regarded as one of the most sensitive issues of national security: in the words of the military specialist, Vitaly Shlykov, the first person to criticize openly the Soviet mobilization system, it was a "sacred cow," defended by all the structures of power.[7] The demise of the USSR brought to an end the elaborate system of planning and financing of mobilization preparation, and all previous legislation (none of which had ever been published) lost its force. However, enterprises were not given permission to reduce Soviet-era mobilization capacities and stocks, although it appears that in practice mobilization stocks were sold and exported widely in order to cushion the shock of reduced military orders.[8] Work on the preparation of a new law on the mobilization system stimulated a policy debate which revealed that some influential figures within the armed forces and defense industry were reluctant to contemplate radical change even though the security and economic position of the country had been transformed.

Some of the new concerns were spelt out in 1992 by Yury Glybin, first deputy chairman of the Committee for the Defense Branches of Industry. He argued that policy must take account of the break-up of the USSR. A twin-track approach was required. First, efforts must be made to secure bilateral agreements with other states of the former Soviet Union for cooperation in the development and production of military equipment during both peacetime and periods of emergency. Second, recognizing that only partial success will be

5. *Voennaya Mysl'*, 1993, no. 2, p. 8.

6. Notably in the writings of Jacques S. Gansler: see, for example, his book *Affording Defense* (Cambridge, Mass: The MIT Press, 1989), pp. 273–86. Kokoshin's view are discussed at length in the author's article, "Transforming Russia's Defense Industrial Base,: *Survival* (Winter 1993–94), pp.147–62.

7. *Soyuz*, no. 24(76), June 1991, p. 11.

8. This has been claimed by Shlykov. See his article, "Economic Readjustment within the Russian Defense-Industrial Complex," *Security Dialogue*, vol. 26, no. 1 (1995), p. 30.

achieved in this, preparations must be made in peacetime for meeting possible delivery failures—hence the import substitution policy now under way in some fields of military production. Supply uncertainties dictate that mobilizational plans should be drawn up in two variants: the first assuming continuation of supplies from the "near abroad," the second their breakdown. What about concern that conversion would "significantly worsen" the mobilizational possibilities of the defense industry? In Glybin's view, special measures were needed to ensure that mobilizational capacities were retained in the new conditions. This would involve the conservation of specialized production capacities not needed for civil production, the retention and storage at enterprises of special-purpose equipment, and the further development of so-called assimilation—the adaptation to civil purposes of capacities freed from military work in such a way that they could be made available for military production once again in time of need.[9]

Meanwhile, in the absence of a new policy, some enterprises found that they were being prevented from adapting capacity freed from military production on the grounds that it could be required in the future for mobilization purposes. To make matters worse, the system of state budget funding for the maintenance of such reserves had collapsed, leaving the enterprise itself to cover any costs involved. This increasingly serious problem was finally resolved by Yeltsin in July 1994. A presidential order on the mobilization system provided for a substantial reduction in the scale of reserve capacities and stocks to be retained, with their concentration at plants heavily involved in the fulfillment of military orders. Now many enterprises are free to dispose of unwanted equipment and mobilization reserves and fully to convert facilities previously excluded from civilianization.[10] A new consideration which prompted this action was the *privatization of enterprises engaged in military work.*

Long before the October Revolution there was acceptance in Russia that arms factories vital to the country's security should be owned by the state. Given this long-established tradition it is not surprising that the extent to which privatization should develop in the present-day defense complex is a controversial issue. There are fears on the one hand, that privatization may undermine the country's security; on the other, that the success of privatization will be jeopardized if the most advanced enterprises in the country are excluded from the process. Official thinking on this question has evolved gradu-

9. *Voprosy Ekonomiki i Konversii*, 1992, no. 4, pp. 45–50.
10. *Rossiiskaya Gazeta*, 13 July 1994.

ally. A concept of defense industry privatization was developed initially by the former Ministry of Industry, which argued that the enterprises of the defense complex should be divided into three categories. A core group of specialized enterprises considered vital to the country's defense would remain in full state ownership; enterprises with a limited but significant degree of involvement in actual military production would be transformed into joint-stock companies, but with the state retaining a 30-40 percent share; and the remaining factories—those only marginally involved in military production as such—would be permitted to privatize completely.[11] In all of this the watchword was clearly caution.

With the adoption of a policy of mass privatization based on the use of vouchers, those in charge of the process, notably the head of the State Committee for Property, Anatoly Chubais (now first deputy prime minister), began to argue for a reduction to a minimum of the number of enterprises excluded from the process, in particular the defense complex facilities potentially attractive to private investors. This campaign was successful. In February 1993 Chubais declared that privatization would encompass the majority of defense sector enterprises, and Yeltsin instructed Glukhikh, chairman of the defense industry committee, to start privatizing defense plants. "Private enterprises can fulfill military orders no less successfully than state enterprises," Yeltsin informed Glukhikh. "One should not link privatization exclusively to conversion." All limitations on privatization should be reduced to a minimum, he added, calling for the large-scale transfer to private ownership of subdivisions of those enterprises which would remain in the hands of the state. That Yeltsin and Chubais had opponents within the defense industry was immediately demonstrated by the angry riposte of a well known plant director, Georgy Kostin, then leader of the missile-space industry's Voronezh Mechanical Works. "To say that private enterprises can successfully fulfill military orders is stupid and immoral," wrote Kostin, who went on to declare, "The command to separate out and privatize individual subdivisions is a direct order to tear down our high-technology industry. It is a crime against Russia."[12] Kostin, since removed as plant director, was known for his association with the extreme-right National Salvation Front. But in challenging the privatization policy he probably spoke for many in the conservative wing of the defense industry.

During the first half of 1993 the leadership of Goskomoboronprom and other representatives of the defense industry attempted to moderate official

11. *Inzhenernaya Gazeta*, 1992, no. 126–27.

12. BBC, *Summary of World Broadcasts*, SU/1605 C1/1, 5 February 1993; *Sovetskaya Rossiya*, 16 March 1993.

policy on privatization within the military sector. The policy struggle was resolved by a presidential order of 19 August 1993, subsequently modified by a government decree in December, according to which 474 facilities of Goskomoboronprom (214 enterprises, approximately one-fifth of the total number, and 260 R&D organizations, 40 percent of the total) were identified as candidates for full state ownership. The remaining facilities were to be transformed into joint-stock companies and privatized, although the state was to retain an ownership share for at least three years in those enterprises considered important from a national security point of view. In some cases this state participation in some cases was to take the form of a single golden share, giving the authorities the right to veto decisions considered detrimental to state interests.

By August 1994 almost half of the defense industry's enterprises and R&D organizations had become joint-stock companies.[13] It is clear that in practice many managers in the defense industry view privatization as a means of gaining additional freedom to determine the future of their own enterprises. In most cases the so-called second variant of privatization has been chosen, giving the enterprise workforce a majority share. By this means the existing top managers are likely to remain in control, though they may encounter difficulties if they decide to push through radical restructuring policies threatening large-scale redundancies. Among the well-known defense sector plants now privatized are the St Petersburg Kirovskii zavod, Baltic shipyard and Arsenal, the Tula Tulamashzavod (producing anti-tank missiles and guns for aircraft), the Perm Permskie Motory (one of the country's largest builders of aero-engines), the Komsomolsk-na-Amure Amurskii shipbuilding works (until recently a major producer of submarines), and the Moscow-based Vympel corporation (strategic defense systems). The last is unusual, but possibly a harbinger of future developments, in so far as it is multinational, embracing both Russian and Belarussian facilities. Privatization is developing a momentum of its own, but there are still influential figures in the Russian government with a preference for a more controlled restructuring of the defense industry. They want nothing less than a national industrial policy.

In the early months of 1993 there were clear signs that leading representatives of the military sector were seeking to broaden the policy debate. The President of the increasingly influential League for the Support of the Defense Enterprises, Aleksei Shulunov, gave expression to the new thinking when in early March of that year he set out his ideas in an article significantly entitled, "We must forget the word 'conversion' and tackle nationwide tasks." The

13. *Delovie Lyudi*, September 1994, p. 34.

"ideology of conversion has gone too far," he declared; now what was needed was a properly considered national industrial policy.[14] At about the same time, Yeltsin's conversion adviser, Malei, took up the same theme: "Rather than conversion (which is a narrow field of work) we must speak about a cardinal reform of the Russian military-industrial complex."[15]

The real initiator of this new approach was Andrei Kokoshin, who in the autumn of 1992 had put forward proposals for a National Industrial Policy (NIP). The principles behind this policy were drawn up by Kokoshin in association with a group of his former colleagues from the academic community. The central idea was that a restructured defense industry should not only provide for Russia's security, but also act as a locomotive for the country's economic revival. This could be achieved by creating a number of powerful, diversified financial-industrial groups, incorporating the leading research and manufacturing facilities of the defense industry and also some of their civilian counterparts, together with commercial banks, insurance companies and trading organizations. Ownership would be mixed, with both state and private capital, but with the possible scope of foreign participation left unclear. Financial-industrial groups would be structured so that high-technology civil activities would predominate, allowing civil technology to run ahead of military according to a model familiar in Western experience in recent years. A key focus of these organizations would be the development of dual-use technologies, and for this reason Kokoshin has pressed for their creation as a crucial means of restoring the country's mobilizational capability.[16] The first deputy defense minister has made bold claims for his NIP: "We are speaking not only about the maintenance of the defense capability of Russia, but also of the salvation and development of the entire society and the state, the achievement by our country of a worthy place in the world hierarchy of developed countries."[17]

Kokoshin's vision gained powerful backing in the government, and also found favor with the League for Support of Defense Enterprises. An order on the creation of financial-industrial groups was approved by Yeltsin in December 1993. Quite stringent conditions were set out for the registration of such groups, but official registration renders them eligible for privileges, including tax concessions and credits at preferential interest rates. Additional measures to promote their formation were adopted by the government in January 1995

14. *Krasnaya Zvezda*, 6 March 1993.

15. *Moscow News*, 1993, no. 8, p. 4.

16. *Krasnaya Zvezda*, 29 October 1992; 12 December 1992; *Megapolis Express*, 27 January 1993, p. 12; *Delovye Lyudi*, April 1993, p. 14.

17. *Ekonomika i Zhizn'*, 1993, no. 4, p.4.

in the form of a "program of assistance to the formation of financial-industrial groups."[18] By early 1995, however, only 9 groups had been registered. The new program envisages the creation of a further 10–15 in 1995 and 50–70 in 1996, including approximately 20 in the defense industry. Several of the newly created groups incorporate enterprises of the defense complex, in particular Uralskie zavody in the republic of Udmurtiya. In early 1995 legislation for the creation of financial-industrial groups was adopted in Ukraine, and similar legislation was at that time in an advanced stage of drafting in Kazakhstan, offering new possibilities for organizing multinational groups as a means of restoring some of the links within the defense sector broken by the collapse of the USSR.[19] An intergovernmental agreement in February 1995 for the creation of a joint Ukrainian-Russian group, International Aircraft Engines may prove to be the first of a series of such initiatives.

The envisaged restructuring of part of the Russian defense industry into financial-industrial groups is not without problems and potential dangers. It is not clear that it is wholly compatible with the policy of privatization; indeed one opponent of the creation of the groups has been the state privatization committee, which has expressed concern that new monopolies will be created.[20] As defense sector enterprises privatize, will they be prepared to forgo their new independence and enter voluntarily into the financial-industrial groups? Can the financial-industrial groups achieve their intended purpose? Some doubts must be expressed on that count. At present there is only a weak domestic market for the civilian high technologies which they will develop. A strong export orientation will be essential, but it will not be easy for Russia to enter this highly competitive market, especially if the new groups are relatively closed to Western participation. There is another danger. Advocates of the new policy have seized upon the concept of dual-use technology, justified on the grounds that it represents the latest trend in the West. However, as noted above, there is nothing new for Russia about dual-use technology, though it may have run in the past on a lower level of development than currently envisaged. Given the still considerable strength of the military interest in Russia, there must be a real danger that the civil facilities drawn into the orbit of the new groups will be obliged to adapt to military requirements; that, as before, the civil economy will have no choice but to accept dual-use items

18. *Delovoi Mir*, 8 February 1995.

19. *Ukrainskie Delovye Novosti*, no. 4, 1995, p. 11; *Kazakhstanskaya Pravda*, 20 January 1995.

20. See David A.Dyker and Michael Barrow, *Monopoly and Competition Policy in Russia*, Post-Soviet Business Forum (RIIA, 1994).

essentially serving the interests of defense and the nation's potential for mobilization. In the absence of strong civilian control over Russia's emerging industrial strategy, a post-*konversiya* policy could bring about a partial remilitarization of the civilian economy. An additional danger is that the groups will become quasi-ministerial structures able to extract resources and privileges from the state, with negative consequences for Russia's emergent market economy.

It was becoming clear by the end of 1994 that a new slimmed-down defense industry is taking shape in Russia. At its heart will be a set of state-owned facilities specializing in military production—so-called treasury enterprises. Research, and the development of new weapons, will be concentrated at state scientific and production centers. Some of the facilities will enter into financial-industrial groups. But many enterprises previously involved in military work will be free to privatize and switch to the civil economy. A restructuring of this type, advocated during the second half of 1994 by the League in Support of Defense Enterprises, was set out in a government decree on measures to stabilize the defense industry adopted in late December 1994.[21] In the absence of substantial state funding, the realization of this restructuring will be difficult and painful, but the prospect is now emerging that the scaling down of the vast Soviet military-industrial complex will be successfully achieved.

21. *Ekonomika i Zhizn'*, no.1, 1995 (supplement *Vash Partner*, p. 7).

CHAPTER SEVEN

Can the West Help?

The restructuring of the former Soviet defense industry is a formidable undertaking, which is likely to entail social costs on a scale that could threaten the political stability of Russia and, possibly, of Ukraine. There is general acceptance that a successful downsizing of the vast military inheritance of the Soviet regime would enhance international security. A smoothly executed process of conversion would also reduce the risks of the emigration of specialists willing to put their knowledge of weapons of mass destruction at the disposal of potentially troublesome regimes. These are good reasons for Western participation to facilitate demilitarization. But Western involvement also offers genuine opportunities for profitable business, at the same time furthering the integration of the newly independent states into the global economy.

At the level of international agencies and national governments there are possibilities for assisting conversion by financing activities designed to create a more favorable environment for private-sector involvement. There is an almost unlimited requirement for technical assistance in a multitude of forms, including training in management skills, accounting, marketing, privatization and business restructuring, small business creation, and strategies for urban renewal. Such technical assistance is all the more useful if it extends beyond the major cities to the more remote regions of Russia, including some of the hitherto closed communities. Certain specialized forms of technical assistance are particularly valuable, including financial support for the secondment to Russia and other states of experienced personnel, including retired managers, willing to spend time at particular enterprises to assist in restructuring. Any relationship extending over a period of time is preferable to the brief consultancy visits that are unfortunately all too common.

One form of Western financial involvement in conversion which has the potential to generate significant externalities is grants or credits for infrastructure, including the development of telecommunications, transport, and environmental projects. Projects of this type are especially valuable if they can involve Russian-defense sector enterprises in the supply of equipment. This also applies to projects for the exploitation of Russia's energy and mineral wealth. Resentment at what was perceived as inadequate involvement of domestic suppliers in the proposals of foreign companies was a major factor in the Russian government's decision to create the Rosshelf joint-stock company to exploit the Stockmann gas deposits off Novaya Zemlya. (See paper in this volume by David Humphreys.) Rosshelf involves major defense sector organizations, including the Severodvinsk submarine yard, and it is expected to place orders for equipment with enterprises undergoing conversion. The Rosshelf episode underlines an important point: Russian national pride is at stake in major projects relating not only to the country's natural wealth, but also to its intellectual wealth. There are many in the defense industry and also in the Russian government, not to speak of society at large, who are suspicious of the motives of Western companies seeking to set up deals designed to reap commercial advantage from the scientific and technical talents of the military sector. These talents are widely regarded as Russia's gold and silver. Seeking to hoard that gold and silver may seem neomercantilist, but Western firms and organizations need to be aware of the sensibilities of their potential Russian partners. Experience suggests that business relationships need to be built up gradually, offering genuine advantage to both parties at every stage, and permitting the development of the mutual trust vital for success.

Notwithstanding all the obstacles and problems, many foreign companies have become involved in projects with organizations of the former Soviet defense industry, including facilities located in the closed towns of the nuclear weapons industry. Some examples are given in box 7-1 below. There are diverse forms of business links. Some companies are commercializing hitherto classified advanced technologies developed in the defense sector. Here there are genuine business opportunities, but effort and patience is required in seeking suitable technologies and partners. Others are setting up joint manufacture, sometimes beginning with the assembly of imported components as a prelude to eventual full domestic production. This is the basis, for example, on which a number of ventures involving South Korean companies are establishing the manufacture of electronic consumer goods at defense plants, not only in Russia, but also in Kazakhstan and Central Asian countries. Similarly, the Polaroid company has organized the Svetozor joint venture with enterprises of the nuclear industry, to assemble cameras for both export and the domestic market. Some projects involve the employment of defense sector R&D personnel to undertake work on behalf of foreign companies. Examples include the US Sun Microsystems company, which is hiring Russians to design software and microchips, and the Boeing corporation, which has set up an office in Russia to organize joint research activities.

In the defense sector the creation of joint ventures with Western firms has been on a modest but growing scale. By late 1992 there were 180 joint ventures involving organizations of the Russian defense complex, and 220 for the whole of the CIS. In terms of total number of joint ventures directly linked with conversion activities, US firms led (29 companies involved), followed by German (27), British (16), and Italian (10).[1] American companies have been particularly active in finding Russian partners with original advanced technologies awaiting commercialization. By the end of 1993 the number of joint ventures involving the Russian defense industry had risen to 300, with an annual output of approximately $500 million.[2]

There are still many obstacles to more active Western participation in former Soviet defense industry conversion. Some are familiar to all those who are attempting to do business with Russia and the other eastern states. The legal framework for foreign investment is inadequate, and liable to change at short notice (see paper in this volume by William Butler), the tax regime is unattractive and unstable, basic market institutions are weak or absent, and the currencies are nonconvertible. In the military sector there are additional specific problems. In Russia there is still no proper legal framework for military secrecy. The former KGB, now called the Russian Security Service, is still active in the defense industry, and there is a tendency to justify the retention of much of the old security regime on the grounds that it is required to protect commercial secrecy. There is no doubt that Russia needs a legal framework for the protection of commercial secrets, but it is striking how old state structures seek to turn the new circumstances to their own advantage. This issue of secrecy is important for Western companies because strict enforcement of security rules could curtail access to partner enterprises or institutes. There is also the problem of the remaining former-COCOM constraints in relation to high-technology sales to, or high-tech cooperation with, the states of the former USSR. In the United States, in particular, security concerns are still very much to the fore—in Western Europe attitudes are generally more relaxed. In

1. *Voprosy Ekonomiki i Konversii*, 1992, special issue, pp. 22-3.
2. *Izvestiya*, 30 December 1993.

Box 7-1. *Western Participation in Russian Conversion:*
Some Examples

Ekaterinburg "Urals electro-mechanical works" (instrumentation for the nuclear
weapons industry)
   Philips is involved in the assembly of video recorders and compact-disc players;
   plus planned volume production of television sets and tubes.

Chelyabinsk-65 (materials for nuclear weapons)
   Amersham International is purchasing radioactive isotopes.

Nizhny Novgorod Research Institute of Measuring Systems (MIIS) nuclear weapons
industry)
   A Finnish company is assisting in the organization of large-volume production of
   integrated circuits and computer equipment.

Sverdlovsk-44 (Verkhne-Ivinsk) (uranium enrichment for the nuclear weapons industry)
   A project with a US company for production of catalytic converters for motor vehicles.

St. Petersburg "Impuls" association (missile-space control systems)
   Assembly of microwave ovens (with South Korean and Italian involvement), elec-
   tric ovens (with an Italian firm), and computers, the latter a joint venture with a
   US company.

Khimki "Energomash" (principal Russian organization for the development of liquid-
fuel missile-rocket engines)
   A joint venture with the US Pratt & Whitney company involving use of the RD-
   170 engine, the most powerful in the world.

Kaliningrad "Fakel" design bureau (space equipment)
   A joint venture with a US company for the development of its electric plasma
   thrusters for space vehicles.

Moscow "Saturn" association (design of engines for combat aircraft)
   Rolls Royce is involved in joint work on engine development for civil transport
   aircraft.

Russia, many people in the defense sector and in government circles suspect
that US companies are attempting to limit potential Russian competition in
high-technology markets. These suspicions were reinforced in 1992 when the
Missile Technology Control Regime was invoked in an attempt to dissuade
Russia from selling cryogenic rocket engine technology to India. Such incidents tend to strengthen nationalist sentiment in Russia, and can lead to increased wariness of business involvement with Western partners.

   Russian organizations would have greater success in finding Western partners if more attention were paid to the elementary rules of business life. The

problems were illustrated at the Conversion–93 exhibition held at the Birmingham National Exhibition Center in May 1993. This exhibition was organized on behalf of the Russian defense industry committee, which paid for the display. The results will have disappointed the Russian organizations involved. But the time, and budget, allowed for the promotion of the exhibition was totally inadequate; the exhibits were organized on a basis incomprehensible to almost all visitors (i.e. by branch, according to the old Soviet ministerial system); many exhibits were of an unimpressive technological level,;publicity materials were inadequate (with the exception of the nuclear industry); and the Russian delegation was characteristically top-heavy, dominated by directors and chief designers, the majority of whom had no working knowledge of English. The exhibition also illustrated another basic problem: there is an expectation that Western companies will be interested in Russian technologies simply because they are advanced. It will take time for the leaders of the Russian defense industry to appreciate fully that technology alone, however impressive from a scientific and engineering point of view, is not enough. In the past their markets were guaranteed; now they have to be won.

CHAPTER EIGHT

Conclusion

The partial demilitarization of the former Soviet economies, above all that of Russia, is an immense problem, the solution of which is in the interests not only of the local populations, but also of the world at large. Military production has been reduced sharply, but there has been only limited progress in finding alternative uses for the resources released.

Taking advantage of the new possibilities offered by economic transformation and the weakening of the once all-powerful central institutions of the state, many enterprises and institutes of the defense industry in Russia are showing initiative in finding alternatives to military work. Given the incomplete state of marketization, in particular the still distorted price structure, high rates of inflation, and the weakness of domestic demand, many of these new ventures may turn out to be unprofitable. However, pragmatism is essential. The conversion projects now under way are not only helping to reduce the social costs of the transition by keeping specialists and workers in employment, but are also providing valuable experience of adaptation to new market conditions. What is in progress is a vast collective learning process. As experience is gained, so also the willingness grows to contemplate more radical solutions.

For understandable reasons, in Russia, Ukraine and the other newly independent states, there is a reluctance to recognize that successful conversion may entail more drastic restructuring than has so far been contemplated. The existing complex of defense industry enterprises and R&D organizations was built up over decades. The facilities of the defense industry are of an unusually large average size. They are not simply production units, but social institutions, often central to the existence of local communities and even whole towns. It is highly unlikely that all will be viable in the new conditions. Closures will be necessary, and large enterprises may have no choice but to break up, with parts separating out as independent companies. Indeed, the latter process has already started with privatization. In these circumstances the generation of alternative employment will be essential. The increasing emphasis on city, regional and republican conversion programs is encouraging, as the adoption of a local focus provides hope that the problems of the defense industry will be tackled within the broader context of regional economic renewal. The most valuable inheritance of the former Soviet armaments industry is not its physical plant, but its human resources. Young, highly educated personnel are already leaving the defense industry, finding new opportunities in the emerging market economy. For older workers, however, there are still substantial obstacles to mobility. The Russian government and local authorities need to give more thought to measures to facilitate the redeployment of the skilled personnel of the military sector, and also to promoting new business formation more actively.

Domestic economic pressures and the new post–Cold War international situation are working in the direction of a substantial reduction in the scale of the Russian defense sector. However, there are those in Russia who wish to see the maintenance of a very strong military industry. It is not only ardent nationalists who want Russia to remain a great power, and great-power status tends to be interpreted in terms of military strength. As the defense industry of the former Soviet Union was the strongest part of the economy, the only sector able to generate really advanced technologies, there is also a tendency, both within and outside the industry, to regard the maintenance of a strong defense sector as an essential condition if Russia is to possess a high-technology capability. Associated with these attitudes is a fetishism of advanced technology: the economic and social benefits to be derived from it take second place to national prestige considerations—it is an attribute of a great power that it is able to reach the frontiers of world technology. Russia is undergoing a profound crisis of national identity, and in these uncertain conditions it is perhaps not surprising that many are unable to appreciate that a truly great power is one that possesses a dynamic, prosperous economy able to secure a decent standard of living for all its citizens.

The restructuring of the defense industry will remain near the top of the Russian policy agenda for several years, as it will in Ukraine and to a lesser extent in the other newly independent states of the former USSR. It is a process in which the West has a vital interest, and there are many ways in which governments, international organizations and the business community can assist. Until recently, in both East and West, conversion has been a facile slogan, perhaps best regarded now as an epiphenomenon of the Cold War.[1] In the new postcommunist world the practical experience of demilitarization in Russia and other Eastern countries has induced greater realism. This new realism provides a good basis for collaborative efforts to find workable solutions and even, for the enterprising, opportunities for profitable business.

---

1. This point is developed by the author elsewhere; see "Conversion is Dead, Long Live Conversion!" *Journal of Peace Research*, vol. 32, no. 2 (1995), pp. 129–32.

Select Bibliography

Kenneth Adelman and Norman Augustine, "Defense Conversion: Bulldozing the Management," *Foreign Affairs*, Spring 1992.

Ian Anthony (ed.), *The Future of the Defense Industries in Central and Eastern Europe*, Oxford University Press/SIPRI, 1994.

David Bernstein (ed.), *Defense Industry Restructuring in Russia: Case Studies and Analysis*, Center for International Security and Arms Control, Stanford University, December 1994.

David Bernstein and William J. Perry, *Defense Conversion. A Strategic Imperative for Russia*, Center for International Security and Arms Control, Stanford University, 1992.

Michael P. Claudon and Kathryn Wittneben, (eds), *After the Cold War: Russian–American Defence Conversion for Economic Renewal,* Geonomics Institute, New York University Press, 1993.

Julian Cooper, *The Soviet Defence Industry: Conversion and Reform*, Pinter/Royal Institute of International Affairs, London, 1991.

Julian Cooper, "Defence Industry Conversion in the East: The Relevance of Western Experience," in R. Weichhardt (ed.), *External Economic Relations of the Central and East European Countries*, NATO, Brussels, 1992.

Julian Cooper, "The Soviet Union and the successor republics: coming to terms with disunion," in H. Wulf, (ed.), *Arms Industry Limited* Oxford University Press/SIPRI, 1993, pp. 87–108.

Julian Cooper, "Transforming Russia's Defence Industrial Base," *Survival*, vol. 35, no. 4, Winter 1993–4, pp. 147–62.

Julian Cooper, "Transformation of the Russian Defence Industry," *Jane's Intelligence Review*, vol. 6, no. 10, October 1994, pp. 445–47.

Tarja Cronberg, *The Price of Peace. Military Conversion on the Enterprise Level in Russia*, Technical University of Denmark, Unit of Technology Assessment, Technology Assessment Texts no. 10, Lyngby, 1992.

Taras Kuzio, "Ukraine's Military Industrial Plan," *Jane's Intelligence Review*, vol. 6, no. 8, August 1994, pp. 352–55.

Michael McFaul and David Bernstein, *Industrial Demilitarization, Privatization, Economic Reform, and Investment in Russia: Analysis and Recommendations*, Project Status Report, Center for International Security and Arms Control, Stanford University, March 1993.

Thierry Malleret, *Conversion of the Defense Industry in the Former Soviet Union*, Institute for East-West Security Studies, Occasional Paper Series, no. 23, New York, 1992.

Petra Opitz and Wolfgang Pfaffenberger (eds), *Adjustment Processes in Russian Defence Enterprises within the Framework of Conversion and Transition*, Lit Verlag, Münster and Hamburg, 1994.

Henry S. Rowen, C. Wolf Jr, D. Zlotnick (eds), *Defense Conversion, Economic Reform, and the Outlook for the Russian and Ukrainian Economies*, RAND/Macmillan, London, 1994.

Jacques Sapir, *Les Bases Futures de La Puissance Militaire Russe*, Ecoles des Hautes Etudes en Sciences Sociales, Cahiers d'Etudes Stratégiques, no. 16, Paris, 1993.

US Central Intelligence Agency, Directorate of Intelligence, *The Defense Industries of the Newly Independent States of Eurasia*, January 1993.

Lars B. Wallin (ed.), *The Post-Soviet Military-Industrial Complex*, Swedish National Defence Research Establishment (FOA), Stockholm, 1994.

Part 4

COMPANIES AND CONTRACTS IN RUSSIA AND THE CIS

William E. Butler

The successful introduction of the market economy into the countries of the Commonwealth of Independent States that composed the Soviet Union will ultimately turn on the ability of those states to adapt and assimilate the corporate structures and principles used elsewhere in the world. This part argues, first, that although the legal foundations of a market economy are generally in place in the CIS countries, the legacy of Soviet legal concepts, rules, and institutions remains a unique and critical obstacle to meaningful levels of foreign investment and domestic economic regeneration; and, second, that law reform assistance can help eliminate this obstacle only if intelligently directed toward the enduring strengths of the legal culture to be reformed.

CHAPTER ONE

Introduction to Part Four

Anyone who ever doubted whether Soviet law existed need do no more than examine in detail a single contemporary investment transaction to discover how deeply the Soviet legal heritage of rules and institutions remains embedded in the consciousness of those who inhabit these countries. More often than not, where related obstacles are encountered by the Western party, they are unseen or not understood by the parties in the CIS state concerned, who, after all, have inherited their legal tradition as it is and are endeavoring to cope with it as best as they can.

These are not propositions which have gripped the imagination of the popular media: judging from the coverage by the latter, foreign investors are deterred, depending upon the individual state concerned, by political instability, by civil strife, by the crime rate, by the lack of amenities, or by transport, construction, raw materials, labor, capital, or other infrastructural shortcomings. Any law firm with a reputable CIS practice knows, certainly, that transactions are proceeding, and that the level of activity is substantial. Unseen, however, are those transactions which founder upon the substance of CIS state legislation, or the lack thereof, or upon the ambiguities or inadequacies of that legislation, despite the keen desire of the investing parties to complete the transaction. Creative structuring enables some transactions to be consummated, but all too many are never closed because of legal risks unacceptable to the investing parties. The laconic phrase "capital is not available" usually conceals the unwillingness of financial institutions to lend for reasons of legal uncertainty rather than the absence of funds in the capital market (the same, it should be said, also applies to Russian banks, which are rightly sensitive to legal risk).

Thus the matters treated in this paper, while squarely within the field of law and properly the concern of a trained lawyer, reach beyond to touch every entrepreneur, businessman, banker or investor, and indeed any government or international institution rendering assistance to the CIS countries in any form.

As for law reform assistance, it must bring the legal systems of the former Soviet states not merely up to the basic level of market economies in the advanced industrial countries, but well into the twenty-first century. In principle the legislator in the CIS has expressed a willingness to draw upon legal experience from any relevant source—an openness quite remarkable when one considers that only a few years ago bourgeois law was dismissed as having nothing to contribute to a socialist legal system. In my view, those advising on law reform have a responsibility to introduce an advanced standard of draft legislation which both incorporates the virtues of Western law and has regard to our relevant experience—the lessons of which have not always been absorbed yet by our own parliaments—in the implementation of that law.

But whether one is investing now or later in the former Soviet states, the creative structuring of complicated transactions, or the simple conclusion of straightforward transactions, involves the use of Russian law and legal institutions—what might for our purposes be called, in more general social science terms, Russian structures. To a considerable extent those structures will be of recent origin, introduced since 1987 to facilitate market economic relations. But it should be borne in mind that not all of the Soviet legal legacy is pernicious. There do exist legal concepts, institutions, and values which, if effectively adapted, can ease the introduction of Western market institutions or even improve on them. The Soviet model of civil procedure, for example, contains elements which, on paper at least, are simpler, more expeditious, and less expensive than their Western counterparts. The Soviet practice of an uncontested proceeding will endear itself to Western financial institutions and has useful implications for pledge transactions. The vast Soviet apparatus for the notarization and registration of transactions would seem to lend itself to being creatively adapted to market concepts of registration, or in any event to the reinforcement of a legal mentality which is accustomed to registration formalities when market circumstances so dictate. The relatively simple and straightforward style of legal drafting inherited from the Soviet period has much to commend it: Western investors find, for example, the Russian Labor Code to be vastly more accessible to the layman than its equivalents in the West, a veritable manual comprehensible to worker and manager alike.

There are dozens of other examples, but the lesson is clear: law reform has a greater chance of succeeding when it draws upon the positive strengths, culture, terminology, and legal consciousness of the domestic legal system being reformed. The same is true for transactions. Those investing in the CIS as a rule create juridical persons within those states, which are creatures of the local legal system. The insensitive imposition of Western corporate models contains the seeds of considerable legal risk which can be minimized by effective assimilation of local rules and institutions on the part of the Western party.

CHAPTER TWO

Companies in Russia and the Other CIS States

"Company," as literally translated into Russian, is a misnomer for the subject of this paper. For reasons set out below, the term continues to bedevil the work of entrepreneurs, lawyers, and translators alike. Rather, what we have in view is the "enterprise" in its sundry forms as laid down in the legislation of the former Soviet Union and the CIS countries. Our inquiry begins with the state enterprise, for that creature continues to exist, and continues to exert an inordinate degree of legal influence on all other types of enterprise.

The state enterprise

The history of the state enterprise is absorbing, but for our purposes peripheral. At August 1986, when the Communist Party of the Soviet Union authorized the creation of joint enterprises with foreign participation on Soviet territory, the state enterprise in its sundry forms dominated the Soviet economy. Its essential features, so characteristic of the planned economy and so pernicious to the market economy, included the following:

—Nomenclature

The appellations of state enterprises include: production association, scientific-production association, agroindustrial production association, state enterprise, concern, association, trust, economically accountable (*khozraschetnoe*) foreign economic association, and others. The words "company" and "corporation" were never used; in the Soviet lexicon these last two terms applied only to entities in capitalist countries.

—Assets

The state enterprise, whatever it was called, was created and owned by the state. Its assets were in state ownership. Legally and administratively speaking, this meant that the state enterprise was created by government or ministerial decree and was allocated physical assets owned by the state, including land, buildings, office equipment and raw materials. These assets remained in the ownership of the state even though they were transferred to the balance sheet of the state enterprise. Once recorded on the balance sheet after being formally handed over, the assets were in the operative management of the state enterprise.

"Operative management" meant that the state enterprise had the right to possess, use, and dispose of the assets in the ownership of the state in accordance with legislation and Plan. The right to possession was exclusive and protected by law against any other unlawful possessor, including the state itself unless the assets were properly withdrawn from the state enterprise. Use was also, as a rule, exclusive; the improper use of enterprise assets was a serious, potentially criminal, offense.

Disposition, on the other hand, was extremely restricted, for any other course would invite the alienation of state property on a massive scale. For all practical purposes a state enterprise could dispose of most assets only with the express authorization of a superior ministry acting on behalf of the state. At the same time that same ministry had immense scope for interfering in the activities of the state enterprise by withdrawing or reallocating assets on the balance sheet of the state enterprise. In November 1989 the Soviet authorities introduced a new concept of ownership intended to broaden the dispositive rights of the state enterprise. Called "full economic jurisdiction" (*polnoe khosraschetmoe vedenie*), this concept enabled state enterprises to dispose of certain categories of state-owned assets of their own volition.

—Legal capacity

What has been said above with respect to assets is evidence of the limited legal capacity of the state enterprise. It was, as a rule, a juridical person having the right to possess, use, and dispose of its property, to sue and be sued, and was not liable for the obligations of the state, nor was the state liable for its obligations. But the state enterprise did not have title to its property; and while it could sue and be sued, its assets enjoyed significant immunities. Its true ability to answer for its liabilities was drastically reduced by the fact that very few assets were unequivocally available for that purpose.

The legal capacity of the state enterprise was, and is, governed by certain elements of legislation of the former Soviet Union still in force over much of the CIS, and by more recent laws on enterprises. Most state enterprises have a Statute or a Charter which sets out their rights and duties, functions, management structure, and the like. As a rule, these are pro forma documents which replicate provisions laid down in legislative acts and fill in the blanks. By Western standards such charters or statutes are opaque in the extreme. In many cases they fail to give express authorization to the state enterprise to engage in foreign economic activity, to issue guarantees, to borrow money, to conclude contracts of lease, to acquire hard currency, to open special types of bank accounts, to pledge assets, and so on. Prior to 1986 such transactions on the part of state enterprises would, of course, have been unthinkable, indeed illegal and contrary to the very foundations of the planned economy. As perestroika proceeded, state enterprises were given the right to enter into foreign economic relations, only to find themselves either frustrated in their activities by charter provisions utterly incompatible with market relations, or inadvertently deceiving themselves and their foreign partners as to their true *vires*.

—*Immunity*

From the very outset Western investors were generally aware that concluding contracts with Soviet partners enjoying the status of an "agency of state power or administration" meant that full state immunity would be engaged and there would be no legal recourse, for all practical purposes, in the event of a dispute. Soviet state partners generally understood the position and appointed Soviet juridical persons within the respective administrative systems to act on their behalf. These juridical persons, often but not always state enterprises, did not enjoy immunity from suit. But the Western partners did not always appreciate that even though they were concluding a contract with a Soviet juridical person, that juridical person had the same limited legal capacity as set out above: i.e., the assets which could be reached were extremely limited.

But another danger for the foreign investor was lurking in the wings—and still is. Assuming that a satisfactory transaction was concluded and that the transaction generated genuine cooperation and profit, the venture undertaken by the Western and Soviet partner remained legally vulnerable at several key points. The first was the obverse side of state immunity. Creditors of the Soviet state, of which there are many in the West, or of the Russian state, which has incurred its own debts as well as being the legal successor to those of the former USSR, have the right in principle to proceed against state property wherever they may find it. This would include property in the full economic jurisdiction or operative management of state enterprises, as the state is the owner of that property. Creditors of state enterprises, or Western partners in ventures to which state enterprises have contributed, may find assets which they believed to be in the exclusive possession of their partner to be subject to enforcement proceedings by the creditor of the state.

A second point of practical vulnerability has been the displacement of the Soviet state as owner by other owners. The tale is a complicated one, but the ending foreseeable, at least to an alert student of Soviet law, and we shall return to it below. Suffice it to observe here that many early ventures created with Western investors involved Soviet juridical persons which did not own their assets. When the Soviet Union disappeared, another owner succeeded to the rights of the relevant Soviet party; usually such succession occurred in the Russian Federation, so that the legal successor was the Russian State Property Fund. In September 1992 many joint enterprises received letters from the State Property Fund advising that the Fund was the legal successor to the participatory share previously held by a Soviet party and requesting full particulars of the entity, any dividends due for distribution, full records, and the like. In effect, the Western investor had acquired a new partner whose true interest, expertise, and intentions with respect to future activity were unknown—all because of the legal principles of ownership then in operation, and the legal status of the state enterprise concerned.

—Management

Despite the enhanced role of the labor collective, the state enterprise has remained the epitome of one-man-management. However selected, whether by the superior ministry, as in the past, or elected by the labor collective, as still happens pursuant to the 1983 USSR law on labor collectives in force in most states of the former Soviet Union, the manager, or general director, is given remarkable scope to administer the state enterprise as he or she deems best. The price of failure, however, is removal from office, whether by the superior ministry or by the labor collective. Boards of directors, stockholder meetings, executive councils, and the like have not been a central feature of the management style of state enterprises inherited by the CIS countries from the former Soviet Union.

The Audit Commission, an internal body of each state enterprise of whose workings in practice we know little, seems to have had a negligible impact on management style. The jurisconsult, or legal adviser, whose visa is required in a state enterprise before certain legal documents can be passed, and the chief book-keeper, whose counter-signature is a mandatory requirement of most financial transactions in a state enterprise, seem never to have found a place in management proper.

As for liquidation, economic insolvency and bankruptcy were recognized only in the final days of economic reform in the former Soviet Union. Nonetheless, liquidations were common, as an administrative disposition of state enterprises suffering reorganization, merger, shut-down, hiving-off, or a similar fate. A liquidation commission was appointed to verify the assets on the balance sheet, receive and dispose of any liabilities, settle claims, and capitalize continuing liabilities within the ministry budget—a tidy exercise, usually to be completed within sixty to ninety days. Concepts of sanation were unknown.

In September 1986 it was announced that joint enterprises with participants from capitalist countries might be created in the Soviet Union. There followed an autumn of frenetic negotiations by Soviet and Western enterprises alike, culminating in the signing of Protocols of Intent. No one was precisely sure what a joint enterprise should or could be. The answer unfolded on 13 January 1987, with the adoption of an enabling Edict by the Presidium of the USSR Supreme Soviet, authorizing the creation of joint enterprises and the enactment of the famous Decree No. 49 of the USSR Council of Ministers elaborating the essential features of a joint enterprise.[1]

The joint enterprise

In retrospect it is plain that the legal model of the joint enterprise laid down by Decree 49 was not an invention of the day. As documents have come to light concerning Comecon structures and Soviet relations with, for example, Vietnam,[2] the indebtedness of Decree 49 to those arrangements is seen to be immense. Had that been evident at the time, perhaps the danger signals in relation to certain legal features of the joint enterprise would have come through more strongly. Bearing in mind everything that was said above about the state enterprise, let us now look at the configuration of the joint enterprise.

1. Translated in W. E. Butler, *Basic Documents on the Soviet Legal System* (3d ed., 1992), pp. 471–83.

2. See the Agreement of 29 October 1987 between the government of the Union of Soviet Socialist Republics and the Government of the Socialist Republic of Vietnam on the Basic Principles of the Creation and Activity of Joint Enterprises, International Associations, and Organizations, and its predecessors.

—Nomenclature

The Russian expression for joint enterprise is *Sovmestnoe predpriyatie*. Almost at once it was mistranslated as "joint venture." Seldom has a pure and blatant error of legal translation served the Western commercial and legal community so ill, with countless pernicious consequences for many individual Western companies. Quite apart from the multiple meanings of "venture" in Anglo-American commercial practice, all of which should themselves have cautioned against corrupting the word for "enterprise" into "venture," what translators and investors alike failed to appreciate was that Decree 49 authorized the creation of a *very particular* model of legal entity with very particular legal features based to a considerable extent upon the state enterprise. As the number of corporate vehicles with foreign participation which were possible under Soviet law increased (joint-stock societies, limited responsibility societies and partnerships)—*all of which* were in the generic sense joint ventures—the virtues and especially the limitations of the joint enterprise were ever more exposed.

—Assets

Most Western investors assumed that when they created a joint enterprise and made contributions to the charter fund, the joint enterprise became the owner of the charter fund contributions. Decree 49 provided that the joint enterprise had "possession, use, and disposition" of its property—but to anyone familiar with the state enterprise and Soviet concepts of ownership, this was not the language of title, but of operative management. As a matter of law, the contributors to the charter fund of the joint enterprise retained ownership of what they had contributed, which carried several implications. First, it followed that what the Soviet participant contributed, it could also withdraw. Second, since the Soviet participant as a rule was not itself the owner of what it contributed to the charter fund of the joint enterprise, the true owner of the property (the state) could also withdraw the contribution.[3]

When some joint enterprises failed with debts owing to the Western part-

---

3. It is said that the original draft legislation authorizing the creation of joint enterprises on Soviet territory provided that the joint enterprise might be the owner of its assets. This issue was so sensitive that it reportedly went to the Central Committee of the CPSU for discussion, at which level all references to such ownership were deleted in favor of the language of operative management. There is, it should be added, no verb "to own" in the Russian language. The word "to possess" [*vladet'*] is often wrongly translated as "to own."

ners, the latter were suddenly aware that property in the joint enterprise against which they would ordinarily expect to receive satisfaction was not available for that purpose. Banks learned the same lesson to their cost. And, in the end, so too did the Russian Federation, for when the Soviet Union disappeared and legal succession to its assets occurred, many joint enterprises faced extinction because their Soviet participants had disappeared and their Russian legal successors preferred to withdraw their newly acquired assets from the joint enterprise. The Supreme Arbitrazh Court of the Russian Federation finally issued a decree which directed that where the Soviet state had contributed assets to the charter fund of a joint enterprise, those assets came under the ownership of the joint enterprise.[4]

It also followed from Decree 49 that although the joint enterprise was granted much greater rights of disposition than the state enterprise enjoyed, those rights of disposition were not necessarily unlimited. In fact, Decree 49 should be read, in my view, as laying down the limits of disposition, rather than simply allowing free discretion.

—Legal capacity

It is clear from the above that the joint enterprise also had a limited legal capacity, albeit greater than that of the state enterprise. It enjoyed the rights of a juridical person (which is not precisely the same as being a juridical person), could sue and be sued, and was responsible for its liabilities with its assets. As in the case of the state enterprise, though, the extent to which the joint enterprise owned its assets was subject to doubt.

Decree 49, and model charters developed in accordance with its provisions, in practice gave the parties who created the joint enterprise considerable flexibility to shape it in accordance with their interests. It was an opportunity of which few Western participants took full advantage, principally because they failed fully to appreciate the extent to which the model incorporated the premises of the state enterprise. In the early days of joint enterprises difficulties were compounded by the fact that the Soviet legal system was itself experiencing the pangs of transition from the principle: "everything not expressly permitted is prohibited" to the principle: "everything not expressly prohibited is permitted." Attentive drafting of foundation documents for a joint enterprise

4. See Decree No. 13 of the Plenum of the Supreme Arbitrazh Court of the Russian Federation of 17 September 1992, "On Certain Questions of the Practice of Settling Disputes Connected with the Application of Legislation on Ownership," *Vestnik Vysshego arbitrazhnogo suda Rossiiskoi Federatsii*, no. 1 (1993), pp. 78–82.

should have expressly empowered it to borrow, pledge, lease, own bank accounts abroad, and so on.

—Immunity

This issue was largely lost from view on the part of Western investors. The joint enterprise itself enjoyed no state immunity. It was not regarded as a state-owned entity in any way, although neither was the expression "private" applied to it. At best the state was the owner, directly or indirectly, of a participatory share in the joint enterprise, as was the foreign participant. If state immunity were to arise, it would be in connection with the state continuing to have title with respect to contributions in kind to the charter fund of the state enterprise. For the unwary investor, depending upon what the specific contribution was, either the charter fund contribution in the ownership of the state might be withdrawn by the owner or state immunity might be invoked by the owner against a party seeking to recover liabilities against the assets of the joint enterprise.

—Management

Decree 49 departed from the traditional state enterprise in that it permitted the establishment of a board of the joint enterprise through which representatives of the participants could take decisions. Western participants were quick to equate the board with their own concept of a board of directors. In practice, Decree 49 gave the participants a virtually free hand to structure management as they preferred, and readily accepted most management structures embodied in the feasibility studies submitted by the parties. Below board level, though, Decree 49 seemed to presuppose a general director who would exercise one-person-leadership within the scope allowed by the board.

Voting patterns varied. Unanimity was required for certain decisions, majority votes were deemed sufficient for others, depending on the equity contributions of the parties. Some Western participants equated members of the board with directors in the Western sense, wondering whether directors' liability existed, and, in some cases, themselves making independent provision for such liability in the foundation agreements.

The Audit Commission was retained, to the bewilderment of most Western investors, who usually made provision to augment the Audit Commission with an outside independent auditor. Only exceptionally were other management organs improvised.

The ultimate legal fate of Decree 49 is not recorded. The Decree does not appear to have been repealed in the Russian Federation or any other former

Soviet state.[5] Some 3,000 joint enterprises were registered during the nearly five years of its operation within the Soviet Union. Long before the USSR disappeared, the Russian Federation had begun to refuse to register Decree 49 joint enterprises, requiring instead that juridical persons be created in accordance with Russian Federation rather than the USSR legislation. The actual practice varied widely from one locality to another.

The true demise of the Decree 49 joint enterprise dated from an Edict of the President of the USSR, issued on 26 October 1990, which permitted the creation of "enterprises with foreign investment" on Soviet territory.[6] The joint enterprise was now merely one type of enterprise with foreign participation. Two other principal types emerged, rapidly overtaking the joint enterprise in popularity. At the USSR level they were called joint-stock societies and limited responsibility societies; in the Russian Federation, joint-stock societies and limited responsibility partnerships. When the Russian Federation began to encourage Decree 49 joint enterprises to re-register in Russian clothing, and in cases where the joint enterprise wished to re-register without in any way changing its form, the question arose: what was a joint enterprise, juridically speaking? Given the innate legal characteristics of the joint enterprise, there could only be one answer under Russian concepts: a limited responsibility partnership. The belated realization of this was a most sobering experience for many Western investors.

By late 1990 Russia and the other Soviet republics had set about the enactment of their own first-generation laws and statutes on enterprises generally and, in greater detail, on individual types of enterprise. The USSR was operating in parallel, leaving legal advisers with a bewildering diversity of corporate vehicles. More often than not, the ultimate choice of vehicle depended upon what could be registered within each independent state, or union republic as it then still was. Nevertheless, this corpus of legislation represented the first effort to begin to establish corporate forms familiar to Western legal systems side-by-side with long-standing Soviet corporate models. Continental lawyers perhaps found the early models chosen more familiar than did their Anglo-American counterparts, although so too did students of prerevolutionary Russian law. But the Soviet legacy remained paramount.

5. On 27 September 1993 the President of the Russian Federation issued an Edict on improving work with foreign investment which invoked the archaic terminology of "foreign and joint enterprises" (point 1). See *SA RF* (1993), no. 40, item 3740.

6. Translated in M. I. Braginskii, W. E. Butler, A. A. Rubanov (commentary), *Fundamental Principles of Legislation on Investment Activity in the USSR and Republics* (1991), pp. 261–62.

Economic partnerships and societies

The terminology chosen for this subhead is that of the republic of the Russian Federation, amongst others. Some former Soviet states reversed the equation and referred to "economic societies and partnerships." The 1991 Fundamental Principles of Civil Legislation of the USSR and Republics (FPCivL), scheduled to enter into force on 1 January 1992 had the USSR survived to that date, contained an analogous category.[7] The 1994 Civil Code of Kazakhstan has virtually eliminated the word "society," reserving it only for the joint-stock society, and in fact treating such a society as a species of partnership; the 1994 Russian Civil Code preserves both terms. Practice varies as to whether state enterprises, cooperatives, and other survivals of the Soviet past are placed into this category or not.

—Nomenclature
The corporate vehicle perhaps most widely used by foreign investors is the joint-stock society. There are two types: open (in which the stock is publicly offered and may be acquired by anyone) and closed (in which the number of stockholders may not exceed a specified number and, as a rule, stocks must first be offered to other stockholders before sale to a nonstockholder). "Society" [*obshchestvo*] is the proper translation, not company, although many translators replicate the mistake widely made in English and American texts when translating "société" from the French or "Gesellschaft" from the German. The word "company" [*kompaniya*] in Russian has usually meant a foreign entity (although before the 1917 Revolution the word enjoyed domestic currency). Kazakhstan has had the final word, perhaps, amending its legislation to introduce both the joint-stock society and the joint-stock company— the latter constituting a joint-stock entity in which the State holds a golden stock or a stipulated minimum stockholding. To translate "joint-stock society" as "joint-stock company" would make it impossible to describe a key distinction in Kazakh legislation.

---

7. The 1991 Fundamental Principles have since been brought into force in the Russian Federation (3 August 1992) and Kazakhstan (30 January 1993) pending the enactment of new civil codes. On 19 October 1994 the State Duma of the Russian Federation adopted Part One of the Civil Code, which for the most entered into force on 1 January 1995. Portions of the 1991 Fundamental Principles remain in force pending the enactment of Part Two of the Civil Code during 1995 or 1996. Kazakhstan adopted the General Part of its Civil Code on 30 December 1994, with effect from 1 March 1995. The status of the 1991 Fundamental Principles after 1 March 1995 is the same as in Russia.

Next in popularity is the limited responsibility partnership, analogous in most respects to the USSR version of the limited responsibility society. Legislation in CIS countries also makes provision for additional responsibility partnerships, *kommandit* partnerships (adapted from the continent, in which some are full partners and others are limited partners), full partnerships, simple partnerships (contract of joint activity), and others. These are not the same from one sovereign state to another; investors will need to follow with special care the finer points of each piece of relevant legislation.

While each of the corporate vehicles mentioned above continues to retain features of the Soviet model of state enterprise, it must also be observed that several states are experimenting with hybrid corporate vehicles which deliberately incorporate elements of the state enterprise and what might loosely be called a market-orientated enterprise model. Anyone doing business with such hybrid entities needs to proceed with special caution. Examples include the state joint-stock company (introduced in 1993 in Kazakhstan, such an entity may be 100 percent state-owned, or the state may hold 51 percent of the voting stocks, or the state may own a golden stock); the commercial production enterprise; and others. In Uzbekistan the national airline is simultaneously a state enterprise and an agency of the state administration.[8]

It should be noted, moreover, that in most former Soviet states corporate vehicles may be either 100 percent foreign-owned or partly foreign/partly domestically owned. Of course, all the latter instances are, broadly speaking, joint ventures, this demonstrating yet again how unfortunate it was to translate "joint enterprise" as "joint venture."

—Assets

The same problem which afflicted the joint enterprise plagues the joint-stock societies. While not entirely categorical in this respect, the legislation of the former USSR and most of the CIS states with respect to joint-stock societies preserves the terminology of "contribution" to the charter capital. The participant contributes or makes a contribution to the charter capital, with the implication that the stock received is evidence of the contribution. On that premise, the joint-stock society does not acquire title to the assets received in exchange for the stock, and the participant retains the right to withdraw his/her contribution at a later stage. Taken literally, this concept destroys the notion of a joint-

8. See the Edict of the President of the Republic Uzbekistan, 28 January 1992, No. UP-326, "On the Creation of the National Air Company Uzbekistan" and the Decree of the Cabinet of Ministers attached to the President of the Republic Uzbekistan, No. 44, adopted 4 February 1992 "On the System of Administration of Air Transport on the Territory of the Republic Uzbekistan."

stock society, undermines its creditworthiness, and makes it vulnerable to un-foreseeable partitions of assets. A joint-stock society of the closed type, on this scenario, is nothing more than a limited responsibility partnership with stock certificates. For American companies the taxation implications could be hor-rific if the Internal Revenue Service were to determine that the joint enter-prise, both open- and closed-type societies, and the limited responsibility partnership all met its test of a partnership for tax purposes.

In fact, the terminology of "contribution" permeates much of the CIS first-generation legislation, most notably the USSR and union republic laws on in-vestment activity. The affinities with the role of the state in the state enterprise are obvious.

The better view, which also finds support in the terminology of the legisla-tion, is that the founder of a joint stock society purchases the stock with his monetary or in-kind contribution, becomes the owner of the stock (which may be alienated in accordance with the provisions of the Society Charter and rele-vant legislation), and exercises the rights in the society which a stockholder may exercise. The society acquires full title to any moneys, property, or prop-erty rights received as payment for the stock. In amendments to its Law on Economic Partnerships and Joint-Stock Societies adopted in April 1993, Kazakhstan expressly provided that a joint-stock society becomes the owner of everything received in payment for stock (Article 15).[9]

—Legal capacity

Old forms die hard. In the planned economy, as we saw earlier, it was com-mon practice for the state enterprise to have its own charter or statute based on a model handed down from above. Each enterprise essentially filled in the blank spaces (such as name, legal address and bank account numbers). Legal capacity was deliberately limited in the interests of state ownership and eco-nomic planning.

At present lawyers are caught betwixt and between. CIS countries' legisla-tion on individual corporate vehicles is drafted as though it were a veritable manual for the entrepreneur. In a very real sense lawyers are expected to repli-cate most of the statutory provisions in the actual charter; often model charters are published as annexes to legislation. While creative structuring can do much to smooth the rough edges, lawyers nonetheless have to resolve the ex-tent to which, as a matter of drafting principle, they should replicate statutory

9. Translated in W. E. Butler, M. E. Gashi-Butler (intro.), *Foreign Investment and Privatiza-tion in Kazakhstan: Collected Legislation* (1993).

provisions in the charter, or mostly supplement or modify those statutory provisions with formulations required by their particular client. To put the issue more broadly, to what extent must they make express provision for the legal capacity of the corporate vehicle they are advising, and to what extent can they assume that the said vehicle enjoys all the basic legal capacity provided for by legislation?

In Western legal systems the contours are well-established. The former Soviet states are still developing concepts of *vires* that reflect the mixed nature of corporate vehicles in existence. So long as the classic state enterprise is retained, it cannot be allowed to act other than in accordance with the principle that "everything that is not expressly permitted is prohibited."

—*Immunity*

By their terms, commercial societies and partnerships do not enjoy state immunity against jurisdiction, suit, or levy of execution (although the hybrids mentioned above may do so). However, to the extent that the investor is deemed to retain title in his contribution to the charter capital of the partnership, immunity questions may arise.

—*Management*

The management structures prescribed or permitted by CIS countries' legislation vary substantially with respect to each type of corporate vehicle. From the Western point of view, the management structures prescribed are often indebted to the old state enterprise model.

Let us take the Russian Federation joint-stock society of the closed type as an example of first-generation legislation. There is confusion first between what the legislation calls the Council of Directors and the Board of the Society. The legislation is unnecessarily restrictive with respect to the number of directors required, requiring subterfuges to avoid the difficulty, and vague in the extreme with respect to the duties and liabilities of directors. For small joint-stock societies, or one-man societies, the legislation imposes requirements which are literally impossible to meet. The Audit Commission is retained, and in some states a supervisory council introduced.

Kazakhstan, by contrast, liberalized in spring 1993 its requirements in these respects through the simple expedient of giving the founders of an economic society or partnership greater discretion in devising management structures. This may become the standard for the second generation of CIS legislation governing corporate vehicles.

Stability and inflexibility in the 1994 Civil Codes

The codifications of civil law in Kazakhstan and the Russian Federation enacted in late 1994 have largely removed any autonomy from involved parties in shaping business societies and partnerships. The basic approach is that only those specific types of juridical person mentioned in the codes may be created and registered. In Kazakhstan the business partnership is the sole type of juridical person which a foreign investor can create or participate in. Moreover, the Kazakh code has so structured the various forms of business partnership that all without exception entail retention by the investor of ownership of his investment contribution. The partnership, in whatever form, is at best merely the owner of property created at the expense of contributions of the founders or participants and property produced or acquired by the partnership in the process of its activity.

This rather cumbersome formulation means that the juridical person is not the owner of its charter capital. In cases where it has the right to issue stocks, the stockholder is not in fact the owner of the stock, but the owner of the participatory share in the joint-stock society; the stock is merely evidence of such participation and not an object of property in its own right.

Given the legacy of Soviet law, this approach to structuring partnerships will in many cases impede the development of a secondary securities market and create unusual difficulties for the unwary investor. In purely conceptual terms it is a structure which is deeply indebted to Soviet concepts of the state enterprise.

The observations above relate to the principal route taken by foreign investors setting up within the former Soviet states: the creation of a new corporate vehicle to serve their requirements. From mid-1993 a second route has been made increasingly attractive: the acquisition of a minority or majority stockholding or other equity participation in an existing, operating state enterprise transformed into a joint-stock society.

Destatization, privatization, and corporatization

Destatization is something of a puzzle in the English tongue—and quite a mouthful in Russian: *razgosudarstvlenie*. Most emphatically, it is not denationalization. Rather it refers to the result of transforming state enterprises into joint-stock societies, a procedure no less cumbersomely designated joint-stockization [*aktsionirovanie*]. Denationalization is inapt because destatization leaves the stocks issued through the process of joint-stockization in state ownership. The movement of those stocks into nonstate hands is privatization. The expression destatization, coined in the Soviet period, has mostly disappeared in the Russian Federation, but other states of the CIS, notably Kazakhstan and the Kyrgyz republic, continue to use the term in privatization legislation.

The foreign investor comes in, as a rule, after destatization has occurred and usually in the late stages of privatization; that is, after the labor collective in the state enterprise concerned has been given the opportunity to purchase a substantial block of stocks either with privatization checks or cash by closed subscription. If the foreign investor seeks a stockholding, as will usually be the case, he must be as attentive to the quality of the joint-stockization process and procedures as if he had created the society from the beginning. First, if the joint-stock society has not addressed satisfactorily all of the concerns described above as the legacy of the Soviet era, the stockholder will be at a serious disadvantage, perhaps to the extent that the acquisition of stocks is unattractive. Second, if the procedures for joint-stockization and privatization have not been properly complied with, there is a substantial legal risk that the entire process may be undone.

Corporatization is an expression which first appeared in Ukrainian legislation in April 1993. It means the transformation of joint-stock societies of the closed type into joint-stock societies of the open type. In Ukraine all closed-type joint-stock societies are required to be so transformed.

Contracts in Russia and the Other CIS states

Western students of Soviet law debated whether freedom of contract existed in the Soviet Union. The question was not quite as absolute as it at first sounds. No one doubted that to some extent freedom of contract existed, and that the Civil Code provisions on the law of contract defined the essence of contract in terms familiar to any continental lawyer.

Rather, the issue was the extent to which the so-called economic contracts concluded between state enterprises were truly contracts in our sense of the word or were a legal relationship dictated by Plan. From the mid-1960s, the legal dimension of economic reform in the Soviet Union centered partly around the extent to which the state enterprise should be granted greater discretion and freedom in contractual relations, and partly around how far the administrative-command system should be loosened.

The greater portion of the Civil Code provisions on contract was devoted to various types of economic contracts which could be concluded only by state enterprises. For a time in the 1960s and 1970s it seemed that the Civil Law of Contract might give way to Economic Law administered by planning authorities. With the advent of perestroika, the pendulum swung strongly in the opposite direction. Central planning was abolished, and planning directives were supplanted by state orders whose precise legal nature is somewhat obscure and which appear to be widely circumvented in practice.

Yet, while the transition to a market economy has witnessed a marked decline in the role of economic contracts, the law of contract has changed little. The reason is simple. Under Soviet law and the legal systems of the successor states of the CIS, the parties are free to contract unless expressly prohibited. This means that the parties are likewise at liberty to conclude types of contracts not provided for in the Civil Code—which explains the introduction in Soviet foreign trade during the 1970s and 1980s, for example, of leasing contracts of various types.

Constraints on freedom of contract

State orders constitute at least a potential constraint on the freedom of contract. To the extent that state orders are mandatory for an enterprise, the latter is not at liberty to dispose of its production to other parties, notwithstanding pre-existing contractual obligations. In Kazakhstan the relevant legislation is unequivocal in subjecting most enterprises, irrespective of form of ownership (a euphemism which includes enterprises with foreign participation) to the possibility of state orders.

The Contract of Pledge is, as a rule, conceived in its narrow sense as a means of securing obligations, rather than in its broader sense as a mechanism for deploying assets in order to achieve the future accumulation of capital. State enterprises are prohibited from pledging basic assets without the permission of the owner, i.e. the state. Thus freedom of contract is constrained by a limitation on disposition intended to prevent state enterprises from achieving through pledge what they may not achieve through direct alienation—that is, fictitious pledges as a concealed form of alienation.

Contractual formalities

Notarial formalities in the Soviet period operated as a constraint on the freedom of contract. The requirement that all designated legal transactions had, as a condition of validity, to be notarially certified (and also thereby disclosed to the state) operated as an informal constraint on such transactions occurring at all. Many of these formalities would seem no longer to serve any sensible purpose in a market economy, the more so when they are linked with substantial levels of state duty.

On the other hand, other types of contractual formality essential to a market economy remain underdeveloped in the CIS region. The registration of pledges is an example. In the West pledges are registered above all to enable creditors to ascertain the existence of prior encumbrances on property and to establish the priority of creditors. The former Soviet states have yet to appreciate the legal risks and associated costs when priorities of creditors cannot be established with certainty. Their registration requirements are a throw-back to notarial formality rather than an aid to determining the existence of earlier creditors.

The 1994 Kazakhstan (Article 308) and Russian Federation (Article 339) civil codes both link registration of pledges to the provisions governing state registration of the property which is the subject of pledge. Local registration systems are beginning to come into being; the city of Moscow is amongst those administrative units which have introduced a unified system for pledge registration.[1]

In the domain of contractual formalities, however, no practice from the Soviet era exerts so baneful an influence as the requirement that a transaction relating to foreign economic activity must have two authorized signatures from the party in the respective CIS state; the absence of such signatures renders the transaction void. The requirement dates back more than six decades, its present legislative roots stemming from a Decree of the USSR Council of Ministers dated 12 February 1978.[2] The 1978 Decree has not been repealed, and is believed to be in force in all the states of the former Soviet Union. Whether such a requirement has any place in a market economy must be seriously addressed (how does a one-man company comply with the Decree?), but so long as the classical state enterprise remains in existence, perhaps so too does the rationale for this imperative rule.

Codification and new contracts

The transition to a market economy is introducing new types of contract into the mainstream of Russian economic life. Among them are contracts of indemnity, franchising, distribution, distributorship, production sharing, and various insurance contracts. Although parties are at liberty to conclude these under Russian law, it would be unfortunate if the new generation of civil codes failed to take their existence explicitly into account.

Those experimenting with contractual relationships novel to Russian law

1. See the Statute on the Registration of Pledge on the Territory of the City of Moscow, confirmed on 20 September 1994, by Decree 788 of the Government of Moscow. *Vestnik merii Moskvy*, no. 21 (1994), pp. 42–51.

2. See W. E. Butler, *Soviet Law* (2d ed., 1988).

do run some risk of inadvertently crossing, to their disadvantage, existing contractual models. Two which often catch the foreign investor unawares are the contract of joint economic activity and the preliminary contract.

For various reasons, Western investors sometimes prefer to conclude a set of contractual arrangements with a partner in the CIS state—a true joint venture without a juridical person being created. Depending upon how the arrangement is structured, there is a danger that both the terminology and the substance may be deemed to constitute a simple partnership pursuant to a contract of joint activity (but with certain features unfamiliar to the Western concept of partnership), the more so when the parties use, as they so often do, the language of joint activity. The 1994 Kazakhstan Civil Code actually moves the provisions regulating the contract of joint activity from the chapter on obligations to the chapter on ownership (Chapter 12).

The Western energy industry is, quite justifiably, experiencing difficulty in introducing its concept of an "association agreement" into Russia—not because Russian law is in principle resistant to such an arrangement, but because the word "association" in Russian always connotes the creation of a juridical person (which is precisely what the energy industry does not wish to happen in this case), and no way has yet been discovered of giving linguistic expression to the relationship such as would take it outside the pre-existing Russian models that the energy industry finds undesirable. On the other hand, the language of a "cooperation agreement" is rather looser than the "association relationship" intended.

The concept of the preliminary contract first appeared in the 1991 FPCivL, and is consequently in force in Russia and Kazakhstan; it has since been expressly incorporated into the 1994 Kazakhstan (Article 390) and Russian Federation (Article 429) civil codes.[3] Although its intellectual pedigree is uncertain, the doctrine would seem to owe much to the concept of economic contract in the planned economy. Parties who conclude a contract but leave certain details to be mutually agreed in future would, in the event that they fail to reach agreement on those details, have the right to bring suit in court, in which case the court would write the details for them. While it is doubtful that the parties can conclude a preliminary contract without expressly intending to do so, the parallels between the preliminary contract and, for example, a tender or competition contract have caused the lights to burn late in many law offices. When tendering for a project, the applicant is normally required to af-

---

3. See W. E. Butler, M. E. Gashi-Butler, *Legal Aspects of Doing Business in Russia* (1993), pp. 13–14.

firm in writing that the offer being made is a legally binding offer, even though in most tender or competition situations certain details will be negotiated with the winning party after the award is made. Suppose the winning party cannot accept the ultimate conditions? Is he bound by the principle that his original offer and its acceptance constitute a preliminary contract which the court is at liberty to complete should the parties be unable to do so?

On balance, however, issues arising out of the Soviet legacy of contract are proving to be less intractable than has been the case with the legislation regulating enterprises. For Anglo-American lawyers there are novelties in approach to be assimilated. As a rule, contracts drafted in the Russian model are shorter, more stylized, and vastly less verbose than English and American documents. Industry models for guidance purposes are often approved by government agencies, even for the private sector. Vast bodies of subordinate normative acts are routinely read into the contractual provisions by reference and sometimes by simple replication.

The general terminology of contract is another matter, and falls outside the scope of this chapter. In passing, one need merely observe that much of the contractual terminology of English and American law, even when translated accurately into Russian or other indigenous languages, has virtually *no legal meaning* in that system.[4] Likewise, such terminology misses important legal concepts under local law which need to be covered. And the reasons lie with us, not with the Russians or the other nationalities of the former Soviet Union, or with their languages.

Conclusions

This chapter began by alluding to unseen obstacles to the successful introduction of a market economy in the countries of the Commonwealth of Independent States. The Anglo-American legal system is a historical system of law, fashioned incrementally over centuries of trial and error, mostly the latter. Only in retrospect are we able to discern how we have identified fundamental problems and contrived to muddle through.

The Russian science of law prefers to see everything laid out neatly, prop-

4. The same problem plagues law reform efforts. The classic case is the conceptual and terminological discrepancies between the EBRD Model Law on Secured Transactions [sic] and the Russian version, which translates back as the Model Law on Operations with Security. In the Russian language one does not secure a "transaction"—one secures the performance of an obligation.

erly classified, integrated—all legal relations in their respective place harmoniously regulated by rational rules of law laid down in normative acts. The Soviet legal system aspired to that objective, and failed miserably. It is the unraveling of that very considerable structure which challenges us. Such an unraveling is an exercise in legal engineering no less momentous than that undertaken by the Soviet leadership in the late 1920s, for we require not to destroy, but to replace, to improve, dare we say to perfect. The measure of our success or failure will be the ultimate fate of the revolution which continues within the states of the former Soviet Union.

Part 5

THE RUSSIAN FAR EAST

Sergci Manezhev

During the years of Soviet rule the Russian Far East was exploited in a wasteful way as a source of primary products. Overspecialization and underinvestment have left it ill equipped to cope with the emerging new market economy in Russia. The region has gained, however, from the liberalization of external economic relations, as demand for its exports from the rapidly expanding North-West Pacific market has grown.

Political reform in Russia has transferred substantial powers to regional and local authorities, and politicians in the Far East have managed to extract significant concessions from Moscow. Among other things, they have won greater freedom to control the export of local products. Relations with the center remain tense, however, and the distribution of powers between the two levels of government is still unclear.

The Far East contains a large proportion of Russia's coal, oil and natural gas deposits, and possesses rich mineral reserves and substantial potential in forestry and fishing. Currently under discussion is a new regional development strategy which envisages priority development for processing capacity

I would like to thank Dmitri Zhogolev and Tamara Milian of the Institute of Far Eastern Studies of the Russian Academy of Sciences, Moscow, as well as Shyama Iyer, Russian and CIS Program at the Royal Institute of International Affairs for help in the preparation of this paper. Special gratitude is due to Dr. Neil Malcolm (Royal Institute of International Affairs) and Dr. Margot Light (London School of Economics), who took an active interest in the paper and contributed significantly to it.

in forestry and minerals, fishing and fish farming, transport facilities, conversion of the arms industry, tourism, food processing, and the social and industrial infrastructure. Local and regional authorities and businessmen have set up a string of agencies to promote trade and investment. Obstacles to development include the high level of sensitivity to ecological issues provoked by recent abuses, lack of clarity concerning the prerogatives of the different arms of local government, and the legacy of past neglect of infrastructural development.

Three `Free Economic Zones' have been established in the Far East, but their impact has been negligible. Moscow is reviewing policy in this area. The likely outcome is a reduction in the size of such zones, and the imposition of stronger central control.

Foreign economic exchange can have a substantial impact on the development of the Far East. Trade, and investment activity is growing rapidly and developing new forms. At present, however, there is an overemphasis on raw material exports, and the available hard currency is frequently not being used in ways which support long-term development. Foreign investment is increasing. As many as 72 percent of all joint ventures in the Russian Far East are registered with partners from the Asia-Pacific region. The legal and financial framework is, however, still only half formed.

Japan has traditionally been the largest trading partner of the Russian Far East. Changes in the pattern of demand are weakening Russia's position in the Japanese market, and there are complicating political factors. But there is a compelling logic to the development of the Sea of Japan Rim economic zone, which will also include Northeast China and Korea. Meanwhile China shows signs of overhauling Japan as a trading partner, and new forms of economic exchange are multiplying, although there are debates within Russia about the benefits they provide. The third main partner is South Korea. There are important complementarities here which promise to make this a key growth area.

In contrast to the promising long-term prospects, the immediate economic situation in the region is bleak, and there are few signs of improvement. Conditions favor the growth of separatism, which could have disastrous consequences. Moscow is sponsoring a new regional development program for the Far East which places a high priority on attracting foreign investment. What is required is a multilateral approach to all these issues by the states of the Asia Pacific region, involving the public as well as the private sector.

CHAPTER ONE

Introduction to Part Five

The collapse of the Soviet communist regime, the disintegration of the former USSR and the discrediting of the centrally planned economic system throughout the world have opened the way to the establishment of a new global order, based on cooperation rather than on ideological and political confrontation. The large-scale natural and intellectual resources of the former Soviet states, combined with the potential capacity of their domestic markets, mean that efficient economic integration of these newly independent states could provide a fresh impetus to world economic development. This could in turn contribute to the solution of many economic, political, ecological and humanitarian problems. However, the realization of these prospects is hampered by the deep social and economic crisis which the CIS countries are going through, and by the effects of the closed development model which they have inherited from the communist past. All this is particularly true of Russia, the principal post-Soviet economy.

The problems of the former Soviet states can only be solved by first establishing a decentralized and open-market-type economy in Russia, integrated into the global political and economic system. Because of the vast dimensions of Russia, the size of its economy and its striking diversity, the regional dimension of this process is particularly important in that country. This paper discusses the gradual emergence and opening up of the regional market in the Russian Far East—one of the world's most remote, yet most richly endowed areas.

The Russian Far East contains ten administrative entities: Primorsky and Khabarovsk Territories (*krai,* pl. *kraya*), Amur, Magadan, Kamchatka and Sakhalin Provinces (*oblast,* pl. *oblasti*), the Jewish Autonomous Province, the Chukchi and Koryak Autonomous Districts (*raion,* pl. *raiony*), and the Republic of Sakha (Yakutiya). The processes under way throughout this large geo-

The Russian Far East

State Boundaries
Republic, krai, oblast, autonomous oblast
autonomous okrug

graphical expanse are dynamic but contradictory. The huge mineral wealth of the region, its seaports, and its transcontinental railway lines represent a basis for rapid economic growth. The Russian Far East also enjoys geographical proximity to the prosperous and rapidly developing countries of East and Southeast Asia. Moreover, the breakup of the USSR and the ensuing geopolitical shifts have turned Russia into a predominantly northern country, with limited access to the Black, Mediterranean and Baltic seas. This means that the northern and Pacific territories are now taking on a new national importance. At the same time, the Far East manifests many of the economic, political and social tensions which threaten the national integrity of present-day Russia.

Analyzing major problems of regional development in the Russian Far East in the light of current market transformations, and in a domestic and international context, this paper explores the origins of these problems, discusses future possibilities, and examines conceivable solutions.

The Current Socioeconomic Situation: The Roots and Driving Forces of Far Eastern Regionalism

The profound economic and social changes going on in postcommunist Russia are accompanied by deep intra and interregional conflicts inherited from the centrally planned economy. Imbalances in the spatial development of Russia are rooted in lingering patterns of administrative resource allocation reflecting the precedence of politics over economics and the domination of central interests over regional needs. The same centralized methods were also used in the Soviet period to redistribute resources intersectorally and interregionally, in order to correct—in urgent cases—the imbalances which they themselves had generated. As the machinery of the centrally planned system is dismantled, it is not surprising that crisis situations surface in different parts of Russia, that new regional interests and development priorities emerge, and that there is a radical redistribution of power from central to local authorities.

The long-term development crisis

No region of Russia better illustrates the general trends and processes than the Far East. The post-1917 development of this region depended on the millions of victims of the GULAG, brought in as forced laborers from the better-developed western part of the country by a totalitarian regime. The wasteful Soviet command economy created a persistent resource hunger, and the Russian Far East, with its natural wealth, was turned into a highly specialized raw material-supplying province. The share of extractive industries in the Gross Value of Industrial Output (GVIO) in the region is about 30 percent, almost three times the national average. The Far Eastern economy is extremely dependent on a small number of industries—nonferrous metals, fishery and forestry. Those sectors together account for more than 50 percent of the industry in the region, compared with 10 percent in Russia as a whole.[1] Another special feature of the Far East's economy is its heavy dependence on the arms industry, which accounts for approximately 10 percent of the region's industrial output.

Concentrating on primary industries and supplying raw materials for processing to other regions, the Russian Far East missed out on the profits to be gained in value added. Finished goods are manufactured outside the region and have to be imported for local consumption. The situation has been aggravated by a number of specific factors, including:

— a distorted system of relative prices, with undervalued raw materials and overvalued finished products. For many decades this artificial imbalance in state-fixed prices served as a major instrument of forced industrialization in Russia and the other former Soviet republics.

— the very large share of transport costs in the region's GVIO, exceeding the national average by a factor of 2–2.5. The average freight haul from Russia's major industrial centers to the Russian Far East is 5.2–5.8 thousand km.[2]

— relatively high labor costs. In order to attract labor to the remote and inhospitable Far East, local wages have in the past been set on average 1.5 times higher than elsewhere.

— high production and construction costs on account of extreme climatic conditions.

The profitability of Far Eastern enterprises has accordingly remained substantially (20 percent) lower than the national average.[3] As a result, the Russ-

    1. V. P. Chichkanov, *Dal'nii Vostok: strategiya ekonomicheskogo razvitiya*, Moscow, 1988, p. 19.

    2. V. F. Kurkin, *Vozmozhnosti i tendentsii razvitiya ekonomicheskogo sotrudnichestva mezhdu dal'nevostochnymi raionami SSSR i severo-vostochnymi provintsiyami KNR*, Candidate's Dissertation. Moscow, 1991 (mimeo), pp. 85, 121.

    3. The Mitsubishi Research Center, *Issledovanie v otnoshenii planov razvitiya eksportnykh zon v sovetskom dal'nevostochnom raione*, December 1989 (mimeo), p. 51.

ian Far East occupied a low-priority position in the centralized resource allocation system with regard to practically all sectors falling outside the small number of officially designated areas of local specialization. A chronic lack of investment to meet local needs has resulted in numerous bottlenecks.

Infrastructure. As a developing region, the Russian Far East requires a high level of new urban and industrial construction. However, local construction capacity is only half what is required.[4] Despite its huge fuel reserves, the Russian Far East, with its severe climatic conditions, has a permanent energy deficit. Per capita energy production is only two-thirds of the national average.[5] The density of roads and railways is 1.5–2.5 times lower than in Russia as a whole.

Consumer goods and social services. Farms in the region can supply only about 50 percent of local demand for staple foods. Per capita production of consumer goods is only three-quarters of the low Russian national average. As far as housing and public services are concerned, the Russian Far East is at the bottom of the league of Russia's regions and republics. Low living standards lead to intractable demographic and social problems. About 30 percent of the population of the Russian Far East are recent immigrants. Typically up to 75 to 80 percent of these leave to return to their previous place of residence elsewhere in Russia within three to five years of arrival.[6] There was a sharp increase in the number of out-migrants from the region in 1993—66,100, 6.9 times the number of out-migrants in 1992. The outflow of population from the Far East in 1993 exceeded the regional rate of natural increase by 24,000. Population trends like these mean high labor turnover, skill shortages, high absenteeism and in general low labor productivity—about 70 percent of the overall level in the former Soviet Union.[7] All in all, lopsided development has left the Russian Far East economy in a structural impasse, and under the threat of general economic and social decay.

The situation is not much better as regards the development of the high-priority extractive industries. With the gradual exhaustion of the most accessible and profitable deposits from the beginning of the 1980s, the need for technological upgrading and new equipment suitable for poorer geological conditions has become increasingly urgent. By the 1980s, however, the stagnating Soviet economy was in no position to reallocate large-scale resources to the

4. V. P. Chichkanov, *Dal'nii Vostok*, p. 27.

5. *Dal'nii Vostok Rossii. Ekonomicheskii ezhegodnik.* 1991, Khabarovsk, 1992 (mimeo), p. 108.

6. E. Motrich, "Demografiya i ekonomika", *Problemy Dal'nego Vostoka*, 1991, no. 6, p. 32.

7. V. F. Kurkin, *op. cit.*, p. 101.

Table 2-1. *Index of Industrial Production, 1986–93*
previous year = 100

Year	Russian Federation	Russian Far East
1986	104.5	104.3
1987	103.5	104.4
1988	103.8	103.7
1989	101.4	102.2
1990	99.8	98.0
1991	97.8	97.3
1992	82.3	85.6
1993	85.9	87.7

Sources: *Dal'nii Vostok Rossii. Ekonomicheskii ezhegodnik 1991*, Khabarovsk, 1992 (mimeo), p. 281; *Ekonomicheskaya reforma na Dal'nem Vostoke: rezul'taty, problemy, kontseptsiya razvitiya*, Khabarovsk, 1993 (mimeo), pp. 46, 51; *Ekonomika I zhizn'*, 1992, no. 4, p. 4; p. 13; *Rossiiskii statisticheskii ezhegodnik 1994*, Moscow, 1994, pp. 296, 615.

Russian Far East—at the expense of other regions—to meet higher investment costs per unit of output. As a result, the Far Eastern economy began to experience a slowdown, and its share in the GVIO of the former Soviet Union—and of Russia—began to fall steadily.

The last attempt by the planners to rectify the situation was the long-term State Program of Economic and Social Development of the Far East, adopted in 1987. The Program envisaged substantially increased central investment in regional development. However, the mounting state budget deficit meant that it was never implemented in practice. The main central resource distributors— ministries and departments—evaded their obligations under the Program on the pretext that, with the introduction of market relations, enterprises were now responsible for planning their own investments. No more than 20 percent of the planned industrial, infrastructural and social programs could be supported out of the region's own resources.[8] Thus at the beginning of the 1990s the Far Eastern economy was facing not only a general crisis of the command system, but also its own local structural crisis. The region is now in the grip of a protracted economic recession. The local housing program has collapsed, incomes have declined relative to other regions and there are general shortages, reflected in rationing of consumer goods and foodstuffs. This picture of economic decay is particularly depressing when contrasted with the flourishing economies of resource-poor neighbors—Japan, Korea, Taiwan and Hong Kong. Dissatisfaction with the traditional relationship with the center in the

8. The Mitsubishi Research Center, *Issledovanie* p. 51.

region is widespread. The evident urgent need to pursue a development policy attuned to local realities has helped to encourage an emerging Far Eastern regionalism.

Far Eastern regionalism and the current reform program

The present market reform program in Russia, with its goals of overall price deregulation, privatization, liberalization of foreign trade and so on, is introducing substantial changes to relations between the regions and center. As far as the Russian Far East is concerned the overall effect is to stimulate economic autonomization, the formation of a regional Far Eastern market, and the emergence of specific geographical and sectoral development priorities. A range of factors encourages economic regionalism.

1. *The shrinking position of the Far East in Russian and CIS domestic market.* The dramatic increase in transport charges (up by 30 times in 1992 alone) has sharply undermined the region's competitiveness on the Russian market. The disintegration of the USSR and the consequent disruption of the Russian Far East's business ties with Kazakhstan, Central Asia and other regions has caused a further, painful shrinking of traditional markets. All this has meant idle manufacturing capacity, a shorter working week and holidays without pay for many workers, financial losses of many millions of rubles for producers and growing pressure on local budgets.

2. *Deteriorating interregional terms of trade, payments crisis.* Many commodities exported from the Far East to central regions of Russia (diamonds, precious metals, coal, certain raw materials) were still being sold at state-controlled prices in early 1995. However, machinery and equipment, spare parts and consumer goods, accounting for over 50 percent of the Russian Far East's imports from other regions of Russia, have been sold at free-market prices for several years now. All this has further damaged competitiveness. It is not clear how the price deregulatory measures of March 1995 will, on balance, affect the Far East.

Additional problems are caused by the seasonal nature of trade in the northern part of the Russian Far East. Remote settlements in the far north are supplied with the greater part of their foodstuffs, fuel and raw materials for the following year during the few months of the summer when navigation is possible. Because of the huge size of the region and its undeveloped transport network, the vast majority of goods are in transit or storage for one or two years, which leads to extensive reliance on credit.[9] All this made the Russian Far East highly vulnerable to the 1992 price liberalization and the high inflation which followed. Thus the payments crisis which came to a head in Russia in mid-1992 proved especially painful in the Russian Far East. The share of Far Eastern enterprises in total arrears in Russia around this time was twice as high as their share of the GVIO.[10] As early as May 1992, two months before the Russian government issued its decision on the mutual clearing of accumulated debt held by state enterprises, attempts were already being made to achieve a local solution to the crisis in the Russian Far East, by setting up regional clearing houses.[11] These efforts were, however, of little avail. In 1994, as many as 42.8 percent of all enterprises in the Far East were making losses, and the region accounted for nearly one quarter of all the losses generated in the Russian economy in that year.[12]

3. *Cash shortages*. From early 1992 shortages of cash began to appear throughout Russia, as a result of soaring inflation and failure by the Russian government to judge the correct level of money emission. The Russian Far East was in a particularly vulnerable position for a number of reasons:

— the relatively high prices of consumer goods in the region. Because of sectoral imbalances the prices of 70 basic foodstuffs increased 21 times in 1992, compared with 17.5 times for Russia as a whole, leaving the price of the minimum consumer-goods basket in the Russian Far East standing at 1.4 times the national average;[13]

— higher wage levels, on account of the preservation of regional differentials;

— a permanent cash drain from the region caused by the high emigration rate, the high rate of outflow of seasonal workers, and so on.[14]

9. M. Nikolayev, "Nuzhen li Rossii sever?" *Sovety Yakutii* (Yakutsk), 26 June 1992.

10. Calculated from the data on Primorsky and Khabarovsk Territories, amounting to 55 percent of the GVIO of the Russian Far East: *Utro Rossii* (Vladivostok), 27 October 1992; *Tikhookeanskaya zvezda* (Khabarovsk), 8 July 1992; *Rossiiskie vesti*, 14 April 1992; *Delovoi mir*, 15 January 1993.

11. This was done under the auspices of the Vladivostok Commodity Stock Exchange and Eastnet Limited in Khabarovsk, *Utro Rossii* (Vladivostok), 29 September 1992; *Tikhookeanskaya zvezda* (Khabarovsk), 28 May 1992.

12. *Ekonomika i zhizn'*, 1995, no. 5, p. 2

13. *Izvestiya*, 10 December 1992; 29 December 1992.

14. P. A. Minakir, *Ekonomicheskaya reforma na Dal'nem Vostoke*, Paper prepared for the Bureau of the Department of Economics, Russian Academy of Sciences, Moscow, 26 May 1992 (mimeo), p. 8.

The seriousness of the cash crisis in the Russian Far East is demonstrated by the fact that Yakutiya (which accounts for only 0.7 percent of Russia's population—1 million people) was responsible for approximately 15 percent of nonpayments of wages, pensions and welfare benefits by the state in the January to June 1992 period. In order to avoid social unrest the local authorities in several areas—and even large enterprises—in the Russian Far East began to issue various substitutes for money. This further eroded local confidence in Moscow.

4. *The transport factor.* While state-controlled transport charges have rocketed, they continue to lag behind the freely formed prices of transport equipment, construction materials, lubricants and (to some extent) fuel. This makes heavy losses for Russian transport enterprises inevitable. As a rule the level of the losses is proportional to distance, which puts the Russian Far East in an unfavorable position. The fuel consumed by an airplane flying from Khabarovsk to Moscow costs 1.5 million rubles, while the airfares generated amount to only half-a-million rubles. Every time a ferry plies between the mainland and the island of Sakhalin it incurs losses equal to one-and-a-half times the transport charges. All this has led to a progressive weakening of economic contacts between the Russian Far East and the rest of the country.

5. *The liberalization of foreign economic ties.* The abolition of the state monopoly on Russian external economic relations has helped to reveal the international comparative advantages of different regions and different enterprises. Here the Russian Far East turns out to be one of the major beneficiaries, in view of its favorable geographical position and its large reserves of raw materials that are in high demand internationally. In addition, the dramatic devaluation of the ruble has helped to encourage rapid growth in the numbers of local foreign trading companies and to boost exports.

External factors are gradually reshaping the labor market. The breakup of the USSR has turned about 800,000 local people (almost 10 percent of the population of the region) into foreign nationals. The new citizenship regulations being introduced in many CIS countries encourage such people to return to their places of permanent residence. Yakutiya, Magadan Province and Primorsky Territory have recently all recorded an absolute reduction in their populations. In 1992 local authorities in the Russian Far East were given powers to make special provisions to attract workers from abroad. This has had impressive results. By late 1992 there were approximately 10,000 foreign workers (70 percent of them Chinese) in Primorsky Territory, compared with only 4,000 in early 1992. In the course of 1994 the Russian Federal Migration Service granted work permits to 26,366 Chinese workers—the great majority of them bound for the Far East.

Outward reorientation of the Far Eastern economy has to some extent alleviated the effects of the Russian economic crisis. Industrial production figures for 1992 and 1993 were markedly better than those for Russia as a whole, and in 1993 exports from the Far East increased by 18.4 percent, as compared to just 4.5 percent for Russia as a whole. It seems likely that external development factors will become even more influential in the region.

Political Aspects of Far Eastern Regionalism

The Soviet economy was based on strict centralist principles. The vast majority of state enterprises were exempt from local control, wherever they were located. Enterprises subordinated to local authorities accounted for less than 10 percent of the GVIO in the Russian Far East.[1] As a result, local revenues were vulnerable to factors beyond local control and local budgets depended essentially on central subsidies. The regional authorities found themselves obliged continually to petition for funds, and had little choice but to act simply as the executors of commands emanating from Moscow.

Such a system of decisionmaking was clearly inappropriate to the size and regional diversity of Russia. In the Russian Far East it meant that economic resources were not used effectively, environmental problems were aggravated, and so on. The kinds of tensions in central–regional relations which helped to destroy the USSR continue, today, to threaten the national unity and integrity of Russia. There are a number of new political organizations in the region—the Far Eastern Republican Party of Freedom, the Party of Revival, and so on—which call for separation from Russia and the setting up of an independent Far Eastern Republic.[2] Thus a vital aspect of the current reform process in Russia and in the Russian Far East is the reallocation of powers between the different levels of government.

1. V. P. Chichkanov, *Dal'nii Vostok*, p. 226.
2. I. Ilyushin, "Kto zhelaet porulit?" *Utro Rossii* (Vladivostok), 11 April 1992.

The new Russian system of territorial administration

Recent Russian legislation has substantially transformed the existing administrative system and created a rather complicated system of institutions. It comprises:

— the President of Russia and the President's administration. The President issues decrees and other instructions which are legally binding throughout the country. He has the right to make significant changes in the existing system of territorial administration.

— the State Duma of the Federal Parliament. The Duma has the right to introduce amendments to the Constitution and other basic laws, and to vote on new laws determining the powers of administrative agencies and enterprises. In April 1992 the Sixth Congress of People's Deputies of the Russian Federation, the predecessor of the State Duma, passed the Federal Treaty, which laid down the basic principles of the distribution of powers between the center and the local and regional authorities. The Treaty was then more or less incorporated into the new constitution of December 1993.

— the Federation Council (upper house) of the Federal Parliament. Composed of representatives from each of the 89 territories of the Russian Federation, it elaborates and adopts laws defining in detail the rights and obligations of local and regional authorities.

— the federal government. In accordance with the President's instructions and the decisions of Parliament, the government has the right to take decisions regarding local economic, environmental and development issues in particular regions.

— ministries, departments and committees (including territorial branches). These are responsible for the promotion of regional economic activity on the basis of government decisions.

— regional and territorial elected assemblies and executive bodies, local authorities in cities, and in small towns. All these operate on the basis of federal legislation, presidential decrees and government decisions.[3]

In the early 1990s the powers and responsibilities of regional authorities and their capacity to influence local social and economic affairs were substantially upgraded, as part of the general decentralization of administration in

---

[3] *Reforma bez shoka. Vybor sotsial'no-priemlemykh reshenii*, Moscow-San Francisco, 1992, pp. 62-3.

Russia, and the new pattern was largely consolidated by the December 1993 constitution. As a result, first, the economic base of the local authorities has now been expanded through the establishment of municipal and regional property—land holdings, enterprises, financial assets, and so on. Second, local authorities are now legally responsible for ensuring comprehensive economic stabilization in their area. They have the power to approve (or forbid) the setting up of, or substantial alteration to, any economic or social entity having regard to the possible demographic, ecological or other local consequences. They have the same powers over the business activities of existing enterprises.[4] Third, in addition to managing their own property, local authorities have certain responsibilities in regard to locally situated federal enterprises (concerning environmental protection, the social security of local residents, and so on).[5]

The expanded economic functions of local authorities are backed up by a set of new rights. These include the right

— to dispose of municipal and regional property, retaining not less than 50 percent of the receipts for the local budget;

— to establish joint ventures with foreign companies;

— to fix regional taxes and duties as well as tax and economic incentives within their territory;

— to decide independently on price fixing and subsidization from the local budget of commodities sold locally;

— to create local commodity stocks, in agreement with enterprises, by levying taxes in kind instead of in cash;

— to cooperate freely with other regions on the basis of bilateral agreements, interregional associations and mutual financial funds;

— to distribute regional export quotas and license local export transactions, and to form regional hard-currency funds. In July 1991 state enterprises in the Russian Far East were provisionally granted the right to export freely up to 30 percent of their output, surrendering 40 percent of their gross export earnings to the local hard-currency funds.

4. V. Leksin, E. Andreeva, "Territorial'naya dezintegratsiya Rossii," *Rossiiskii ekonomicheskii zhurnal*, 1992, no. 8, p. 40.

5. Zakon o kraevom, oblastnom sovete narodnykh deputatov i kraevoi, oblastnoi administratsii, art., 11. *Vedomosti S"ezda Narodnykh Deputatov Rossiiskoi Federatsii i Verkhovnogo Soveta Rossiiskoi Federatsii*, 1992, no. 13, p. 869.

The regional drive for resources and autonomy

The local authorities in the Russian Far East have made energetic use of these rights. In 1990 they established the Far Eastern Association for Economic Cooperation, intended to coordinate economic policy in different territories and relations with the center. Direct interterritorial[6] business contacts are gaining momentum. A number of bilateral economic agreements were signed in 1992 (e.g. between Khabarovsk and Primorsky Territories, between Yakutiya and Sakhalin Province, etc.). Direct interterritorial supplies under contracts signed by the Khabarovsk Territorial Administration account for 80 percent of local sales of Russian products. Such interterritorial contracts are normally arranged on a counter-trade basis, which makes active use of local commodity stocks.[7] All this reinforces the position of the local authorities and increases their role in regional economic stabilization.

However, the serious economic and social problems of the Russian Far East cannot be viewed in a purely regional context. The inevitable continuation of the Far East's long-established dependence on federal financial support means that it is particularly vulnerable to the effects of national economic policies. GNP consumed in the Far East has consistently exceeded locally produced GNP by 3-4 billion rubles (in 1991 prices), which is equivalent to about 15 percent of the regional GVIO.[8] Disregarding the effect of irrational relative prices, this gap is accounted for by the sectoral structure of the local economy, by low productivity and high production costs. Redistribution of powers between Moscow and the Russian Far East is scarcely likely, of itself, to resolve the region's serious long-term development problems.

The price liberalization policy and the associated fall in living standards, and the increase of social tensions in the Russian Far East, have introduced new elements into the social and economic activity of the local authorities as well as into their relations with the center. Attempting to control its own budget, the federal government has tried to transfer the bulk of welfare and other social expenditures to the regional level. For example, in 1992 price subsidies and welfare expenditures amounted to 71 percent of the local budget in Primorsky Territory, as against 22 percent of projected federal expenditures.[9]

6. The word "territory" is used here to refer to any of the administrative units mentioned above which make up the larger Far East region.

7. *Tikhookeanskaya zvezda* (Khabarovsk), 11 March 1992; 26 May 1992.

8. P. Baklanov, "Kontseptsiya razvitiya sovetskogo Dal'nego Vostoka," *Problemy Dal'nego Vostoka*, 191, no. 3, p. 4; *Dal'nii Vostok Rossii* (1992), p. 269.

9. Calculated from *Utro Rossii* (Vladivostok), 28 March 1992; *Vedomosti S"ezda*, 1992, no. 34, pp. 2602–04.

Hence the ever-growing pressure on local budgets in the Russian Far East. In Yakutiya the proportion of welfare expenditure in the 1992 budget increased almost ninefold compared with 1990.[10]

Meanwhile, local revenues are lagging behind desperately, owing to the slow pace of privatization and the irregular behavior of state enterprises. The general trend to falling labor productivity and declining volume of production is accompanied by an expansion of wage costs and a shrinking of profits. The result is a narrowing of the local tax base. Not surprisingly, in 1992, many Far Eastern territories (e. g. Khabarovsk Territory, Yakutiya, Sakhalin Province) were unable to cover more than 50–70 percent of local expenditures without direct or indirect federal subsidies.[11] The continued high incidence of loss-making in Far Eastern industry means that the problem remains essentially unresolved at the present time. New powers given to local authorities by the State Duma in January 1995 allow them to increase local profits tax within broader limits than previously permitted. But this measure is unlikely in practice to be of much help to regions like the Far East, since higher rates of tax would only strengthen the regional budget at the cost of penalizing enterprises that do manage to make some profits, and generally weakening already weak local industry even further.

Since 1992, the regions and territories of the Russian Far East have sent to Moscow a multitude of requests and proposals on these matters. They fall broadly into the following categories:

—*Financial claims.* These have been mainly requests for urgent lump-sum federal support (both credit and budgetary) to cover soaring transport costs, subsidies to power generators and fuel suppliers, wage payments, construction costs of local development projects, etc. In some cases the proposal has been for a share of foreign loans drawn by the federal government, assuming a 50:50 division of debt repayments. The most far-reaching proposals have involved a radical change in the existing scheme of revenue-sharing between federal and local budgets, by permitting all locally collected taxes to be retained. Such a measure could expand local revenues by a factor of 3–3.5.

— *Property rights and disposal of local produce.* Local natural resources are readily exchangeable for hard currency, and regional authorities in the Russian Far East have frequently demanded the right to own, use and dispose of all natural resources on their territory. Less ambitious proposals include ones for the retention of 10–30 percent of locally mined precious metals for

---

10. Calculated from *Sovety Yakutii* (Yakutsk), 13 October 1992.

11. *Tikhookeanskaya zvezda* (Khabarovsk), 30 April 1992; *Sovetskii Sakhalin* (Yuzhno-Sakhalinsk), 19 September 1992; *Sovety Yakutii* (Yakutsk), 19 June 1992.

local jewelry production, and for regional mortgage funds to be set up to attract foreign investment.

— *Additional managerial rights*. claimed by local authorities include: (a) the right independently to attract foreign investment into the gold-mining industry under concession or product-sharing agreements; (b) the right to establish free economic zones; (c) the indefinite prolongation of a preferential right to export independently up to 30 percent of local produce.

4. *General economic proposals*. have included demands on the government to act to attract skilled labor to the area, to implement federal development programs for the fuel and power industries in the Russian Far East, to convert local defense plants, etc.[12]

The general scope for regional/central conflict has been widened by the continuing division of state property into federal property and the property of territorial authorities.

Instruments of regional political pressure

As the economic and legal functions of local government multiply, contacts with superior administrative bodies become more frequent, and the regions become stronger *vis-à-vis* the center. As a result there has gradually grown up a relatively comprehensive system for exerting pressure on federal policymakers. It consists of the following basic elements.

— *Legislative activities and lobbying*. The right of legislative initiative granted to local authorities under the Law on the Territorial and Regional Council of People's Deputies and the Territorial and Regional Administration of March 1992 is frequently exercised. Locally initiated drafts of Presidential decrees, government regulations, and so on are channeled to Moscow, either through the formal procedure or through personal and political contacts. For example, in late 1992 a draft decree on Measures to Deal with the Critical Economic Condition of the Economy of Magadan Province was passed to the federal government through the Magadan branch of the People's Party of Free Russia, of which Aleksandr Rutskoi, then vice-president of the Russian Federation, was Chairman.[13]

12. *Utro Rossii* (Vladivostok), 18 March 1992; 28 March 1992; 1 August 1992; 29 September 1992; *Tikhookeanskaya zvezda* (Khabarovsk), 16 June 1992; 9 September 1992; *Magadanskaya pravda* (Magadan), 19 November 1992; *Sovetskii Sakhalin* (Yuzhno-Sakhalinsk), 3 December 1992.

13. *Magadanskaya pravda* (Magadan), 19 November 1992.

In Moscow local drafts are lobbied for either by regional groups in the State Duma and Federation Council, or by regional offices established by the Far Eastern authorities in 1992 to represent their interests.[14] Active pressure is exercised during visits to Moscow by local 'governors' (heads of administration) or their deputies. Collectively agreed drafts are supported by the Far Eastern Association of Economic Cooperation.[15]

As the drafts pass through the relevant federal representative bodies and administrative agencies, some of the initial local proposals are of course amended or even excised. However, the regional authorities have succeeded in obtaining a string of federal decisions concerning practical steps for Far Eastern development: supplementary financial allocations, transport subsidies, development programs in the energy sector and for environmental protection, etc.

—*Direct political pressure.* Various instruments of direct political pressure are employed by the Far Eastern territories in their relations with the center. The most obvious are appeals, petitions and open letters directed to the President, the State Duma or the federal government, by regional authorities or public organizations (e.g. by the territory's trade union council). These documents typically refer to the dangerous rise in social tension which has occurred in the region, and demand an immediate allocation of additional funds from the federal budget.

A more subtle means of applying political pressure derives from the exclusive right of regional authorities to permit or forbid any business activity on their territory, 'in the interests of the local population'. No large development project can be initiated in the Far East without prolonged bargaining between the federal and territorial authorities. For example, to obtain local approval of international bids to exploit gold fields in Khabarovsk Territory, the federal government has felt obliged to transfer control of 49 percent of all gold-mining licenses to the territorial authorities.[16]

The conditions attached to center–regional deals can be politically far reaching. For example, in March 1992, by a special resolution of the Primorsky Territorial Council of People's Deputies, the chairman of that body, D. Grigorovich, was instructed not to sign the Federal Treaty unless certain amendments of principle were introduced. Among the changes demanded was

14. I. Shkol'nikov, "Nashi lyudi v Moskve," *Tikhookeanskaya zvezda* (Khabarovsk), 21 February 1992.

15. I. Shkol'nikov, "Prezident daleko ot Moskvy," *Tikhookeanskaya zvezda* (Khabarovsk), 2 February 1992.

16. *Tikhookeanskaya zvezda* (Khabarovsk), 15 July 1992; *Finansovye izvestiya*, 30 December 1992.

acceptance of the principle that territories and regions would be treated as independent subjects of the Russian Federation, endowed with the right to own and dispose of local natural resources.[17] The Sakhalin provincial authority has intervened in the Russian-Japanese negotiations over the disputed Kurile Islands, adopting a more hard-line approach than Moscow with regard to the possible return of territory to Japan, but letting it be understood that it is prepared to moderate its position in return for financial, tax and other economic concessions by the center.

The Republic of Sakha (Yakutiya), which declared sovereignty within Russia as early as July 1990, has been particularly active in setting political conditions. A special Yakut-Russian economic agreement was signed on 31 March 1992, just a few hours before the official acceptance of the Federal Treaty by all subjects of the Russian Federation. The treaty yielded to Yakutiya long-sought sovereign rights over its land and natural resources, combined with retention rights to 11.5 percent of all locally mined gold, 20 percent of diamonds, 100 percent of industrial diamonds and 40 percent of hard-currency proceeds from the export of precious stones. At the same time, Russia committed itself to providing Yakutiya more generously with producer and consumer goods, including foodstuffs.[18] Subsequently the republic concluded a series of important bilateral agreements with Russia (on budgetary relations, on royalty payments, on the distribution of property and on the establishment of the joint-stock company Russia-Sakha Diamonds). Yakutiya now retains 100 percent of locally collected taxes in its regional budget, compared with a national average of 30 percent.[19]

The high level of economic autonomy enjoyed by the Republic of Sakha has provoked moves to emulate it in the neighboring Far Eastern territories. In July 1993 the Primorsky Territorial Congress of People's Deputies adopted a declaration demanding that Primorsky Territory be granted republic status. It also decided to call a local referendum on the issue, to Moscow's evident annoyance.

Competing with one another for greater economic concessions from the federal government, local authorities tend to act in an uncoordinated manner, which inevitably reduces the overall impact of their efforts. Nevertheless, the current trends in center-regional relations mean that the social and economic environment in the Russian Far East is more and more affected by the policies pursued by the local authorities. Local regulations in certain parts of the Far

17. *Utro Rossii* (Vladivostok), 18 March 1992.
18. *Sovety Yakutii* (Yakutsk), 30 October 1992; *Federatsiya*, 1992, no. 18, p. 6.
19. *Ekonomika i zhizn'*, 1993, no. 5, p. 5; *Moskovskie novosti*, 1993, no. 28, p. 8.

East (in Khabarovsk Territory, Amur and Magadan Provinces and Yakutiya, for example) introducing additional local taxes, restricting exports to other regions of Russia and so on, are contrary to federal legislation, but enjoy the support of the local judiciary.[20] Despite intervention by the Supreme Court of Russia, which periodically nullifies illegal local decisions, the trend to greater autonomy in the Russian Far East is gaining momentum.

20. *Ekonomika i zhizn'*, 1992, no. 37, p. 1; *Tikhookeanskaya zvezda* (Khabarovsk), 26 May 1992; *Sovety Yakutii* (Yakutsk), 31 October 1992.

CHAPTER FOUR

The Emerging
Far Eastern Market

The Russian Far East has many special characteristics, and yet it is one of the least investigated areas in the country. Its huge, sparsely populated territory is still at an early stage of development, and the volume of production and manufacturing facilities is relatively modest. The natural wealth and the economic potential of the Russian Far East have been only partially explored. Potential mineral reserves here are in many cases several times greater than verified ones.

Regional development—supply and demand factors

The basis of the region's economic development must be its very large natural resources. The Far East contains over 30 percent of explored coal reserves on the territory of the former USSR, and its offshore oil and natural gas deposits represent approximately 30 percent of the corresponding Russian total. There are deposits of over 70 kinds of mineral resources, including iron ore, nonferrous and precious metals (gold, silver, zinc, lead, tin, copper, etc.), diamonds, chemical raw materials, building materials, etc. Yakutiya alone boasts around 1,000 deposits of mineral resources, estimated to be worth about $10 trillion at current market prices.[1]

The forests of the Far East account for 35 percent of the afforested area and 28 percent of the timber stock of the former USSR.[2] The region provides

1. *Federatsiya*, 1992, no 18, p. 6.
2. V. P. Chichkanov, *Dal'nii Vostok*, p. 11.

about one-third of Russian furs (sable, ermine, blue fox, etc.), and 12 percent of pharmaceutical raw materials and medicinal herbs, including ginseng and eleutherococcus. The marine life in the Russian Far East's 200-mile offshore zone is estimated at about 30 million tons, or approximately 17 percent of total resources in the Pacific.[3]

The Far East is a major Russian supplier of nonferrous and precious metals, timber, minerals, fish and other items (table 4-1). The mining industry, fishery and forestry are markedly export-oriented, and the region provides over 40 percent of Russian lumber exports, 7 percent of wood pulp, 5 percent of woodworking products, 28 percent of fish, 30 percent of tinned fish and 20 percent of coal. Other sectors (such as iron and steel, engineering, chemicals, light industry) are less important, and as a rule fall far short of meeting even local demand.

For many decades one of the main stimuli for forced industrial development was the fact that in Russia natural resources could be used free of charge. In the Russian Far East a "frontal development" model was followed. This meant beginning with rapid exploitation of the most convenient and most valuable resources. In the end this approach damages the natural-resource potential of the territory concerned. The richest ore deposits become exhausted, unit production costs soar, growth rates fall, and finally an absolute decline of production sets in. This is precisely the stage which has been reached in the Russian Far East. There is a crying need for new production technology and substantial expenditure on infrastructure (especially power-supply and transport networks) and environmental protection. Further economic development in the Russian Far East is hampered by a lack of investment at both regional and federal levels.[4] This has led to a radical reassessment of external development factors and their potential value in the Russian Far East, and, indeed, to consideration of a new regional economic policy.

The new model of economic development which is being discussed for the region is based on two assumptions. First, while natural resources should form the basis for economic growth, new resource-saving and technology-intensive styles of exploitation should replace the current extensive, irrational approach. Second, regional growth should be geared to enhancing economic cooperation with the Pacific Rim countries—through foreign trade, technology transfer and inward investment.[5] The development goal is to bring about the kinds of

3. *Dal'nii Vostok Rossii*, p. 21.
4. V. Karakin, A. Sheingauz. "Priorodopol'zovanie: problemy i perspektivy," *Problemy Dal'nego Vostoka*, 1991, no. 6, p. 41; P. Minakir, "Ekonomika sovetskogo Dal'nego Vostoka: vyzov krizisu," *Problemy Dal'nego Vostoka*, 1991, no. 5, p. 7; *Ekonomika i Zhizn'*, 1995, no. 4, p.2
5. *Dal'nii Vostok Rossii*, pp. 201-2.

Table 4-1. *The Far East within the Russian Economy*

Sector	Percent of total output for Russia as a whole	Remarks
I Industry	4.7	Principal industrial regions include
of which extractive	15.0	Primorsky Territory (29% of GVIO
manufacturing	3.6	in the Far East), Khabarovsk Territory (25%), Yakutiya (13%)
(1) Mining		
(non-ferrous metals)	12.7	
of which lead and zinc	10.0	Mainly in Primorsky and Khabarovsk Territories
tungsten	14.0	Primorsky, Khabarovsk and Magadan
gold	50.0	Yakutiya, Magadan, Khabarovsk
tin	80.0	
diamonds	98.0	Western Yakutiya
(2) Food industry	11.4	Including 60-70% of the national catch
of which fish and marine products	58.7	of herring, 99.5% of salmon, 100% of crabs
(3) Forestry	7.4	Mostly larch and pine. In the southern
of which lumber	9.7	areas timber resources are nearing
wood products	6.0	exhaustion
(4) Fuels	3.4	
of which coal	12.0	90% of potential and 33% of confirmed reserves located in Yakutiya
(5) Engineering	2.8	Electrical equipment and machinery, instruments and measuring equipment, agricultural equipment, military equipment
(6) Building materials industry	8.8	Meets from 14% (metal structures) to 68% (bricks) of regional demand
(7) Light industry	1.6	Mainly clothing industry, relying on imported materials
II Agriculture	3.2	90% of sown area concentrated in the souther part of the region
of which soybeans	90.0	Primorsky, southern parts of Khabarovsk and Amur territories
honey	11.0	
III Construction	5.0[a]	Highly depreciated equipment, high proportion of manual labour
IV Transport (freight and passenger traffic)	7.2[a]	Mainly railway and sea freight. 75% of railways and highways located in the souther part of the region

Sources: Dal'nii vostok Rossii. Ekonomicheskii yezhegodnik 1991, Khabarovsk (mineo), 1992; V.F. Kurkin, *Vozmozhnosti I tendentsii razvitiya ekonomicheskogo sotrudnichestva mezhdu dal'nevostochnymi rayonami SSSR I severo-vostochnymi provintsiyami KNR*, Candidate's dissertation, Moscow, 1991; *Ekonomicheskaya reforma na Dal'nem Vostoke; rezul'taty, problemy, kontseptsiya razvitiya*, Khabarovsk (mimeo), 1993.
    [a] Data for the former USSR.

structural adjustment of the local economy which will improve its international competitive edge.

In the light of world market trends, and taking into account the existing potential comparative advantages of the Russian Far East, the region will probably seek to promote investment over the next ten to fifteen years in the following areas.

Setting up processing facilities in forestry and the mining industry. The multicomponent character of Far Eastern ores, combined with the value of many of the byproducts, mean that comprehensive processing can be highly profitable. For instance, the ores excavated at the Solnechny Mining and Dressing Integrated Works (Khabarovsk Territory) contain up to 9 industrially extractable components. However, due to the absence of appropriate processing technology, 40–50 percent of the mined tin, 40 percent of the copper, 60 percent of the tungsten, and 65–75 percent of the lead and zinc is discarded. To produce manufactured goods using such waste products is reported to be in many cases only half the cost it would be with specially mined raw materials.[6]

Poor production techniques in lumber processing result in the wastage of up to 60 percent of timber during logging and woodworking. Moreover, about 50 percent of sawn timber is lost during transport to other parts of Russia. Thus comprehensive processing of timber inside the Russian Far East (to produce high-quality plywood, manufactured sawn goods, hydrolyzed yeasts, etc.) could increase the economic efficiency of the local forestry sector two or three times over.[7]

A promising though technically complicated field of business activity in the Russian Far East is jewelry production. It is reported that Israel is making $0.6–$1 billion every year by faceting Yakutiya's diamonds. It is not surprising that as soon as it acquired retention rights to local gold and diamonds, Yakutiya immediately set up joint jewelry ventures with American, Israeli and Japanese firms. The new Sakha-Japan Diamond Company, for example, has been authorized to process 10 percent of Yakutiya's diamonds.[8] The company plans to build 12 jewelry factories and to produce up to 300 thousand carats of processed diamonds a year.

Development of the fishing and fish-processing complex and mariculture on a technologically advanced basis: utilization of nonwood forest resources. The traditional North Pacific fishing areas are gradually becoming depleted,

6. P. Minakir, O. Renzin, V. Chichkanov, *Ekonomika Dal'nego Vostoka: perspektivy uskoreniya*, Khabarovsk, 1986, pp. 37-9.

7. V. P. Chichkanov, *Dal'nii Vostok*, p. 21.

8. *Sovety Yakutii* (Yakutsk), 8 September 1992; 14 October 1992.

and equipment is obsolete. There is a pressing need to reequip the Far Eastern fishing and fish-processing fleet in order to expand deep-sea trawling. It is calculated that the productivity of fishery operations could be increased by 20–35 percent.[9] At the same time, the bays and islands of the Far Eastern coast of Russia offer promising sites for marine agriculture, including fish farming and the cultivation of marine invertebrates and seaweeds as delicacy foods. The experience of existing farming operations suggests that every ruble invested in marine agriculture can yield up to 10 rubles in profit.[10]

A November 1992 government program for manufacturing new types of medicines in the Far East was based on making fuller use of waste products from the processing of fish and other sea animals, and on the cultivation of medicinal herbs. The program envisaged investments totaling 1 billion rubles (in 1991 prices), and an annual rate of output of 3.5 billion rubles' worth of medicaments (in late 1992 prices) within four years.[11] In September 1993 the Russian government approved a "Federal Program for the Socioeconomic Development of the Kurile Islands over the Period 1993–5 and up to the Year 2000." The Federal Program envisages the development on the Kuriles of a biological and pharmaceutical complex, within the structure of the biological and pharmaceutical complex of the Far Eastern region as a whole, with the participation of foreign capital. In practice, however, the Program has failed to get off the ground, on account of a shortage of budgetary resources.

Modernization and transformation of the ship-repairing and ship-building industry, with the goal of upgrading the Far Eastern merchant, passenger and fishing fleets, and enhancing the importance of the region for through traffic. The Russian Far East has a long coastline, and it accounts for 17 percent of Russian sea cargo shipments. Russian Pacific seaports serve as terminals for a transcontinental container line running between Western Europe and Japan. By using more of certain specialized types of vessel (container carriers, "roro" ships, lighter ships, etc.) unit transport costs could be reduced by 30–50 percent and competitiveness sharply improved.

Conversion of the arms industry. At present 70–80 percent of the machinery and equipment used in the Russian Far East has to be brought in from other parts of Russia, while nearly all local machine-tool output is shipped in the opposite direction. In view of the substantial proportion of munitions plants among local mechanical engineering enterprises (about 50 percent by

9. P. Minakir, *Kontseptsiya dolgovremennogo razitiya Dal'nego Vostoka*, Vladivostok, 1990 (mimeo), p. 13.
    10. P. Minakir, O. Renzin, V. Chichkanov, *Ekonomika Dal'nego Vostoka*, p. 131.
    11. *Izvestiya*, 13 November 1992.

value of output), converting the arms industry could play an important part in
the regional reorganization of engineering production. The most promising projects envisage setting up production of machinery specially designed for local
conditions, and of equipment for forestry, fishery and mining. There are high
hopes of attracting foreign investment to around 20 military-industrial factories,
employing a total of over 30,000 people, in Khabarovsk Territory alone.[12]

Setting up large- and small-scale tourist centers. The region has extensive
recreational resources, including beach and coastal water recreation zones, opportunities for fishing, hunting and winter sports, and therapeutic mineral and
thermal springs. It is estimated that these facilities could attract over 8 million
customers every year to the Russian Far East.[13] In 1992 Yakutiya set up a
Ministry of Tourism and Youth Affairs, and launched a tourism-development
program. There has been a rapid growth of publicly owned and private tourist
agencies, including the first joint ventures in the field. So far, in the absence of
a tourist infrastructure, most of them specialize in exclusive safari tours for
sportsmen from the United States, Germany, Japan and other countries.

Upgrading of the food industry and development of agribusiness. About
80 percent of the Far East is characterized by average annual temperatures
below 0°C and underground permafrost. However, provided that suitable technology is applied (e.g. Dutch potato-cultivation technology) even the northern
areas of the Russian Far East could be 90 percent self-sufficient in eggs and
potatoes and 50 percent self-sufficient in vegetables, meat, milk, and other
products.[14] Export-oriented industrial cultivation of ginseng and other valuable plants also appears promising.

Upgrading and development of the social and industrial infrastructure. A
long-term program for developing the regional infrastructure has been worked
out jointly by the federal and local authorities. It is based on large interterritorial projects in transport and power supply. Local and foreign companies are
increasingly active in such fields as electric power (including wind energy),
local civil aviation and international telecommunications.

New institutional and commercial structures

If new regional policies are to be implemented, the Far Eastern territorial
authorities will have to make a coordinated effort to channel funds into prior-

12. *Nikkei Weekly*, 2 May 1992.
13. *Dal'nii Vostok Rossii*, pp. 27, 28.
14. *Tikhookeanskaya zvezda* (Khabarovsk), 29 October 1992.

ity development programs, and to promote independent business activity in the most promising sectors. Intraregional business ties and coordinated action by the Far Eastern territories in domestic and world markets are vital. The system of interterritorial institutional structures in the Russian Far East is now expanding, as follows.

The Far Eastern Association of Economic Cooperation (FEAEC) was established in mid-1990 with its headquarters in Khabarovsk. Its Coordinating Committee includes the chairmen of local dumas and heads of administration of all the Far Eastern territories. The principal functions of FEAEC include:

> working out a policy for developing major onshore and offshore mineral deposits and related development projects;
> voluntary pooling of funds for joint development of the energy sector, the agroindustrial complex, transport and communications in the Russian Far East, establishing regional commercial institutions and dealing with major interterritorial environmental problems;
> working out and implementing a common foreign economic policy;
> setting up interterritorial funds for foreign economic activity, research and development, etc.;
> establishing an interterritorial business information network, etc.[15]

FEAEC has a staff of twenty-five, including many former members of the previous Soviet administrative elite, or *nomenklatura*, with a network of region-wide informal connections at their disposal. The association activity is financed from a fund contributed to every year by the member territories.[16] FEAEC has been involved in a number of large projects, including the renovation of the Pacific port of Vanino and the Vanino-Komsomol'sk railway, developing free economic zones (see below) and establishing a regional ship-building association.[17]

The Far Eastern Branch of the Russian Union of Governors, bringing together heads of administration throughout the Russian Far East, was established in October 1992. Meeting at least once a month, the heads of local executives try to find cooperative solutions to practical problems (e.g. facilitating food distribution, coping with high transport costs, organizing interterritorial banking services and supplies). If necessary, the governors can apply for help directly to the federal authorities.[18]

15. P. Baklanov, *op. cit.*, p. 5.
16. *Tikhookeanskaya zvezda* (Khabarovsk), 7 February 1992.
17. *Ibid*, 20 October 1992.
18. 2. *Ibid*, 24 October 1992.

The local business community also plays its part. In some territories (for example in Khabarovsk Territory) local Councils of Entrepreneurs have been set up. They act as permanent consultative bodies for local governors, and their recommendations feed directly into the local decisionmaking process. Local businessmen have also consolidated their political influence on a panregional basis. A Far Eastern Federation of Entrepreneurs was established at the Far Eastern Regional Conference of Entrepreneurs held in June 1992 in Khabarovsk. At their bimonthly meetings Federation members work out common positions and take decisions on matters of urgency. The Federation seeks to influence the decisions of both local and federal authorities.[19]

The political weight of the Far Eastern business community is enhanced by the emergence of more and more panregional bodies. The most important are:

The Far Eastern Trading Corporation (FETC), established in late 1991 as a joint-stock company with authorized capital of 100 million rubles. The parties to the FETC are the leading commodity exchanges in the Far East, including the Yakutiya, Kamchatka, Magadan, Sakhalin and Khabarovsk exchanges. FETC is registered in the Sakhalin Free Economic Zone and has its headquarters in Khabarovsk. Boasting a wide network of commercial outlets in major cities of the Russian Far East, as well as in other regions of Russia, the CIS and even Northern China, FETC holds regular (twice weekly) integrated trading sessions.[20]

The Asian Exchange Finance and Commercial Group is one of the largest commodity exchanges in Russia. The Asian Exchange (AE) (registered in Ulan Ude, Buryatia) was established in July 1991 as a limited liability company with a registered capital of 50 million rubles. The participants in the AE are major state enterprises in the Russian Far East and Siberia, including aluminum plants, gold- and diamond-mining works, etc. At its centers in 18 major cities in Russia, Mongolia and China, the AE holds regular interregional computer-aided trading sessions. In December 1991 the AE became a major partner in the largest operation of its kind in Eastern Russia, the Asian Trading House, a joint-stock company with authorized capital of 50 million rubles, engaged in wholesale and retail commodity trading in the Russian Far East and Siberia. In early 1992, together with the Russian Commodity and Raw Materials Exchange, the AE set up the Asian Investment Company (AIC), a joint-stock company with authorized capital of 4 billion rubles. Other partners in the AIC include the Siberian branch of the Russian Academy of Sciences, ter-

19. *Ibid*, 5, June 1992; 16 June 1992.
20. *Ibid*, 31 March 1992; 11 July 1992; 19 December 1992.

ritorial state property committees from the Urals, Siberia and the Far East, and the Asian Trading House. The AIC's activities are targeted at mobilizing substantial nonstate investment funds for the all-round economic development of Siberia and the Russian Far East. AIC investment projects are concentrated in the mining industry (gold, precious stones, coal) and in conversion. The Asian Exchange Finance and Commercial Group also includes the Asian Bank.[21]

Current problems of regional economic policy

There are a number of special problems associated with the implementation of a new regional economic policy of the kind under discussion. The key role to be played by natural resource exploitation means that ecological concerns are likely to be aroused. According to a recent opinion poll, 21 percent of Far Eastern residents consider that pollution of the natural environment is one of the most serious social problems, compared with 11 percent of Russia's population as a whole.[22] The green movement in the Far East, moreover, is acquiring an increasingly xenophobic character, after unfortunate incidents arising from the use of foreign labor in forestry. It has been reported that, as a result of poaching by North Korean timber workers who have been working in Khabarovsk Territory since 1966, the number of rare birds and animals in local forests has fallen to half the level of 25 years ago.[23]

The green movement in the Russian Far East is concerned, too, with threats to the survival of the small number of far Northern national-minority communities. Many areas have now been officially assigned as ethnic territories to the aboriginal peoples. Any use of ethnic territories for business purposes not connected with the traditional activities of the local population requires the consent of the residents. This helps to increase the potential for conflict between public opinion in the Far East and Russian and foreign businessmen who are eager to develop the region's resources. In late 1992 environmental damage caused by the logging activities of the Hyundai Corporation of South Korea, and the potential ecological threat posed by an aluminum plant project put forward by Comelco Limited of Australia, produced an upsurge of protest in Primorsky Territory. There were declarations by members of the local academic community, and armed picketing of timber-felling areas by Ussuri Cossacks.

21. *Sovetskii Sakhalin* (Yuzhno-Sakhalinsk), 28 April 1992.
22. *Tikhookeanskaya zvezda* (Khabarovsk), 1 May 1992.
23. *Ibid*, 16 June 1992.

It is clear that entrepreneurs and local authorities need to pay greater attention to the social aspects of resource development.

Problems are also created by lack of clarity in the division of powers between local legislative and executive bodies. The Law on Territorial and Regional Councils of People's Deputies (now local dumas) and Territorial and Regional Administration indicates at least nine instances in which elected deputies can exercise control over the operating principles and the day-to-day activities of local executive authorities. According to P. Minakir, Vice-Governor (Deputy Head of Administration) of Khabarovsk Territory, strict adherence to this law would make it impossible to run an effective administration.[24] This situation encourages disputes between local dumas and their executives. One example is the long-running argument between the Primorsky Territory CPD/local duma and the administration of the territory regarding the allotting of a timber-felling area to the Svetlaya joint venture and the Hyundai Corporation.[25] All this undoubtedly hinders the working out and implementing of a well-coordinated regional development policy.

Finally, securing stable and dynamic growth in an area such as the Far East requires higher than average initial investment. Capital is urgently needed if the region's comparative advantages are to be exploited. There must be continuing federal support, albeit supplied in quite different forms to those common in the past, for the economic development of the Far East. By providing selective structural adjustment project financing, the federal government can facilitate the region's reorientation to new economic principles, and to sustainable development as part of a new domestic and international division of labor. For potential foreign investors, state support for the region's economic development would serve as an important indicator of Russia's serious intentions concerning the Far East.

24. *Ibid*, 29 May 1992
25. D. Gainutdinov, "A zatevali khoroshee delo...," *Utro Rossii* (Vladivostok), 20 October 1992.

CHAPTER FIVE

Free Economic Zones

Although there is a vital need to open up the Far Eastern economy, the investment environment in the region falls short of international standards. Hence the special importance of regional efforts to set up free economic zones (FEZs), which envisage the establishment in certain favorably located areas of attractive conditions for foreign investment.

In establishing FEZs, the Far East has emulated many Pacific Rim economies (Taiwan, South Korea, Malaysia, etc.) which have export processing zones (EPZs). Particularly influential, however, have been the Chinese special economic zones (SEZs), which have proved effective in promoting marketization and the opening up of the centrally planned economy. The Russian Far Eastern FEZs, like the SEZs in China, are intended not only to promote exports, but also to resolve a number of general development problems. In 1990–91 the Russian government approved regulations governing FEZs in Nakhodka (Primorsky Territory), Sakhalin and the Jewish Autonomous Region.

Incentives for foreign investors

The official aims of the FEZs include facilitating technology transfer and foreign investment; encouraging balanced regional development and the growth of employment; promoting exports and import substitution; increasing foreign exchange earnings; developing transcontinental transit communications; upgrading management and training; and initiating different approaches to transition from a centrally planned, closed economic system to a market-type open economy.[1]

Full legal guarantees are provided with regard to foreign investment in FEZs, and any discrimination against foreign investment is ruled out. To secure a beneficial investment environment within the zones important incentives have been offered:

— Simplified export-import procedures. Exports of local produce and imports for local needs are exempted from quotas and licenses.
— Simplified registration procedures for enterprises bringing in foreign investment.
— Tax incentives. Joint ventures (JVs) and wholly foreign-owned enterprises pay income tax at 10 percent. The repatriated profits of foreign investors are taxed at a rate of 10 percent of the remitted amount. Enterprises with foreign investment can be exempted from income tax for the first five profitmaking years. If the enterprise reinvests its profit in developing the infrastructure of the FEZ, the income tax paid on the reinvested portion is refunded.
— Preferential customs treatment. Goods and other property imported and exported by enterprises in FEZs are exempt from customs duties. If products of the enterprises are sold in other regions of Russia, custom duties are charged only on that portion of the products that originates abroad.
— Preferential tariffs for infrastructure and public services, including power and water supply, communications, municipal and transport services. Reduced rents are charged for manufacturing facilities and reduced land use fees are charged for long leases (up to 70 years), which embody sublease rights.
— Simplified entry and exit procedures for foreign entrepreneurs and other personnel.[2]

Enterprises in FEZs can employ labor from other territories of the Russian Far East and Russia, or from abroad. Labor relations are regulated by collective or individual labor contracts. Wage payments in foreign exchange are allowed.

1. *Svobodnye ekonomicheskie zony i zony svobodnogo predprinimatel'stva v RSFSR. Sbornik dokumentov*. Moscow, 1991 (mimeo), pp. 2, 12.
2. *Svobodnye ekonomicheskie zony i zony svobodnogo predprinimatel'stva v RSFSR*, pp. 2–28.

On the whole, the investment incentives offered in the Far Eastern FEZs are, therefore, comparable to those in the EPZs of the neighboring Pacific Rim economies. The Russian FEZs do, however, offer the foreign investor rather more than the EPZs in a number of important dimensions.

The political economy of FEZs

Ever since the idea of FEZs was first discussed, in the late 1980s, it has been a focus of conflict between central government and local authorities. Decisions regarding FEZs also turned into a weapon in the political struggle between the center and the Union republics in the lead-up to the dissolution of the USSR.

Within Russia, the FEZ instrument has been actively used both by federal authorities and by influential regional leaders. In legalizing FEZs from 1990, the Russian government delegated to local authorities a wide range of important administrative functions and economic privileges which had previously belonged to, or been in the gift of, Union government bodies. Among them were:

— a five-year tax credit, which implied that locally collected taxes would be retained within the regional budget;
— exemption from the mandatory surrender of 40 percent of gross export earnings to the central budget;
— the retention of up to 30 percent of gross export earnings for five years;
— removal of restrictions on barter transactions in foreign trade;
— local autonomy in the development of natural resources and in the implementation of economic reform, including privatization, autonomous determination of effective tax rates, etc.

At the same time, the Russian government and the corresponding regional authorities applied for the transfer of all state enterprises of Union ministries located in the FEZs to republican administrative subordination. Thus the greater the number of newly established FEZs and the larger their territory and their economic resources, the weaker was the economic control of the central Union authorities of the USSR and the stronger was that of both the corresponding regional authorities and the republican government of Russia. The result was that Russian zone policy developed rapidly and involved large administrative units, with insufficient attention paid to location and other comparative advantages of the designated territories.[3] In other words, political considerations led in Russia to an underestimation of some basic economic, legal and institutional problems associated with the establishment of FEZs.

LIMITED ABSORPTIVE CAPACITY. Despite the high demand for foreign investment, a range of structural, technological and financial problems in the domestic economy limits the volume of external resources that can currently be efficiently absorbed in Russia. These limitations are particularly acute within the FEZs, because the tax breaks and other benefits for foreign investors restrict the share of profits that the Russian side can take. The problem can be dealt with by through the selection of a relatively small number of high-priority areas for foreign investment, capable of acting as a catalyst for the entire economy and thus increasing its capacity to absorb external resources. On this argument, the number and the size of FEZs should be limited at first, and they should have clearly defined sectoral development priorities aimed at maximum financial payoffs.

In the Far East, however, as in the rest of Russia, no long-term FEZ development strategy has been elaborated. The regulations for the FEZs in Nakhodka and Sakhalin, for example, do not specify which sectors of the local economy should have priority for foreign investment. This impedes the operation of a goal-oriented selective tax policy and other instruments for the regulation of foreign investment. In the Nakhodka FEZ, for example, the same level of tax benefits is offered to all JVs with 30 percent or more foreign participation, irrespective of sectoral specialization, export potential or technological capacity.[4]

LACK OF FINANCE. If FEZs are to work properly, they require a good power supply, extensive transport and communications facilities, comfortable accommodation and other elements of infrastructure. In the Third World it costs $25 to $40 million to develop one square km of EPZ territory, and in China up to $70 million per square km of SEZ. In the deregulated prices of early 1993, the development requirements of the Nakhodka FEZ alone are estimated at between 16 and 90 billion rubles over the next five years.[5] Where is this

3. S. Manezhev, "Free Economic Zones in the Context of Economic Changes in Russia," *Europe-Asia Studies*, vol. 45, no. 4 (1993), p. 613.

4. *Ibid*, p. 615.

5. T. Bondarenko, "Svobodnye ot nalogov i zdravogo smysla?" *Delovoi mir*, 7 May 1991; *Ekonomika i zhizn'*, 1993, no. 4, p. 13.

money to come from? The large budget deficit in Russia makes it unlikely that it will come from the state, while the self-financing capacity of the FEZs, especially at the initial stage, is limited. Estimates of the infrastructural requirements of Nakhodka suggest that the tax credit granted by the Russian government to FEZs is unlikely to cover more than 20 percent of their costs.[6]

BALANCING CENTRAL AND LOCAL CONTROL. On the one hand, the extensive economic autonomy granted to the FEZs is designed to exploit new resources and factors of regional development, as well as to create more flexible conditions for local enterprises to operate on the international market. On the other hand, the redistribution of central funds in favor of the FEZs (through state budget allocations, tax credits, etc.) is sanctioned because the central authorities hope also to satisfy broader, national interests. Finding a rational balance between central coordination and local initiative presents one of the key problems in setting up and running FEZs.

Unfortunately, the current FEZ schemes do not pay sufficient attention to this issue. There is no requirement, for example, that Nakhodka should supply the domestic market, even though it is an important regional industrial center. Similarly, the regulations on the Sakhalin FEZ make it difficult for the federal government to influence local development programs or to regulate the activities of foreign investors.

Experience and current prospects

FEZ development has, not surprisingly, made little progress in Russia. About 150 JVs and wholly foreign-owned enterprises are registered in the Far Eastern FEZs.[7] However, the number of enterprises actually operating is only 25–30 percent of that, and the foreign investors (for example the Chinese in Nakhodka) are hardly the most promising. The export efficiency of FEZ JVs is about 20 percent higher than the corresponding figure for the whole of Russia—but that corresponding figure is rather low.[8] Moreover, in some cases uncertainties surrounding the administrative and financial relationship between FEZs and Moscow has held up promising foreign investment projects like the multi-billion dollar offshore oil and gas development project in

6. S. Manezhev, "Free Economic Zones," p. 618.

7. Calculated from *Nakhodkinskii rabochii* (Nakhodka), 6 October 1992; *Rossiiskie vesti*, 5 June 1992.

8. *Izvestiya*, 6 March 1992.

Sakhalin.[9] As a result, unlike in China, FEZs in the Russian Far East have not emerged as regional economic growth centers. Indeed the social and economic situation inside the FEZs is sometimes worse than outside them.

Thus, the economic role of FEZs in post-Soviet Russia has never been properly defined. Not surprisingly, the FEZs are highly vulnerable to any changes in the political climate. Moreover, the general trend in the political climate has been unfavorable to them.

First, the disappearance of the Soviet Union has deprived the Russian government of its incentive to try to increase the financial resources and the functions of the FEZs at the expense of the central Union government. Regional pressure for more funds and more autonomy is now aimed directly at the Russian government itself, at a time when it is increasingly concerned about the danger of regional fragmentation.

Secondly, the abrupt disintegration of the USSR brought with it the destruction of many state institutions, and the further erosion of executive power seems to have been one of the reasons why the Russian government tried to follow the Polish strategy of economic reform, rather than the Chinese model of incremental market transformation, which, it has been argued, may be more appropriate to the Russian situation. Such a trend has inevitably undermine the prospects of the FEZs: The once-and-for-all approach to price deregulation entails much stricter requirements in terms of budgetary balance and limitations on bank credit than the Chinese policy of step-by-step progress toward economic liberalization. Hence the nation's ability to pay for the development of FEZs is reduced.

Radical national economic reform policies mean that FEZs are less able to play the role of 'laboratories of reform' that they play in China. Many economic measures recently considered as special FEZ incentives for foreign companies have now been introduced throughout the territory of Russia. This is true for price liberalization, for the introduction of a simplified registration regime for foreign investment, for the removal of the excess-profit tax, and for the moves to free barter transactions in foreign trade, and to make it possible to establish wholly foreign-owned companies and joint venture banks and to open ruble-denominated bank accounts on behalf of JVs, etc.

The third major factor is the general decline in economic performance and the increasing social tensions which are accompanying the current reforms in

9. In October 1991 the representatives of the Sakhalin FEZ wrecked negotiations on the project by making additional demands on potential investors for supplementary outlays of $15 billion on the development of local infrastructure. Such additional sums would have been larger than the development cost itself (*Nikkei Weekly*, 9 November 1991).

Russia. FEZs are simply being overshadowed by more acute and urgent policy issues. Against this background of crisis, the government seems now to be more concerned with averting social unrest in the different parts of the country than with long-term economic strategy, when it comes to consider requests from the regions. The April 1992 Presidential decree on foreign economic concessions to the Far Eastern territories, for example, put the FEZs in Sakhalin, Nakhodka and the Jewish Autonomous Province on the same footing as non-FEZ areas in Khabarovsk Territory, and Magadan and Kamchatka Provinces.

For all these reasons a FEZ policy, at least as originally conceived, is irrelevant to the needs of present-day Russia. In 1992 the process of approving new FEZ projects in the Far East (proposed for Greater Vladivostok and Ussuriisk) came to a halt. Moreover, the principal Russian laws and regulations of 1992 which define the country's new economic system do not refer to the special status of FEZs at all. They are not mentioned, for example, in the Law on the Basic Principles of the Fiscal System of Russia, the Law on Value Added Tax, the Law on Underground Mineral Wealth, the Regulation on the Splitting up of State Property in the Russian Federation into Federal Property and State Property of Republics, Territories, Provinces, etc., or in the 1992 Privatization Program. The implementation of these legal documents has dramatically undermined the financial, resource and production basis of FEZs.

The initial FEZ concept seems, then, to be gradually disappearing in the whirlpool of Russian economic and political development, before it has even had a chance to be implemented. Given the distorted and impractical nature of the original projects, this is probably a good thing from an economic point of view, and it does provide an opportunity for a pragmatic reassessment of zone policy. Some elements of a new approach were evident in the Presidential Decree on "Certain Measures With Regard to the Development of FEZs" (June 1992). Confirming the economic significance and special status of FEZs, the decree stated that a draft law on FEZs should be worked out by the federal government in the near future. It should (a) embody a revision of the existing regulations on FEZs concerning such basic points as conditionality of the promised tax credits, the proportion of privatization receipts shared between federal and local budgets, and the local customs regime; (b) assert a decisive role for the central government and in general centralize management of the zones; and (c) affirm the absolute precedence of federal laws in regulating foreign investment in both onshore and offshore development of natural resources.[10]

10. *Zakon*, 1992, no. 11, p. 5.

It is clear that the Far Eastern FEZs must undergo fundamental transformation if they are to survive. First, practically all of them (excluding, perhaps, Nakhodka) now need to reduce their territory and carry out a more realistic assessment of what they can achieve with the resources available. The Presidential decree on the Socioeconomic Development of the Kurile Islands (December 1992) called for the carving out of a Kuriles subzone within the Sakhalin FEZ, and undertook to provide it with resources from the federal budget for infrastructure development in 1993–95.[11]

In addition, the development strategy of the FEZs must be reviewed. A new concept for the Nakhodka FEZ suggests subdividing the development process into stages with clearly articulated priorities, stressing trade and transit-transport activities in 1993–97, high-tech industrial production in 1997–2006, and so on.[12] Combined with more active involvement by foreign investment, these refinements could facilitate the transformation of the ailing FEZs into viable functional zones with more sharply defined development targets and diversified investment incentives calculated to enhance their international comparative advantage.

In March 1995 the Russian government finally placed before the State Duma a bill on Free Economic Zones. The bill proposes the abandonment of the idea of large-scale FEZs, primarily on the basis of cost considerations. It has been estimated, for instance, that it would cost Rb6.6 trn plus $5 bn to create a FEZ coextensive with the island of Sakhalin. The notion that funding on such a level might be raised primarily within the private sector has been demonstrated to be unrealistic. The idea behind the new law is that domestic and foreign funding could be attracted to the formation of compact (no more than a few hundred square kilometers) export and customs-free zones.

11. *Sobranie Aktov Prezidenta i Pravitel'stva Rossiiskoi Federatsii*, 1992, no. 24, pp. 2210-2.
12. *Sovetskoe Primor'e* (Nakhodka), 19 September 1992.

CHAPTER SIX

Foreign Economic Relations

The Far East is one of the regions of Russia where foreign economic exchange can have a really substantial impact on development. It is further from Russia's main industrial regions than it is from a number of rapidly developing Pacific countries. As a result, foreign trade transactions can be far more attractive for the Russian Far East than economic exchange with other parts of Russia. The transport cost of delivering one ton of produce from Japan to the region, for example, is only 20–30 percent what it costs to bring it from European Russia.[1] Second, the Far Eastern economy is connected to the rest of the Russian economy mainly through broad intersectoral exchange, rather than through more specific forms of technology-related production cooperation. Third, the structures of production and consumption in the Russian Far East are, in most cases, complementary with those of its Asia-Pacific neighbors

The evolving foreign economic exchange system

During the years of Soviet rule the centralized system of foreign trade administered by the Ministry of Foreign Economic Relations (MFER) in Moscow within the framework of intergovernmental agreements was supplemented in the Russian Far East by coastal/border trade agreements and direct barter transactions. Coastal and border trade transactions were conducted through the 'Dalintorg' trade association in Nakhodka. Far Eastern enterprises were expected to export items from their stock which were not included in na-

---

1. Yu. S. Stolyarov, "The Soviet Far East: The Economy and Foreign Economic Relations," *The Journal of East and West Studies*, vol. 20, no. 1 (April 1991), p. 9.

tional foreign trade agreements. In order to preserve a local balance, export receipts were allocated to cover the import of goods to meet local demand. This system has largely survived to the present day.

The partners of Far Eastern enterprises in this kind of trade are usually small and medium-sized enterprises in Japan (80 percent of the coastal trade turnover) and in China (17 percent). As far as direct counter-trade transactions are concerned, enterprises in the Far East usually trade with enterprises and organizations in the Northeastern provinces of China. This form of trade began in the late 1980s. The legal framework for it is laid down in the Agreement on Developing Trade and Economic Relations between Regions, Ministries, and Enterprises of the USSR, on the one hand, and Provinces, Autonomous Regions, and Cities of China, on the other, signed in 1988.

Since 1992 more wide-ranging autonomy has been given to the region to dispose of its own products. Foreign economic activities have been liberalized, the territorial export quota has been split up among local authorities, and centralized 'state orders' to fulfill Russia's international economic commitments have been reduced. This makes it easier to reorient foreign ties in the Far East toward direct contacts. A number of substantial innovations have recently been introduced in Far Eastern trade:

— International economic agreements have been signed at regional level. In 1992 cooperation agreements were concluded between Khabarovsk Territory and Heilonjiang province in the People's Republic of China, and between Primorsky Territory and the province of British Columbia in Canada.[2]
— Long-term international economic agreements have been signed at enterprise level—for example a ten-year agreement on trade and economic cooperation between the Sunginsky Mayak Association of Yakutsk and the Heilongjiang Provincial Industry-Trade Export-Import Company.
— Bodies have been set up to regulate bilateral economic ties between the region and foreign countries and regions (for example, the Committee for Economic Cooperation between the Republic of Korea and the Russian Far East; the Committee for Business Cooperation between Australia and the Pacific Region of Russia).[3]
— A network of local representatives of foreign business firms has been established. In Khabarovsk alone, more than 30 offices have been set up.

2. *Tikhookeanskaya zvezda* (Khabarovsk), 14 January 1992; 26 May 1992; *Utro Rossii* (Vladivostok), 17 March 1992.

3. *Sovetskii Sakhalin* (Yuzhno-Sakhalinsk), 30 November 1992; *Utro Rossii* (Vladivostok), 25 March 1992; *Ekonomika i zhizn'*, 1992, no. 48, p. 2.

— Consulates-General of neighboring countries (including Japan, United States, Korea and China) have been established in the region.
— Foreign investors have been permitted to participate in the privatization of municipal property in a number of major cities in the Russian Far East (e.g., Vladivostok, Nakhodka, Artem).
— Local commercial foreign trade banks have been set up (for example, Regiovneshbank in Khabarovsk and Primorsky Regional Bank for Foreign Trade).

All these changes serve to create better conditions for integrating the Russian Far East into the free economic exchange of goods, capital, and labor in the region.

Foreign trade

Exports from the Russian Far East include a wide range of products (approximately 100 different items), but three industries (timber, fishery, fuel) dominate, providing 80–85 percent of the total volume. Per capita timber production in the region is 19 times the world average, and local timber enterprises export 25 percent of their output.[4] However, owing to mounting problems of depletion and quality in forestry, the share of lumber and woodworking products in total regional exports declined from 43.5 percent in the mid-1980s to about 25 percent in the early 1990s. This has been compensated for by increased exports from Far Eastern fisheries, which exported more than 13 percent of their total output in 1992. As a result, fish and fish products now account for over 40 percent of the region's exports, compared with about 20 percent in 1985. Mineral fuels (mainly coal, as well as oil and oil products) account for a further 20 percent.[5] Other exports include hunting and livestock farming products, machinery and equipment, ferrous metals, chemical products, and construction materials. The main exporting enterprises are in the Primorsky and Khabarovsk Territories, and also in Yakutiya. Together these areas account for 75 percent of exports from the region.

Exports from the Far East consist primarily, then, of raw materials. Moreover, in the past two decades the proportion of unprocessed raw materials within total Far Eastern exports has increased from 60 percent to 70 percent.[6]

4. *Dal'nii Vostok Rossii*, p. 214.
5. A. G. Ivanshikov, *op. cit.*
6. *Dal'nii Vostok Rossii*, p. 213.

Table 6-1. *Organization of foreign trade in the Russian Far East,*
1988–92

Percent of total exports[a]

Channels of export	1988	1989	1990	1991	1992
Ministry of Foreign Economic Relations	94.4	75.4	73.9	63.6	25.5
Coastal/border trade	2.6	2.0	2.3	0.7	4.9
Direct enterprise-to-enterprise transactions	3.0	22.6	18.7	33.6	69.6
Total exports	100	100	100	100	100

Source: Statistical administrations of the territories and provinces of the Russian Far East.
a. Excluding exports by wholly or partly foreign-owned enterprises

This puts the region in an unfavorable position. Its exports are vulnerable to fluctuations in world prices. The tendency in the structure of exports runs counter to trends in trade in the Asia-Pacific region as a whole, where the most dynamic sector is machinery, equipment and components. There will have to be a radical shift in the export structure of the Russian Far East (and in the sectoral structure of the region's economy) if it is to integrate into the Asia-Pacific international market.

As can be seen from table 6-1, the rapid growth of Far Eastern exports in the early 1990s was stimulated mainly by the dynamic expansion of direct commercial transactions at grassroots level.

The sharp upturn of interest in the foreign market which has accompanied the decentralization and liberalization of foreign economic ties is to be explained principally by the disparity between pricing systems (and prices) at home and abroad. Enterprises have a direct interest in dumping their goods and converting the hard currency they earn into rubles. For example, in 1992 timber was being exported at a price 30 percent lower than the world market level; export prices were 35 percent below world market levels for metals, with corresponding figures of 50 percent for machines and fertilizers and 50 percent for fish. The profit exporters made on these transactions nevertheless amounted to 150–200 percent.[7]

There are also problems with imports. They certainly help to stabilize the domestic market. According to the Khabarovsk Economics Research Institute, 7–8 percent of demand for consumer goods, including food, is met by imports.[8] In this sphere, a substantial role is being played by local authorities, as well as by enterprises importing consumer goods to resell or to distribute to

7. *Tikhookeanskaya zvezda* (Khabarovsk), 27 October 1992.
8. *Dal'nii Vostok Rossii*, p. 218.

Table 6-2. *Foreign investment projects in the Russian Far East by country origin of foreign partner, 1993*
Percent of total exports[a]

Country origin	Joint ventures
United States	21
Japan	20
People's Republic of China	17
Others	42
Total	100

the workforce. However, local hard-currency funds are frequently misused. According to the former Russian Control Department, up to 87 percent of the foreign currency received by local authorities is spent on foreign trips for officials, the purchase of imported cars, and so on.[9]

As a result, the share of machinery and equipment in total direct imports to the Primorsky and Khabarovsk Territories is only 15–20 percent, i.e. less than half the average for the Russian Federation. In territories where industry is less developed (for example Sakhalin and Amur Provinces), machinery and equipment makes up only 1–3 percent of imports.[10] The raw material and extractive industries are the main recipients of machinery and equipment. The share of imported machinery and equipment within total machinery and equipment purchases is 70 percent in the Far Eastern timber industry, 30 percent in wood processing, but only 6 percent in engineering.[11]

Thus foreign trade does not yet play the role that it should play in restructuring the Far Eastern economy and making it more competitive. High hopes are pinned on the effects of novel forms of foreign economic cooperation in the spheres of production and services.

Foreign investment

The economic transformation which has been taking place in the Asia-Pacific region has tended increasingly to replace international trade in primary and finished goods by the internationalization of production. This represents a serious challenge to the Russian Far East. Since 1992 local authorities have

9. *Sovetskaya Rossiya*, 15 September 1992.
10. *Vneshneekonomicheskaya deyatel'nost Dal'nego Vostoka*, p. 4.
11. *Dal'nii Vostok Rossii*, p. 218.

Table 6-3. *Foreign investment projects in the Russian Far East by sector of activity, 1993*

Industry	Number	Percent
Fishing	70	16
Forestry	30	7
Services	141	32
Construction	46	10
Other	158	35
Total	445	100

been permitted to register joint ventures with a nominal capital of up to 100 million rubles. As a result, by mid-1992, 445 enterprises with foreign participation were registered in the region, compared with 128 in late 1991. Most of the JVs are in the Primorsky Territory (38 percent of joint venture registrations), the Khabarovsk Territory (23 percent), and in Sakhalin (14 percent) and the Kamchatka Region (8 percent).[12] American investors have been the most active. Japanese companies are maintaining their traditionally strong position in the region. Chinese activity has also increased since 1992. For example, 20 percent of all foreign investments in Khabarovsk Territory today are mainland Chinese. Investors from the Asia-Pacific region account for 72 percent of all joint venture registrations.

By 1992 the Far Eastern region's share of the total number of operational JVs in Russia exceeded 10 percent, compared with just 2 percent in 1989.[13] As Table 5 shows, the JVs concerned are engaged mainly in services, in fishery, and, to a lesser extent, in the timber industry.

Trade, catering and entertainment are the main areas for JV investment within the services sector. Many of these services are directed at the growing number of foreign clients, but they also address the needs of the local population. With the upsurge of car imports, for example, a network of service stations is being developed in Vladivostok and Khabarovsk by Toyota, Honda, Nissan and other companies.[14] Foreign telecommunications firms are also expanding their activities. Cable and Wireless, a UK-based telecommunications carrier with a strong presence in Hong Kong, has established two joint ven-

12. *Ekonomicheskaya reforma na Dal'nem Vostoke: rezul'taty, problemy, kontseptsiya razvitiya*, Khabarovsk, 1993 (mimeo), pp. 73, 74.

13. *Vneshneekonomicheskaya deyatel'nost Dal'nego Vostoka*, p. 7; *Inostrannyie investitsii: tendentsii, problemy, perspektivy*. Assosiatsiya sovmestnykh predpriyatii, mezhdunarodnykh ob"edinenii i organizatsii, Moscow, 1992, p. 7.

14. *Tikhookeanskaya zvezda* (Khabarovsk), 16 September 1992.

tures in Sakhalin and Nakhodka to offer digital telecommunications services to FEZs sited there. Another major project is being planned by Vostoktelecom Co. (Vladivostok), a joint venture set up by Primorsky Territory telecommunications organizations and KDD, Japan's largest international telecommunications carrier. Japanese investment in this project will amount to $7.5 million.[15]

Capital-intensive hotel projects are less attractive to foreign investors because of infrastructure problems and the lack of hard currency in the Russian Far East. The absence of modern hotels is an important constraint on the improvement of the investment environment. Vladivostok, for example, has only one or two hotels that meet international standards.

Japan has the leading position in JVs within the fishing industry. Enjoying access to the fish stocks of the 200-mile Russian coastal zone, these enterprises employ modern Japanese technology and equipment for fishing, fish farming and processing fish and marine products. Soniko Company, one of the first JVs in the field, is engaged in fish breeding, and in the manufacture of high-quality food and industrial fish products. A number of JVs have been set up with Japanese and South Korean companies in the wood processing industries (production of plywood, chipboard, etc.). As in fish processing, most of the output of these enterprises is exported. Imports by JVs are characteristically dominated by machinery and transport equipment, the share of which exceeds 70 percent in a number of cases.[16]

Since the relaxing of foreign trade restrictions in Russia, foreign investors have become more active in exporting from Russia, and their share in Far Eastern exports is growing. In 1992, JVs in the Far East accounted for more than 24 percent of exports from the region, compared with 1.6 percent in 1991. Current legislation allows wholly foreign-owned enterprises, as well as JVs in which the share of foreign partners exceeds 30 percent, to export without a license from the Ministry of Foreign Economic Relations.

Joint exploration of fuel and energy resources on the basis of production-sharing contracts is a promising area of foreign business activity, which would meet the objectives of economic restructuring in the Far East. Such activities normally imply long-term, large-scale, comprehensive projects, with supplementary investment in local transport, communications, and social infrastructure. This is the approach built into the feasibility study of an offshore oil and gas development project in Sakhalin planned by an international consortium of Mitsui (30 percent of the contracted value), Marathon (30 percent), Mac-

15. *Izvestiya*,8 September 1992; 20 June 1992.16.
16. *Sovetskii Sakhalin* (Yuzhno-Sakhalinsk), 3 November 1992.

dermott International Incorporated (20 percent) and Shell (20 percent). Deposits in Sakhalin are estimated at more than 1.5 billion barrels of crude oil, and natural gas equivalent to 18 billion barrels of crude oil. The planned duration of the project is 20 years, and total development costs are expected to be $10–12 billion.[17] By April 1995, however, the project still had not passed the feasibility study stage, with the Western partners hanging on for passage by the State Duma of, *inter alia*, key legislation on production sharing, expected in mid-1995. The earliest date for oil production from the field is 2001, and for gas production 2003.

Further foreign investment in the development of natural resources in the Russian Far East would be stimulated by a clearer division of property rights between administrative bodies at various levels. In order to provide for the normal functioning of capital-intensive foreign-financed projects, the Far Eastern territorial authorities are developing a project to set up a regional mortgage fund which would enable local administrations to offer deposits of natural resources to foreign banks or intermediaries as collateral against bank credits.[18]

17. *Nikkei Weekly*, 9 November 1991; *Finansovye izvestiya*, 29 October 1992.
18. *Dal'nii Vostok Rossii*, p. 242.

CHAPTER SEVEN

Principal Business Partners

The foreign economic ties of the Russian Far East extend to 50 countries, of which 13 are in the Pacific basin. In the former CMEA the tradition was that member states purchased mainly finished goods from one another. The same is true of the trade with the Middle East. The Asia-Pacific countries, in contrast, have tended to import primary goods. The bulk (more than 85 percent) of exports from the Far East goes to the Asia-Pacific countries.

The Japanese factor in Far Eastern regional development

For many years Japan has been the major trading partner of the Russian Far East. The characteristic feature of economic relations with Japan is the many large-scale compensation agreements that are in operation: Japan supplies machinery, equipment and technology on credit, to be paid through counterpart deliveries of the goods produced by the recipient Far Eastern enterprises, shipped to Japan over an agreed period (up to 20 years). Over the past two decades the two sides have signed ten general compensation agreements, worth several billion dollars, to provide Japan with supplies of dressed timber, wood chips, oil, gas and coal, as well as transport services to enable Japan to deliver cargoes to Europe by railway. Three of these long-term projects are still in operation: an agreement to supply Yakutiya coal to Japan (valid until 2005); an agreement to supply wood chips (valid until 1995); and an agreement on timber, signed in 1992. These long-term compensation agreements reinforce the traditional division of labor between the two countries whereby Russian raw materials are exchanged for Japanese-made finished products. As

Table 7-1. *Russia's trade with Asia-Pacific countries, 1991–93*
Million U.S. dollars

Country	Total			Exports			Imports		
	1991	*1992*	*1993*	*1991*	*1992*	*1993*	*1991*	*1992*	*1993*
Japan	4,047	3,399	3,372	1,881	1,702	2,005	2,166	1,697	1,367
China	3,035	4,654	5,403	1,508	2,864	3,068	1,527	1,790	2,355
South Korea	474	1,044	697	288	366	391	185	778	306
Total	95,384	79,360	71,104	50,911	42,376	44,247	44,473	36,984	26,807

far as the Far East is concerned, Japan has for many years been the major international creditor and the main supplier of the modern equipment needed to develop the region's natural resources.

Most of the export-oriented items produced in the Russian region are meant for particular consumers in Japan, which was taking 65 percent of the Far East's exports in the early 1990s.[1] Hence the level of foreign economic intercourse in the region, generally and sectorally, depends heavily on the state of trade relations with Japan. The main items exported to Japan (1993 data) are: fish and fish products (26 percent of the value of total exports); aluminum (32 percent); industrial wood and timber (25 percent); coal, oil, gold and diamonds. Japan is the Russian Far East's traditional supplier of equipment for turnkey projects, construction and transport equipment, and consumer goods. Purchases of Japanese cars are growing rapidly, making up to 35 percent of the direct imports of some Far Eastern territories.[2] This is the largest imported car market in the CIS. The decision of the Chernomyrdin government in early 1993 to ban the use of right-hand drive cars in Russia after 1994 produced a storm of protest and stirred up a new wave of separatist sentiments in the Far East. Subsequently the decision was rescinded in respect of that region. Pipes of various diameters accounted for 15 percent of Russian imports from Japan in 1993.

There are two contradictory trends in the development of economic relations between Russia and Japan. The two economies have clearly become less complementary in the last decade. The structural reorientation of the Japanese economy toward science-intensive production with lower consumption of materials and energy has resulted in a general decline in Japan's demand for imported fuel and raw materials and greater competition between international raw materials suppliers to the Japanese market. This has revealed Russia's

1. *Dal'nii Vostok Rossii*, p. 219.
2. *Sovetskii Sakhalin* (Yuzhno-Sakhalinsk), 3 November 1992.

weak competitive position, caused by its low industrial standards and poor quality of production. Whereas not so long ago Russia met 12 percent of Japanese demand for timber, today its share has shrunk to only 9 percent, less than that of Australia, New Zealand and other suppliers.

The current economic, legal, and organizational difficulties in Russia have the same negative effect. The crisis in the economy, accompanied by social instability and a sharp decline in Russia's creditworthiness, all make Japanese consider the country a risky partner. Moreover, legislation regarding foreign entrepreneurship in Russia is unclear and patchy; the regulatory framework for Russian foreign economic relationships is confusing. The level of business culture among many Russian partners is low; and there is a shortage of skilled personnel, and so on.

Finally, the Japanese government continues to insist on a linkage between trade and economic relations on the one hand, and the Northern Territories issue on the other. In September 1992 President Yeltsin abruptly canceled a visit to Japan because of disagreements over this issue. The uncompromising positions adopted by both sides undermine the mutual confidence required for developing long-term economic cooperation. Russian-Japanese trade turnover declined by 16 percent in 1992 compared with 1991, with Japan's share of Russia's foreign trade amounting to just 4.3 percent (4.2 percent in 1991).[3] Russian exports to Japan recovered in 1993, growing by 18 percent compared with 1992, but largely on account of a 320 percent increase in aluminum exports as the Russian aluminum industry flooded the world market with its products. Russian imports from Japan fell by 19 percent in 1992–93.

At the same time, because of the globalization of Japan's foreign economic ties through the export of capital, and with the general trend to subregional integration in the Asia-Pacific region, a new local economic area is gradually emerging in Northeast Asia that could act as a bridge between the Pacific Rim economies and the European Community. The end of the Cold War, growing economic contacts between North and South Korea, the decentralization of management in China and, finally, the growing autonomy of Russia's regions, all favor the development of a Japan Sea Rim Economic Zone which would bring together the untapped natural resources of the Russian Far East, the plentiful labor supply of Northeastern China and North Korea, the technology of South Korea and the capital and high-tech knowhow of Japan.[4]

On this perspective Japan has a genuine interest in the easing of social ten-

3. Data from *Goskomstat*.
4. *Nikkei Weekly*, 18 July 1992.

sions in the Russian Far East, demilitarization of the region and its economy, the development of its infrastructure, and the encouragement of local business activity. The rich Far Eastern oil, natural gas, gold, timber and fish resources have not yet been penetrated by Western multinational companies, unlike the resources of West Siberia and European Russia. Finally, political forces in the region's administrations are being brought together by the current political struggle with Moscow, and the Far Eastern territories, in particular the Sakhalin Region, have started to play an independent role in the resolution of the Russian-Japanese territorial dispute.[5] Thus Japan's greater interest in the Far East is a counterweight to the general cooling off of business interest in Russia. While the Far Eastern share of Russian exports to Japan amounted to around 50 percent in the late 1980s, it had increased to about 75 percent by 1992.[6] It is estimated that 55–60 percent of all Russian-Japanese joint ventures are located in the Russian Far East. Japanese companies are involved in discussions about major development projects in the Far East involving investment on a massive scale, such as the Sakhalin Offshore Oil and Gas Development ($10–12 billion), the Sakhalin Paper and Pulp Factory ($0.7 billion), and the Port of Vanino Reconstruction Project ($0.5 billion).[7]

With the current economic recession in Japan, great hopes are placed on more flexible small and medium-sized projects, to be carried out jointly with Japanese companies, for the development of smaller deposits of mineral resources, the utilization of industrial waste products, and the conversion of arms factories. The Japanese government is offering guarantees worth $1.8 billion to Japanese companies willing to invest in the Russian economy. Japanese-Russian joint entrepreneurship at the grassroots level is also being stimulated by new economic cooperation organizations established by local businesses in Niigata, Hokkaido and other prefectures on the Sea of Japan (e.g. the Soviet Investment Promotion Company in Niigata Prefecture; the Aomori Nisso Koeki Company in Aomori Prefecture, and joint trading ventures in Akita and Toyama Prefectures).[8]

As far as technical assistance is concerned, Japan is prepared to contribute to conversion of defense industry plants, modernization of the distribution system, training specialists for the market economy, developing a securities market, and providing technical expertise and consultancy for individual projects and industries (e.g. the development of free economic zones in the

5. *Nikkei Weekly*, 12 October 1991.
6. Estimated on the basis of *Goskomstat* data.
7. *Nikkei Weekly*, 31 August 1991; 12 October 1991.
8. *Nikkei Weekly*, 7 September 1991.

Russian Far East). Russian–Japanese cooperation based on licensed fishing in the two countries' 200-mile zones is also growing.

However, the unresolved territorial issue has adverse effects on the development of Russian–Japanese economic contacts at the regional level. Since it does not recognize Russian jurisdiction over the four South Kurile islands, the Japanese government not only forbids Japanese businesses to take part in any joint economic projects in the disputed territories, but also puts pressure on other foreign companies to stay out of the islands. In October 1992, for example, after pressure from the Japanese Foreign Ministry, Carleson & Kaplan, a Hong Kong company, canceled a deal with the Sakhalin administration for the long-term lease of 270 hectares on Shikotan island.[9] In response to this, business and political leaders from the Far Eastern territories have been trying to moderate the Japanese domination of their foreign economic contacts, and to develop alternative ties with other countries in Northeast Asia.

China: reshaping the traditional relationship

An important feature of the current pattern of foreign economic relations of the Russian Far East is rapidly growing business cooperation with China. Russia and China share a 4,200 km-long common border and have a tradition of trade based on the natural complementarity of their economies. China's surplus labor, its impressive manufacturing capacities, especially in light industry, and its well-developed agriculture, combine readily with the rich raw-material and fuel resources of the Russian Far East, which suffers from an acute shortage of labor and badly needs to develop its consumer goods supplies and its infrastructure. Other favorable factors include Russia's residual technological influence on China (which stems from Soviet economic assistance in the 1950s), as well as geography—transport costs, for example, can be cut be up to 30 percent by exporting the output of major industrial centers in Northeastern China through Russian Far Eastern ports.[10] In the early 1990s Beijing elaborated a long-term plan for Opening-up to the North, which envisages enhanced business cooperation with Russia so as to accelerate the economic growth of Northeastern China, which lags behind the dynamic Southern and Southeastern provinces with their special economic zones, open coastal cities, and so on.[11]

9. *Izvestiya*, 23 October 1992.
10. *China Market*, 1991, no. 11, p. 17.
11. I. P. Faminsky, S. A. Manezhev, I. N. Korkunov, et al., *Nashi delovye partnery: Kitai*, Moscow, 1992, p. 64.

Chinese economists consider that the current transitional state of the Russian economy provides favorable opportunities for penetrating the Russian market. First, the move from a planned to a market economy reveals the sectoral imbalances in the Russian economy and releases a surge of demand for the consumer goods and food stuffs that bulk large in Chinese exports. Second, the breakdown of the centralized distribution system makes it easier for foreign producers to capture Russian markets. Third, as long as the liberalization of prices in Russia has not been completed, the differences between domestic and foreign prices can be turned to profit through arbitrage.[12] But Chinese economists are also aware that these advantages are transient and will soon vanish. China's economic policy toward Russia, and especially toward the Russian Far East, is accordingly developing in the following directions.

UPDATING THE ORGANIZATIONAL AND LEGAL FRAMEWORK FOR BILATERAL COOPERATION. After the disintegration of the USSR, the USSR-People's Republic of China (PRC) Governmental Commission for Trade, Economic, and Technical-Scientific Cooperation was transformed into the Russian–Chinese Governmental Commission, established in January 1992. On 5 March 1992 Russia and China signed their first government trade agreement providing for mutual most favored nation (MFN) treatment, and declaring that enterprises, rather than the state, would be the main actors in economic relations between the two countries. Finally, during President Yeltsin's visit to China in December 1992, 23 important agreements were signed covering, *inter alia,* economic, scientific and technological cooperation.

INTRODUCING INSTITUTIONAL CHANGES INTO CHINA'S FOREIGN-TRADE SYSTEM.

— A rapid increase in the number of companies with the right to engage in independent trading activities and barter transactions in the Russian market; whereas in 1991 there were 11 such companies in the three Northeastern Chinese provinces bordering Russia, in 1992 there were more than 130 of them in the city of Harbin (Heilongjiang Province) alone.[13]
— The removal of restrictions on the number, itineraries, and activities of trade delegations to Russia.
— More generous support for the annual international border-trade fair in Harbin (the total value of the trade deals signed at the Third Harbin Fair in June 1992 was 2.3 times greater than in the previous year).[14]

12. *Guoji Shangbao,* 10 September 1992.
13. *Ibid,* 1 August 1992.
14. *Jiage Xinxibao,* 26 June 1992.

LIBERALIZATION OF IMPORT TRANSACTIONS WITH RUSSIA. Customs duties and VAT have been reduced on a number of imported goods, and the import procedure for certain products has been simplified.[15]

DIVERSIFICATION OF FORMS AND CHANNELS OF COOPERATION. In early 1992 the PRC State Council issued a special decree allowing major Chinese trading companies to invest in industry, trade and property on Russian territory. Measures are being taken to encourage private trade by creating a network of special trading markets (zones of free economic communication) at the Sino-Russian border.[16] The Chinese side is working to open up new border crossings, and new transport links between the border areas of the two countries are being set up.

THE CREATION OF NEW OPEN ECONOMIC ZONES. The State Council of the PRC has granted the status of open border city to four cities bordering the Russian Far East (Suifenghe, Hungchun, Heihe, and Manzhouli). They benefit from trade and investment incentives similar to those enjoyed by the SEZs in Southern China. Large grants have been allocated from the state budget for the development of free investment and trade zones in the cities concerned (e.g. $1.2 billion in Suifenghe).[17]

China's commercial offensive in 1992 enabled it to overtake Japan as Russia's major trade partner in the Asia-Pacific region. Russian–Chinese trade turnover increased from $3 billion in 1991 to $4.4 billion in 1992, and China's share in Russia foreign trade rose from 3.2 percent to 5.9 percent.[18] In 1993 Russian–Chinese trade turnover increased further to $5.4, with Russian imports from China increasing by 39 percent compared to 1992. The nature of Russian-Chinese trade is also changing. According to estimates made by the Russian Ministry of Foreign Economic Relations, direct transactions between Russian and Chinese enterprises (including border and regional trade) accounted for 90 percent of total Russian–Chinese trade turnover in 1992 (compared with 59 percent in 1991 and 25 percent in 1990). China's share in exports from the Russian Far East has grown sharply (from 17 percent in 1990 to

15. *Shichang Xinxibao*, 2 June 1992.

16. *Vostochny ekspress*, 1992, no. 13, p. 6; *Utro Rossii* (Vladivostok), 21 November 1992.

17. *Utro Rossii* (Vladivostok), 21 November 1992.

18. Data from *Goskomstat*; see *Moskovskie novosti*, 1993, no. 24, p. 12. According to the Ministry of Foreign Economic Relations Russian-Chinese trade increased from $3.9 billion in 1991 to $5 billion in 1992; see *Vneshnyaya torgovlya*, 1993, no. 4, p. 18.

around 30 percent in 1992).[19] The Far East's exports to China include mineral fertilizers, fish products, timber, oil products, agricultural machinery and equipment, and construction materials, while China exports food and consumer goods to the Far East. Almost all Far Eastern–Chinese trade is countertrade. Besides official trade in the border areas, tourist trade in consumer goods is gaining momentum, and the annual volume is estimated by Chinese sources to be several billion yuan.[20]

Bilateral economic links of various kinds have developed, including joint ventures, contract construction, assembling and processing using imported components, etc. In 1992, in addition to the 35 Russian–Chinese joint ventures already operating in Russia, agreements were signed to set up more than 200 joint ventures in fields such as clothing, leather processing, joint construction and management of hotels, hospitals and restaurants, market gardening, timber processing, etc. About 20 shops belonging to major Chinese companies have been given permission to open in Russia. In late 1992 and early 1993 Chinese businessmen started to take a keen interest in the privatization of municipal properties in the Russian Far East and to purchase privatization vouchers from the local population.[21] About 30,000 Chinese workers and specialists are working in construction, in agriculture, in wood processing and in industrial plants in Russia.

The explosive growth of border and regional trade is causing a certain amount of apprehension on the Russian side, mainly centering on the economic efficiency of export-import operations. First, the product mix of the Russian Far East's exports through border and regional trade is marked by a relatively high share of raw materials (90 percent as compared with 65–70 percent in government-to-government trade). As one Russian economist has noted, "Border and regional trade has become a huge pump, draining resources from Russia to China."[22] Thus the rapid growth of local trade brings with it a general deterioration in the product mix of Russian exports to China.

Second, while prices for goods traded through state channels more or less correspond to the corresponding world levels, the terms of border and regional trade are sometimes distorted. Prices for Russian exports are often depressed (sometimes substantially), while imported goods are greatly overpriced. The main reasons are the striking disparities in raw materials prices between Russ-

19. A. G. Ivanshikov, *op. cit.*

20. *China Market*, 1992, no. 4, p. 9.

21. *Izvestiya*, 21 November 1992.

22. Ye. Sprogis, "Dvustoronnyaya torgovlya razvivayetsya. Ne bez problem," *Finansovye vesti*, 1992, no. 50, p. 14.

ian and world markets, and the inadequacy of current Russian regulation of foreign economic activities. Loosening of state controls has resulted in too many incompetent exporters (cooperatives, local foreign-trade associations, etc.) operating in foreign markets. They seek quick profits and compete fiercely to clinch contracts with Chinese partners. The implicit price for a heavy KAMAZ truck in barter transactions with the Chinese dropped from SFr70,000 to 55,000 between January and October 1992.[23] The evidence suggests that the preservation of flexible forms of state regulation and control over foreign economic contacts in the Chinese economic reform model gives Chinese partners an advantage in trade with Russia.

A final consideration is that the often inferior quality of Chinese goods reduces the economic benefits of increased trade. China's technological capabilities are obviously too limited to allow it to play a decisive role in the comprehensive development of the Russian Far East.

South Korea: a dynamic newcomer

Substantial possibilities for building up the Far East's exports as well as increasing the influx of hard currency and modern technology may emerge from the expansion of Russian–South Korean economic relations. A number of economic synergies underpin this expansion. First, Russia is in desperate need of a range of daily necessities and basic electrical and electronic consumer goods. Korea is well positioned to be a major supplier both of relatively cheap consumer goods and of mass production technologies in consumer-oriented industries. Second, Russia is rich in resources, but short of the capital required to exploit them. Korea, on the other hand, is relatively cash-rich but resource-poor—Korea's energy import dependency rate has been increasing steadily, reaching 92.9 percent in 1992.[24] Third, Russia is advanced in basic science and certain areas of high technology, but lacks experience in commercializing that expertise. At the same time, Korea is highly dependent on foreign sources of technology, and is finding that Japanese, American, and European companies are less willing than in the past to issue licenses.

Both government and business circles in South Korea seem ready to cooperate with Russia. In November 1992 President Yeltsin made a visit to Seoul which resulted in the signing of a Russian–Korean treaty, as well as inter–gov-

---

23. V. Medvedev. "Rel'sy pakhnut pivom," *Komsomol'skaya pravda*, 8 December 1992.
24. *Korea Economic Weekly*, 1 June 1992.

ernmental agreements on setting up a cooperation committee on economic matters, science and technology. A joint Russian-Korean committee to promote the development of energy and mineral resources in Russia is also being established. In late 1992 Korea resumed economic aid to Moscow, which had been suspended after the collapse of the former Soviet Union.[25] Undisbursed Korean loans earmarked for Russia amount to about $1 billion.[26] All this contributes to laying an institutional and financial foundation for expanded cooperation. In addition, Korea has a special interest in promoting direct business contacts with the Russian Far East, given its geographic proximity and the large ethnic Korean communities residing there (primarily in Sakhalin). With all this in mind, the Korea Trade Promotion Corporation (KOTRA) opened up a regional office in Vladivostok in July 1992.

In 1992 Russia's aggregate trade turnover with Korea reached $1,044 million, representing a 120 percent increase on the previous year. As a result, Korea's share in Russian foreign trade increased from 0.5 percent to 1.3 percent. In 1993 Russian–Korean trade turnover fell back again to just under $700 million. But Russian exports to Korea continued to grow in that year. Russia exports such items as steel and metal products (35 percent of exports by value), coal and petroleum (20 percent), fishery products (15 percent), while importing such Korean goods as machinery (55 percent), and textiles and garments (25 percent). Korea's share in the foreign trade turnover of the Russian Far East has reached 9 percent.

Fourteen Russian-Korean joint ventures, backed by total investments of $20 million, had been registered in Russia by 1993. So far the largest project is the Svetlaya joint venture set up jointly with the Hyundai Business Group in Primorsky Territory. Producing one million cubic metros of timber per year, this enterprise is expected to meet 20 percent of the total annual demand for sawn timber in Korea.[27] During President Yeltsin's visit to Seoul in 1992, the Russian side proposed 23 major economic projects with a total value of $20–30 billion. Of those, 70 percent involve the Far East. They include tin and gold production in Khabarovsk Territory and in the Amur; oil processing and gas and chemicals production in Khabarovsk Territory and Sakhalin; coal mining in Sakhalin, and the development of sulfur fields in the Kurile Islands. The Russian side also proposed cooperation in forestry and timber processing, erection of cement plants, the construction of modern processing plants for

25. *Korea Economic Weekly*, 1 June 1992, p. 2; 30 November 1992, p. 2.

26. *Izvestiya*, 12 November 1992.

27. *Korea Economic Journal*, 10 June 1991, p. 8.

fishery products in Sakhalin and Kamchatka, and the building and running of a seaport, an airport, highways and railways in Sakhalin.[28]

The two sides have already agreed a number of large cooperative projects. Among these, mention should be made of the participation of Daewoo Group and other major Korean companies in the joint development of the natural gas field in Yakutiya, a project which envisages the construction of a 5000 km gas pipe line to South Korea (the expected development costs are $12 billion). Kohap Limited plans to build a huge light-industrial estate in Nakhodka FEZ, exclusively for Korean plants; it is intended to provide facilities for up to 100 export-oriented enterprises with a total of 10 thousand employees on a territory of 300 hectares.[29] Daewoo and Samsung are involved in the conversion of defense industry plants in Khabarovsk Territory, in exchange for access to Russian technical know-how relating to the production of helicopters, gas-turbine engines and underwater vehicles.[30] Cooperation in the field of science and technology is gaining momentum.

South Korea's relatively comprehensive and long-term approach to cooperation with Russia corresponds to the development needs of the Russian Far East. Indeed it has contributed to the emergence of a 'Korean lobby' in Russia. Vladimir Lukin, former Russian ambassador to the United States and now chairman of the foreign affairs committee of the State Duma, has proposed that the government give more business opportunities to South Korea in order to stimulate Japanese interest in the Far East.[31] However, the effectiveness of such a policy, and indeed the overall scale of Russian-Korean cooperation, appear likely to be limited by problems currently being experienced by the Korean economy, which is passing through a difficult period of structural readjustment and transition from labor-intensive to high value-added production.

28. *Finansovye izvestiya*, 19 November 1992.
29. *Nakhodkinskii rabochii* (Nakhodka), 14 July 1992.
30. *Korea Economic Weekly*, 10 August 1992, p. 3; 17 August 1992.
31. *Korea Business World*, 1992, no. 3, p. 21.

CHAPTER EIGHT

Conclusion

The Russian Far East is taking its first steps toward creating an open regional market integrated into the normal international exchange of goods, capital, and labor. The marketization of the Russian economy is generating a new hierarchy of development interests and priorities in the Far East. Local authorities exert increasing influence on the evolution of the economic environment, and on the behavior of enterprises and other economic actors. New institutional and commercial structures are emerging, encouraging integrative processes in the region. The economy is increasingly open to contacts with neighboring countries. All this exemplifies the growing regionalization of economic, social and political life in Russia, as it strives to build a market economy and a democratic political system.

The growth of economic autonomy in the Russian Far East and other regions of Russia is a natural process with deep roots in history. With its vast size and regional differentiation, Russia had for a long time well-developed regional markets, each with its own special characteristics in terms of supply and demand. Under normal economic and political conditions, the economic diversity of the regions would be a natural basis for the development of a dynamic national market. But conditions in Russia are far from normal. There is a point at which healthy economic regionalization can slip into the kind of economic and political separatism which jeopardizes national integrity. There are clear signs that this is happening today.

The lack of attention paid to the specific needs of the regions was undoubtedly a major shortcoming in the Russian government's economic policy in the early 1990s. In the absence of a well-articulated structural and regional policy, radical market reforms have exacerbated the ills which the Far East's economy inherited from the Soviet system. As one economist expresses it: "As a whole, the region is on the brink of a massive bankruptcy. The question is: who is going to buy it, and for how much? The entire region is desperately short of savings, and the local financial base is extremely weak."[1] In an effort to adapt to the new conditions, Far Eastern enterprises turn to foreign markets. However, partly because of the contradictions and instability of Moscow's economic and foreign economic policy, this rapid opening up is not effective. Too often the region's natural resources appear to have been sold on the cheap. Difficulties in relations with the center provoke sporadic upsurges in local separatist feeling that sometimes express themselves in demands for the creation of an independent Far Eastern republic. In view of the rapid formation of local elites with their own interests and their own instruments of political and economic influence, these sentiments can be dangerous.

The political disintegration of Russia would be a catastrophe. The outcome would be widespread ethnic conflict, dramatic impoverishment of the population, political instability, and a prolonged economic crisis which would block the way to any serious reform or involvement in international economic cooperation. For the rest of the world this would mean not only the loss of the Russian market and the writing off of investments that have already been made. The international community would also be forced to intervene to try to stabilize the situation and to prevent a global Chernobyl. It has an interest, therefore, in helping Russia to construct a new flexible system of economic federalism which would rest on a rational redistribution of resources and authority between the center and the regions, and to design a differentiated federal policy toward the regions in such spheres as finance, investment and foreign economic relations.

According to the program for deepening economic reform adopted by the Russian government in 1992, the state would promote regional programs supported by the federal budget by strategic investment projects and by contracts for the supply of products to meet national needs.[2] It is noteworthy that the initial focus of Russia's new regional policy is the Far East—which is seen as the region most likely to provide the spark for a process of territorial disintegration. The Presidential decree "On Measures for the Development and State Support of the Economy of the Far East and Trans-Baikal Region" of 22 September 1992 instructed the Russian government, together with local au-

1. P. A. Minakir, *Ekonomicheskaya reforma na Dal'nem Vostoke* (1992), p. 8.
2. Granberg, "Regional'nyi aspekt ekonomicheskoi reformy," *Ekonomika i zhizn'*, 1992, no. 40, p. 14.

thorities and the Russian Academy of Sciences, to work out a State Regional Program for the Far East to be adopted in the first half of 1993.[3] An organization has been formed on the basis of the Far Eastern Association for Economic Cooperation to administer the Program.

The decree posits that the Program should lay down the major directions of economic development in the region, select key investment projects that would contribute to structural reform of the Far Eastern economy, and identify federal sources of finance for them. The Program aims to lay a basis for self-sustaining economic development in the region within the framework of an integrated Russian economy. It contains concrete proposals for increasing the appeal of the Far East to investors—a more flexible privatization policy for the region, a favorable foreign-trade, customs and currency regime, tax cuts and credit support for efficient producers, stability in central–regional fiscal arrangements, and investment insurance facilities. It recommends that federal financial support be focused on low-profit major infrastructure projects, such as FEZs.[4]

The Program devotes a good deal of attention to the promotion of foreign economic ties. In particular, it envisages the elaboration of a system of special state guarantees and incentives for foreign investors in key industries. The most promising avenues of international cooperation are seen in fields such as the exploration of marine resources, ferrous and nonferrous metals, timber, fuel and energy, recreation, and the development of transport. The Russian Far East can contribute with its natural resources, its high-technology design skills, its intellectual and industrial potential, and the land to accommodate free economic zones. The Asia-Pacific countries, for their part, would provide finance, technology and marketing experience.

Some of the elements of the State Regional Program for the Far East have been superseded as policy on related issues—e.g. SEZs—has changed. But it remains an important framework document for the articulation of special policies for the Far East.

The limitations of many of the bilateral relationships between the Russian Far East and its principal business partners in Asia and the Pacific suggest that a multilateral approach to international economic cooperation in the region would be appropriate. Moreover, because of the size of the challenge in the Russian Far East, private foreign investment on its own would hardly be suffi-

3. *Vedomosti...*, 1992, no. 39, pp. 2852–54.
4. *Ekonomicheskaya reforma na Dal'nem Vostoke: rezul'taty, problemy, kontseptsiya razvitiya* (1993), pp. 119, 120, 165.

cient. What is needed in the region is not so much individual projects as a comprehensive approach to all aspects of industrial and social development. International economic organizations in the Asia-Pacific region need to be drawn into a cooperative development program. A 'civilized' opening up of the Far Eastern economy, taking account of the interests of all those concerned, could make a substantial contribution to the economic and political stabilization of Russia as a whole.

Index